MEDIATIZED CONFLICT

ISSUES in CULTURAL and MEDIA STUDIES

Series editor: Stuart Allan

Published titles:

MEDIATIZED CONFLICT

Developments in Media and Conflict Studies

Simon Cottle

Open University Press

Open University Press
McGraw-Hill Education
McGraw-Hill House
Shoppenhangers Road
Maidenhead
Berkshire
England
SL6 2QL

email: enquiries@openup.co.uk
world wide web: www.openup.co.uk

and Two Penn Plaza, New York, NY 10121–2289, USA

First published 2006

A catalogue record of this book is available from the British Library

ISBN-10: 0 335 21452 5 (pb)   0 335 21453 3 (hb)
ISBN-13: 978 0 335 21452 5 (pb)   978 0 335 21453 2 (hb)

Library of Congress Cataloging-in-Publication Data
CIP data applied for

Typeset by RefineCatch Limited, Bungay, Suffolk
Printed in the UK by Bell & Bain Ltd, Glasgow

CONTENTS

SERIES EDITOR'S FOREWORD

Walter Lippmann's classic text *Public Opinion*, first published in 1922, opens with an intriguing tale. He sets the scene by describing a remote island where British, French and German expatriates live together in a harmonious community. In the absence of telegraphic cables connecting them with the outside world, the islanders rely on a mail steamer to visit every 60 days with the latest newspaper. In September of 1914, however, the steamer is delayed, making everyone even more anxious for news than usual, not least because coverage of a celebrated court trial is the talk of the island. 'It was, therefore, with more than usual eagerness that the whole colony assembled at the quay on a day in mid-September to hear from the captain what the verdict had been,' Lippmann writes. Instead, what they learn comes as a shock. Britain and France, they discover, are waging war against Germany. What were the islanders to think? 'For six strange weeks they had acted as if they were friends,' Lippmann observes, 'when in fact they were enemies.'

Neatly pinpointed in this tale are a number of issues concerning the mediation of distant conflict, the central theme of Simon Cottle's *Mediatized Conflict*. The phrase 'mediatized conflict', he explains, is used here 'to emphasise the complex ways in which media are often implicated within conflicts while disseminating ideas and images about them.' The media, he proceeds to show, possess the capacity to *enact* or *perform* conflicts – that is, to actively shape their constitutive nature – in the course of defining their realities in representational terms. The opening chapters of the book clarify the theoretical implications of this approach, taking care to elucidate pertinent concepts, perspectives and debates. Building on this foundation, subsequent chapters revolve around different examples to help extend this path of enquiry. Topics under scrutiny include news and racism, war reporting, peace journalism, coverage of environmental risk, treatments of terrorism, and identity politics. In the final chapter, this array of topics unifies around Cottle's commitment to extending new research trajectories for future work in this fascinating area. All in all, this book addresses a significant knowledge gap in our understanding in an original and compelling way.

The *Issues in Cultural and Media Studies* series aims to facilitate a diverse range of critical investigations into pressing questions considered to be central to current thinking and research. In light of the remarkable speed at which the conceptual agendas of cultural and media studies are changing, the series is committed to contributing to what is an ongoing process of re-evaluation and critique. Each of the books is intended to provide a lively, innovative and comprehensive introduction to a specific topical issue from a fresh perspective. The reader is offered a thorough grounding in the most salient debates indicative of the book's subject, as well as important insights into how new modes of enquiry may be established for future explorations. Taken as a whole, then, the series is designed to cover the core components of cultural and media studies courses in an imaginatively distinctive and engaging manner.

Stuart Allan

ACKNOWLEDGEMENTS

This book, in more ways than is usual, is indebted to my family who interrupted their UK lives and friendships to accompany me to Melbourne, Australia. Fortunately great whites, red backs, box jellyfish, tiger snakes, brown snakes, crocs, alligators and screeching possums have all decided to let us return, four years later, to less sunny climes and decidedly tamer shores. I'm for ever in the debt of Lucy, Sam, Theo and Ella for coming with me down-under and for making possible one of the most wonderful times of my/our lives. Thank you! Special thanks to Ella too for the three cups of Earl Grey and five iced cup cakes served while writing this book. Again, I'm indebted to Stuart Allan's indefatigable energies and skills as Series Editor emanating 24/7 from the global hub of the mother of all networks. To colleagues and friends in the Media and Communication Program at Melbourne University and especially Hari (Ramaswami Harindranath), David Nolan and, yet again, Mugdha Rai, I thank you for your invaluable help and respective inputs into this book. I would also like to formally acknowledge the Faculty of Arts and the University of Melbourne for their generous support while working on this and other writing projects across the period 2002 to 2006 and for the provision of a University of Melbourne publication grant that has assisted the publication of this book and its inclusion of numerous media images.

Simon Cottle, Melbourne 2005

MEDIATIZED CONFLICT IN THE WORLD TODAY

The world today is characterized by endemic and multifarious conflicts. Here's just a few of them. Though fewer states are now at war with each other than in the past, many are locked in bloody internal conflicts and internecine struggles. The United States, the strongest power in the world, leads a coalition of the willing post-9/11 in a self-defined 'war against global terror' and the United Nations struggles to maintain an international foothold for peace. The world's poor, marginalized and dispossessed can encounter ruthless violence by local elites when challenging oppression, and trades unions struggle to negotiate terms with transnational corporations operating in the borderless world of global capitalism. Industrial technologies and scientific rationalities produce 'manufactured uncertainties' – potentially catastrophic risks threatening environments and populations – prompting critiques of normative goals of economic growth. Disease, famines and disasters continue to stalk the globe and the hungry and afflicted go to early graves while much of humanity looks on and continues to consume more than its fair share of the planet's resources. Political parties compete and struggle to hold back the tide of growing disillusionment, if not cynicism, of electorates jaundiced by mainstream political processes and practices while 'new-age' religions seek out old remedies and past myths to make sense of contemporary alienated lives. Xenophobia and racism greet the increasing flows of migrants and asylum seekers displaced from their homelands and are resisted by diasporic peoples everywhere who struggle to rebuild lives and communities in distant places. And a plethora of cultural identities and single-issue campaigns now struggle and contend for symbolic space and public recognition – often dissolving as they do so boundaries of the 'personal' and the 'political', the 'public' and 'private' (and problematizing simplistic, Manichean, ideas of a 'clash of cultures'). We live, it hardly needs to be said, in highly conflictual times.

We also live in mediatized times. The collective interests and cultural identities now contending for political legitimacy, social change and cultural recognition do so for the most part in and through available media of communication – whether traditional media of mass publicity, press and broadcasting or new digital and interactive media such as the Internet. Today everyone it seems, from elected presidents to eco-warriors, all look to the media to advance their strategic aims and symbolic claims. Few conflict protagonists shun, most seek, and probably all will acknowledge the communicative power of today's media. Of course, some protagonists have considerable institutional advantages over their opponents and they unashamedly use this to manipulate media agendas to ensure that their preferred message gets across (or, equally, that damaging information never finds its way into the media sphere). The resource-poor and institutionally powerless, for their part, are apt to resort to creative tactics and/or turn to new media and modes of communication in their bid to gain media space and symbolically counter ingrained imbalances of power. Disparate interests and diffuse social movements have become adept at deploying resonate symbols and cultural myths or performing stunning media events – 'dissent events' – to attract the media spotlight. Whether pursued strategically by powerful corporate and government interests, or more tactically by diffuse cultural identities, the media have become a prised arena for the waging of conflict.

Mediatized Conflict: Developments in Media and Conflict Studies sets out to explore the changing relationships, representational forms, powered dynamics and impacts of media performance in disparate fields of contemporary conflict and charts new research departures in this important field. It deliberately pursues a comparative approach. This proves both heuristically and theoretically useful. By examining studies of different mediatized conflicts we can consider the generalities and specifics of media conflict reporting as well as informing theoretical frameworks and methodologies. This comparative approach delivers a deeper understanding of the various dimensions and dynamics, complexities and contingencies of media production and performance in national and international mediatized conflicts today. Selected mediatized conflicts addressed include, for example, major protests and demonstrations; wars from the Crimea to the US-led invasion of Iraq; the reporting of peace initiatives and attempts to develop new forms of 'peace journalism'; mediated terrorism post-9/11 and the politics of spectacle; media scandals and other exceptional 'mediatized public crises' centring on 'race', racism and ethnicity; issues of risk, environment and global ecology; identity politics and the politics of cultural recognition including the progressive capacity of at least some sections of the media to give voice to the voiceless and identity to image in respect of various Others – asylum seekers, indigenous peoples, and victims of war and famine. By these means *Mediatized Conflict* develops a grounded theoretical understanding of production processes, professional practices, political contingencies and media performance and how all impact on the public elaboration and unfolding dynamics of major contemporary conflicts.

We focus principally on the media of journalism: broadcasting and the press as well as the Internet, and other new technologies delivering conflict-focused news and commentary. Conflicts also feature of course in other mediums and genres, and some of these media forms will be considered as we proceed. Nonetheless, historically and to this day, journalism remains the principal convenor and conveyor of conflict images and information, discourses and debates, and for this reason deservedly takes the lion's share of discussion. It is in and through the different mediums, forms and appeals of journalism that most of us come to know about the conflicts and contests waged in the world today and this daily infusion is delivered into the rhythms and routines of our everyday lives – and can do so 24/7 and via real-time modes of communication. Conveyed by the ubiquitous forms of news communications, journalism in the 21st century has become stitched into the fabric of everyday existence and for many of us sutures the 'serious life' of citizenship, governance and public issues with the private 'life-worlds' of daily being and consumption practices.

Journalism should not be presumed, however, to be monolithic – whether in terms of its institutional arrangements, political alignments, social functions or cultural forms of expression. Contemporary journalism exhibits far more complexity, and even diversity, than is often conceded by past and present positions of media theory. We will necessarily take some of these complexities and differentiations into account when pursuing the nature, determinants and impacts of mediatized conflicts today. In the chapters that follow we encounter very different kinds of journalism including: 'peace journalism', 'development journalism', 'public journalism', 'on-line' and 'alternative journalism', and new communicative modes of journalism such as 24/7 reporting and 'video-journalism' as well as more traditional forms of press and broadcasting journalism.

Etched into the self-conception of the journalism profession is a view of itself as public watchdog and provider of information and resources for public opinion formation. This view also inflects, though often in a less self-assured manner, widespread public expectations about the social responsibilities and political function of journalism in democratic societies. Journalism, according to this normative evaluation, should circulate information and ideas deemed essential for sustaining a vibrant civil society and functioning democracy. Conflicts by their very nature can also pose, however, challenges to democratic institutions and processes of democracy; but so too are they often the harbingers of that same democracy and they can play an essential part in revitalizing moribund 'democracies' and extending and deepening democracy within civil society. It is in and through mediatized conflicts, the array of views and voices that surround them and the public spaces that they manage to secure to define and defend their claims and aims, that the state of democracy in today's societies becomes revealed and, in important respects, constituted and open to evaluation.

Mediatized Conflict, then, sets out to develop and deliver a more encompassing understanding of how and why mediatized conflicts are represented and enacted in the ways that they are, and how these could or should be improved so as to deepen their contribution to democratic forms of public engagement in the future. By carefully examining studies of different conflicts, their principal findings, informing theoretical approaches and methodologies, it is hoped that you, the reader, will be better equipped to understand the complex forms and changing dynamics of conflict reporting in today's societies as well as the increasingly central role(s) performed by the media within many of them. The remainder of this introductory chapter now sets the scene for what follows. We briefly consider some basic attributes of 'conflict' and situate the conflicted nature of our times in relation to overarching themes of contemporary social theory. These theoretical coordinates provide some bearings for the course that is steered across later chapters. Some basic research questions follow and, going against the grain of common sense, these intimate how there is considerably more complexity to the study of mediatized conflicts than, say, the study of media representations or the pursuit of media bias, distortion and propaganda. As well as signalling something of the multiple dimensions to mediatized conflicts these basic research questions point to the value of media theory for a deeper engagement with today's media, and these ideas are taken up and developed theoretically in the next chapter. A few words of clarification are also offered in respect of what, exactly, is meant by the powered phrase 'mediatized conflict', the title and subject of this book, before concluding with an outline of the chapters that follow.

Contemporary society, conflict and change

Conflicts originate in social relations (rarely, it has to be said, do they emanate solely from the media) and they are seemingly endemic to all social formations whether local, tradition bound and closed, or globalized, dynamic and relatively open. This said, there are certainly grounds to suggest that the range and forms of conflict in the world today have proliferated and that many of them express underlying processes of change. Themes of 'globalization', 'post-traditionalism', 'socially reflexivity' and 'cultural heterogeneity', for example, all feature prominently in the writings of contemporary social theorists and these often surface across the chapters and case studies that follow. Together they go some way in helping to explain the different fields of contention spawned by late modern, capitalist societies. We shall return to these presently. But first, what are 'conflicts'?

Conflicts can be defined straightforwardly. Essentially they are struggles between opposing interests and outlooks. Thereafter the picture becomes a little less simple. This is because conflicts can be theorized as latent or manifest, structurally determined or purposefully enacted, objectively real or subjectively perceived, raising philosophical issues about origins, determination, social construction and the role of intentionality and agency in their enactment. Some conflicts are rooted in economic contradictions and political structures, others within social attitudes or cultural outlooks, but whatever their source, location and forms of expression, conflicts are necessarily defined, mobilized and populated by people. Thinking, feeling, sentient, human beings define and engage in disputes, prosecute ideologies and interests, participate in forms of struggle, and wage wars. Conflicts involve more than insentient structures; they require agency, and this agency invariably becomes collective, organized and positioned in relation to other agents and opposing interests. For the participants, conflicts are made sense of discursively and culturally – they are often high in meaning and affect – and they are invariably pursued purposefully, strategically and practically. Conflicts can also burn briefly and brightly or smoulder across generations. They can be conducted at the interpersonal level or extend geopolitically to the interstate level and beyond. They are local to global in scope. Conflicts can lead to some of the most inhumane acts of violence including war and genocide; they can also serve, however, humanitarian and emancipatory projects and can act as a vitalizing spur for participatory and deliberative democracy. Some conflicts can be contained by existing political structures or managed through processes of conflict resolution; others escape all attempts at containment and are prosecuted with extreme violence, often entrenching enmities and storing up hatreds for the future. Conflicts are endemic to the known social world.

Contemporary positions of social theory help identify some of the mainsprings of both old and new conflicts – though clearly no single theoretical approach apart from the most generalizing or reductionist can hope to adequately map, much less explain, all the conflicts in the world today. Nonetheless, and in broad strokes, the social theoretical ideas of Anthony Giddens, Manuel Castells and Ulrich Beck, among others, help to map many of today's conflicts and they do so in respect of profound processes of contemporary change. Three interrelated processes in particular – globalization, post-traditionalism and social reflexivity – deserve preliminary mention. Globalization – itself a highly contested term – is often used to refer to the latest stage and expansionist logic of capitalism; of how economic inequalities become exacerbated within and between nation states and extended across the globe, processes recently accelerated by state policies of liberalization, deregulation and privatization (Harvey 2003). The disparities of wealth, income and life opportunities in the world today fuel many, perhaps most, of today's conflicts.

Globalization is also used to refer, however, to other dimensions of change and transformation. The rise of new information and communication technologies (ICTs) contributes, according to Giddens (1994) and others, to the collapsing of space and time and facilitates the stretching and intensification of social relations conducted at a distance, giving rise to an interconnected global 'network society' (Castells 1996 cf. Hassan 2004). Globalization also prompts increased flows of finance, peoples and cultures around the globe (Lash and Urry 1994; Urry 2003) and this contributes both to the reassertion of nationalisms and the undermining of nation states and their ability to manage economic and political processes within territorial borders (Held et al. 1999; Kaldor 2003). Globalization can best be approached, perhaps, as a complex of uneven and often contradictory sets of forces characterized by: the expansionist logic of capitalism, the reconfiguration of spatial politics, the disembedding and re-embedding of social relations conducted at a distance, and the accelerated and technologically assisted flows of culture and peoples around the globe. All of these transformative processes generate new conflicts as well as exacerbating old ones.

In today's globalizing and 'post-traditional' times (Giddens 1994) traditions and belief systems once taken for granted or left unquestioned are now exposed to counter ideas and are expected to defend themselves in reasoned and self-reflective terms. Further fields of social, political and cultural contention have opened up across recent years as traditional solidarities of class and political allegiance rooted in the social relations of mass production have become weakened by new flexible regimes of social production and cultural patterns of consumption. These, in turn, support the rise of new identity politics, new social movements and a cacophony of 'subpolitics' beyond and outside established parliamentary institutions (Beck 1997; Castells 1997). Together these cultural forces of change often make for vibrant, agonistic and potentially 'democratizing' civil societies at the same time as they become increasingly fragmented and internally contested (Hall and Jacques 1989; Mouffe 1996; Beck 1997; Castells 1997). Globalization and detraditionalization contribute to the cacophony of discourses and clash of interests alluded to at the outset of this chapter, with many of them now engaging on the battlefields of the media.

Societies today also exhibit increased 'social reflexivity', and this too feeds into the contested terrain of civil society. Knowledge claims and expertise, as with social traditions, are no longer sacrosanct or beyond the challenge of lay people and non-experts. Decline in deference to social authorities, increased access to education and growing disenchantment with technocratic rationalities and experts systems, whether those of science, medicine or the administration of 'risks', have all undermined systems of trust and established knowledge systems (Beck 1992; Beck et al. 1994). Widespread feelings of 'ontological insecurity' (Giddens 1990) or deep-seated feelings of anxiety about the state of the planet and its future also spring from these new social conditions and fuel the rise of environmental consciousness and grassroots protests. Moreover, powerful states as well as individuals inhabit uncertain times, as the events of 9/11 and its appalling aftermath around the world bear witness (Zelizer and Allan 2002). US military actions, dubbed the 'new imperialism' by some (Harvey 2003), have prompted renewed efforts at an international 'suprapolitics' – a politics of above – which moves to debate and construct a workable framework of international relations and possible emergent 'global civil society' (Kaldor 2003; Keane 2003; Held 2004).

This brief excursive into contemporary social theory simply makes the point that some of the most profound processes of social transformation of our time are often implicated in mediatized conflicts, prompting new research questions and new research directions. We shall revisit many of them in the chapters that follow.

Researching mediatized conflict

The media's relationship to conflict and conflict-related processes, as already suggested, cannot be encapsulated by a narrowly conceived concern with media 'representations'. The complex interactions and processual nature of conflicts as much as the media's interrelationship and participation within many of them, require us to broaden our analytical frame and extend theoretical horizons. Critical sights are prematurely narrowed if we accept, for example, commonsense ideas of media 'bias', 'distortion' or even 'propaganda'. These terms do not have the analytical edge needed to cut into the complex determinations, dynamics, forms and impacts of today's mediatized conflicts – though we may not want to discard them entirely. Terms like 'bias' and 'distortion' can betray an empiricist naïvety in respect of the epistemological issues that surround media conflict representations where opposing parties, by definition, are likely to hold to different beliefs, values, accounts and perceptions of reality. This is not to suggest that media representations are beyond critical analysis or evaluation, or that we cannot develop the critical benchmarks to systematically and incisively analyse forms of media output, but it is to say that notions of 'bias', 'distortion' or even 'propaganda' cannot do all the hard work for us.

As a first step in opening up some of these complexities we can pose some basic research questions about the origins, nature and forms of mediatized representations of conflicts, as well as the methods used by researchers in their analysis:

- Why are some conflicts hidden from public view and 'symbolically annihilated' in the media, while others steal the media spotlight and may do so over a considerable period of time?
- Who gains access to the media stage to promote and discuss conflicts and by what means? In what media forms or arenas are they permitted entry and with what discursive, deliberative or symbolic consequences?
- How have conflicts been shaped and conditioned by different mainstream media forms and genres and what new opportunities now exist within today's 'alternative' and 'new' media? How can old and new media better serve processes of democratic deepening and/or conflict resolution in the future?
- How are conflicts defined, elaborated and evaluated in the media? Why do some conflicts become visualized and dramatized, narrativized and mythologized and imbued with cultural resonance and moral charge, and others not?
- What methods best serve to analyse media representations and recover how they circulate messages and generate meanings?

We can also enquire into the possible explanations, motivations, reasons and other factors, whether intended or unintended, that determine or shape the course of mediatized conflicts as well as their interpretation by audiences:

- What is the relationship between mediatized conflicts and the media's commercial and competitive imperatives and political alignments? When do the media follow, when do they lead, when do they simply report, when do they purposefully perform 'mediatized conflicts'?
- What constraints and controls – political, technological, professional, regulatory, normative and cultural – condition the operations of media professionals and

media organizations in respect of mediatized conflicts, and with what results? Under what circumstances are the media complicit or resistant to various forms of external and internal control, containment and censorship, and why?

- How do diverse media audiences respond to mediatized conflicts? What do we know about the complexities and contingencies of audience reception and the impact and influence of media conflict reporting on audiences? How do audiences influence media representations? When do audiences become 'publics'?

In keeping with the comparative thrust of this book, we can also pose questions about the extent to which it is permissible to extrapolate from, and generalize, past or present research findings whether in respect of different media or different conflicts:

- To what extent is it permissible to generalize about 'the media' and their role(s) in today's conflicts given the variegated nature of contemporary media ecologies composed of competing organizations, mediums, genres, formats and forms, and their distribution by traditional and new media technologies?
- To what extent is it permissible to generalize about conflict reporting given the different natures of different conflicts? What can observed differences of conflict reporting contribute to improved positions of media theory?

Broad questions about media theory can also be raised at the outset, and then developed and refined as we proceed:

- What is the role of media theory in the study of mediatized conflicts? What are the principal theoretical paradigms and approaches that organize the field of media research today and which have direct relevance for the study of mediatized conflicts? What are their respective strengths and insights? What are their respective weaknesses and blind-spots? How, if at all, can current positions of media theory be improved to better accommodate the complexities of mediatized conflicts and provide a more encompassing, multidimensional and convincing explanatory approach?

These basic questions, by no means exhaustive, serve to signal something of the book's intended terrain. Some of them help us to move beyond relatively flat conceptions of 'representation' and encourage empirical investigation of the multiple dimensions and complexities involved in 'mediatized conflicts'. Some point to the necessity of engaging more conceptually and theoretically with this field of study.

Why 'mediatized' conflict?

The phrase, 'mediatized conflict', the chosen title and subject of this book, is deliberate. It is used to emphasize the complex ways in which media are often implicated within conflicts while disseminating ideas and images about them. As such, it signals a much stronger sense of media involvement than, say, 'mediation'. 'Mediation' tends to suggest a view of media as a neutral 'middle-ground', equidistant perhaps between events that the media report on and the audiences that view/read/hear about them. Implicit to this view of 'mediation', then, is a view of media 'conveyance' or 'transmission' as well as, possibly, an 'arbitrating' role – again often neutrally conceived. The terms 'mediated societies', or even 'mediatized societies', are also increasingly heard today, drawing attention to the ways in which the media have infiltrated into the rhythms and practices of everyday life as well as systems of governance and the conduct of societies more generally (Thompson 1990, 1995). These senses of 'mediation' and 'mediated' are useful but here I want to incorporate and augment them with a further level of meaning. 'Mediatization' is used here in a powered sense to deliberately capture something of the more complex, active and performative ways that the media are involved in conflicts today. The media, as we shall see, are capable of enacting and performing conflicts as well as reporting and representing them; that is to say, they are actively 'doing something' over and above disseminating ideas, images and information. The media's relationship to conflict, therefore, is often not best thought of in terms of 'reflection' or even 'representation' given its more active *performative* involvement and *constitutive* role within them. '*Mediatized conflict*', then, as well as referring to different possible media roles, representations and arenas for the public display and deliberation of conflicts, sets out to explore this media performance or '*media doing*' (for more on media performativity see Cottle 2004a). This understanding of 'mediatized conflict', *of how the media do things with conflicts*, necessary for engaging with the media's involvement in conflict reporting today, is elaborated and refined throughout the rest of the book.

Plan of book

Mediatized Conflict is structured into ten carefully sequenced chapters. Each chapter introduces new dimensions and complexities that together build into a more in-depth and encompassing understanding of mediatized conflicts. Chapter 2, 'Getting a Fix on Mediatized Conflict: Paradigms and Perspectives' introduces three overarching theoretical paradigms that currently structure the field of media and communications research and which have particular bearing on the study of media and conflict. Exemplary studies from each are critically reviewed and their respective theoretical insights and blind-spots noted as we move to build a more encompassing and multidimensional approach. With theoretical foundation stones laid in Chapter 2, a series of selected mediatized conflicts and discussions follow. Each examines distinct fields of conflict, reports important research findings and considers their contribution for improved understanding of mediatized conflicts more widely. Each chapter also identifies the latest research trajectories and how these often qualify or challenge widely held theoretical positions. In this way, the book elaborates a more encompassing theoretical understanding which equips us to analyse the complexities and contingencies, mechanisms and meanings of contemporary mediatized conflicts.

Chapter 3, 'Reporting Demonstrations and Protest: Public Sphere(s), Public Screens' begins by examining findings from 'classic' studies of media reporting of demonstrations conducted over 30 years ago. Theoretical frameworks and key findings from these early studies, still influential today, are then supplemented and reconsidered in the light of the most recent studies of mediatized demonstrations. Attending to issues of geopolitics, changing repertoires of protest, ideas of dramaturgy, and activism and the Internet, the discussion opens up important complexities and contingencies in contemporary mediatized protests and considers the conceptual adequacy of current ideas of 'public sphere(s)' and 'public screens' when deployed in this context.

Chapter 4, 'From Moral Panics to Mediatized Public Crises: Moving Stories of "Race" and Racism' focuses on exceptional, often media-driven, phenomena and how these appear to be able to galvanize collective feelings and summon collective solidarities or 'publics'. The chapter discusses a number of highly performative media phenomena, including 'moral panics', 'media events', 'media scandals' and 'mediatized public crises' and how each taps into deep-seated social anxieties and divisions. The discussion considers the transformative as well reactionary possibilities that attend these exceptional mediatized phenomena and does so by demonstrating how exceptional media events contribute 'moving stories' of 'race' and racism – in both emotional and political senses – within contemporary societies.

Chapter 5, 'War Journalism: Disembodied and Embedded' addresses the historically changing relations between state, military and journalism in times of war – probably the most pressurized and fraught journalistic arena of all. Key research findings and important theoretical perspectives are outlined concerning state censorship, military controls and the professional culture of journalism and how these combine to produce sanitized, 'disembodied', views of war. Globalization and debates about the changing theatre of contemporary warfare, including 24/7 real-time news, the military's 'embedding' of journalists in the Iraq invasion of 2003, the public display of 'body horror', and alternative media are then considered as possible destabilizing influences on the media at war and the traditional dominance of state and military perspectives.

Chapter 6, 'Peace Journalism and Other Alternatives: On Hopes and Prayers' considers a range of alternative journalisms that deliberately challenge traditional news values, dominant news agendas, privileged elite access and 'professional' journalist practices. Examining the ideas and ideals of peace journalism, development journalism, public journalism and on-line alternative journalism we appraise their respective politics and prescriptions for change and ask to what extent these largely normatively framed interventions in today's media environment can hope to achieve their aims.

Chapter 7, 'Media, "Risk Society" and the Environment: A Different Story?' explores media performance in respect of the rise of environmental issues and the public concerns and contentions surrounding ecology and the so called 'risk society'. The role of organizational claims makers in building media agendas over time as well as the deep cultural resonances of 'the environment' are explored as possible key explanations for the rise and fall of environmental media coverage. A common 'rhetoric of environmental images' is discerned and discussed and we also examine recent research findings on how audiences actively and selectively respond to the symbolic appeals and arguments structuring media representations of the environment, opening up complexities of audience reception and political response.

Chapter 8, 'From "Terrorism" to the "Global War on Terror": The Media Politics of Outrage' examines how the US war on terror as well as its asymmetric enemies have positioned 'terror' high on global news agendas. Research findings challenge common-sense views about the media's alleged causal relation to terrorism (media as the 'oxygen of terrorism') and point to the semantics and semiotics of 'terror' as potent means of waging propaganda wars. This earlier research finding, in turn, opens up more recent research sensitized to the 'politics of representation' embedded in the media's communicative forms and how these can play an important role in the 'democratization of violence'. The prominent role of symbolic, spectacular and staged media images in the recent war on terror is further addressed as an important development in the media's 'transformation of visibility' in the field of mediatized terror, and one that has recently been made possible by new digital means of communication and global distribution.

Chapter 9, 'Identity Politics and Cultural Difference: On Mediatized Recognition,' the last substantive chapter, sets out important theoretical arguments about the politics of recognition and its enactment in today's media. In keeping with the emphasis on new directions in research it explores how mainstream television, as well as other media, occasionally break the mould of media representations. As documented in countless studies these too often render voiceless and invisible the lives of minorities and oppressed social groups who are thereby symbolically marginalized, denigrated or denied their humanity within media representations. Here we examine the overlooked and undertheorized capacity of mainstream media to play a more progressive role in the politics of recognition and the symbolic rehabilitation of Others – asylum seekers, refugees, indigenous minorities, terrorism suspects, and victims of war and famine. Journalism's established communicative modes of *deliberation* and *display* are found to be powerful communicative allies in processes of cultural recognition and, potentially, political action and change.

Finally, Chapter 10, 'Mediatized Conflict: Conclusions' reviews the principal findings and discussion of the preceding chapters and argues for a considerably more encompassing, multidimensional and multilevelled approach for the study of mediatized conflict than is often entertained in the field of media and communications research or outside it; an approach which can begin to theorize and grapple with the media's complex, often changing, relation to different fields of conflict and contention and how these complexities and contingencies play out over time and circumstances.

When approached thus, we find that today's media not only reproduce the views and voices of the powerful, which they often certainly do, but also contain openings and opportunities for deepening democracy and the democratization of civil societies. The selected conflicts discussed in the various chapters collectively illustrate some of the complexities, contingencies and performative nature of mediatized conflicts today.

2 | GETTING A FIX ON MEDIATIZED CONFLICT: PARADIGMS AND PERSPECTIVES

The field of media and communications research is structured by different traditions of scholarship and draws on a wide range of academic disciplines. Inevitably this makes for a contested field of research and study. In this chapter we discuss three overarching paradigms each of which plays an important part in directing current research practice and the theorization of media and conflicts. I term these, respectively, the '*manufacturing consent*', '*media contest*' and '*media culture*' paradigms. Though sometimes engaged in border skirmishes as well as more substantial disputes, each contributes something of value for an in-depth, multidimensional and encompassing understanding of mediatized conflicts today, and each also provides a particular vantage point from which to better view and understand the media's possible contribution to contemporary 'public sphere(s)' of engaged discourse, deliberation and display.

Paradigms broadly condition the kinds of questions asked, the conceptual and theoretical frameworks guiding research, the methodological approaches deployed, the epistemological assumptions made about what constitutes 'knowledge' and the role of political values and commitments in academic enquiry. At any one time a small number of paradigms only are likely to be influencing research and these will be in varying states of intellectual emergence, consolidation, challenge and decline – and so it is in the field of media and communications scholarship. Here it is useful to address each of our three paradigms by focusing on an exemplary position from each, and making reference to related theoretical approaches, studies and authors as we proceed.

The theoretical approaches used here to exemplify each paradigm provide, I think, particularly eloquent and forceful statements in the field of study today, and each helps sensitize us to important dimensions of mediatized conflict. Each on its own, however, also exhibits deficiencies and blind-spots that limit our field of vision and capacity to engage with the multidimensional complexities involved. Following a critical review of each, the chapter concludes by encapsulating these differences of theoretical approach into diagrammatic form and illuminates how each provides a distinctive take on the media when conceptualized in terms of 'public sphere(s)' – debates which are revisited in the chapters that follow and elaborated in our first substantive discussion of mediatized conflict.

The manufacturing consent paradigm

Ever since the early work of the Frankfurt school in the 1930s and 1940s the critical tradition of media research has viewed the mass media with a sceptical eye. Ideas of the mass media as 'culture industry', that is, as capitalist enterprise and corporate purveyor of cultural commodities, false dreams and dominant ideology have long informed the critical tradition of mass communications research. With the ever-increasing domin-ance of corporate media giants such as News Corporation, Microsoft, Sony and Viacom in the world marketplace, based on their evident powers of production and distribution around the globe, it is perhaps understandable that the original critique of mass media outlined in *Dialectic of Enlightenment* by Theodor Adorno and Max Horkheimer in 1944 (Adorno and Horkheimer 1944/1972) continues to chime, for many, with contemporary circumstances.

Across the 60 years or so following Adorno and Horkheimer's pessimistic account of how the 'culture industry' contributes to the demise of Enlightenment ideals by 'mass deception', theorists have variously emphasized the 'one dimensionality' of capitalist consumer culture and the media's production and reproduction of false needs (Marcuse 1972); the media's functional role as an 'ideological state apparatus' positioning or 'interpellating' subjects within ideology and thereby reproducing capitalist relations (Althusser 1971); and the instrumental use made of the media by the ruling class and media owners who thereby legitimize the capitalist system and delegitimize dissent and opposition (Miliband 1973). Systematic studies of news output seemingly lend some empirical support to such theoretical claims when documenting the media's hierarchy of news access, interpretative frames, linguistic cues and encoding of the 'culturally dominant assumptions of society', especially when unfavourably reporting on workers, trade unionists and protestors (GUMG 1976, 1980, 1985).

The political economy tradition in media research also underpins the manufacturing consent paradigm. Here researchers have sought to explain, for example, the media's privileging of dominant views and values and the marginalization of oppositional voices as the largely unintended outcome of market structures and economic determi-nants. Notable international theorists such as Graham Murdock, Peter Golding, James Curran, Nicholas Garnham, Oliver Boyd-Barrett, Herbert Schiller, Dallas Smyth and Robert McChesney, to name a few, have all variously deployed political economy analyses to explain, and criticize, how the media invariably support domin-ant interests and the perpetuation of an inegalitarian social order (for a review see Mosco 1996).

While not wishing to minimize the internal differences and debates within and between variants of political economy, especially in respect of the explanatory mechanisms thought to explain the media's production and dissemination of 'ideology' and/ or 'dominant discourses', they nonetheless share a common concern with the way in which media are embedded within capitalist structures, are oriented to the pursuit of profit and disseminate images and ideas in support of dominant economic interests and political power.

A particularly influential, and hard-hitting, exposition in this tradition is Edward Herman and Noam Chomsky's *Manufacturing Consent: The Political Economy of the Mass Media* (1988), reissued many times over the years and widely available in bookshops to this day. This serves as our exemplar of the manufacturing consent paradigm and draws, as we shall hear, on many of the critical themes above. The authors clearly state their central argument at the outset:

> The mass media serve as a system for communicating messages and symbols to the general populace. It is their function to amuse, entertain, and inform, and to inculcate individuals with the values, beliefs, and codes of behaviour that will integrate them into the institutional structures of the larger society. In a world of concentrated wealth and major conflicts of class interest, to fulfil this role requires systematic propaganda.
>
> In countries where the levers of power are in the hands of a state bureaucracy, the monopolistic control over the media, often supplemented by official censorship, makes it clear that the media serve the ends of a dominant elite. It is much more difficult to see a propaganda system at work where the media are private and formal censorship is absent. This is especially true where the media actively compete, periodically attack and expose corporate and government malfeasance, and aggressively portray themselves as spokesmen for free speech and the general community interest. What is not evident (and remains undiscussed in the media) is the limited nature of such critiques, as well as the huge inequality in command of resources, and its effects both on access to a private media system and on its behaviour and performance.
>
> A propaganda model focuses on this inequality of wealth and power and its multilevel effects on mass-media interests and choices. It traces the routes by which money and power are able to filter out the news fit to print, marginalize dissent, and allow for the government and dominant private interests to get their message across to the public.
>
> (1988: 1–2)

Manufacturing Consent proceeds to deliver a blistering attack on the state of the US media system, and by inference those in other western liberal democracies. Their provocative formulation of the 'propaganda model' (the term had hitherto largely been associated with communist and fascist regimes, not liberal democracies) is based on five mutually supporting media 'filters'. Together these are said to explain how and why the media systematically propagate the views and values of the dominant political elite and corporate economic interests. They can be briefly summarized:

- Filter 1: *Size, concentrated ownership, owner wealth, and profit orientation of the dominant media firms*. In capitalist societies media industries are essentially businesses organized in pursuit of profits. In a bid to tame costs and control markets, corporations consolidate through mergers and take-overs and this, in turn, squeezes out competition by producing prohibitive start-up costs and unfair market advantages. James Curran and Jean Seaton's *Power Without Responsibility* (1997) and its discussion of the historical rise and emasculation of the radical press in Britain by market forces is used as a classic example of this process of market monopolization. More recently, other authors provide evidence for how this same process is now being played out on a world-wide scale, intensified through digitalization and the increased opportunities for technological and industrial convergence that this has generated (Herman 2000; Thussu 2000; McChesney 2003). The commanding elites of corporate media enterprises, say Herman and Chomsky, wield enormous power and they are fully integrated into the circuits and networks of political and economic power.
- Filter 2: *Advertising as the primary income source of the mass media*. Advertisers exert tremendous power and influence, according to Herman and Chomsky, by selecting and supporting 'sympathetic' media outlets to advertise their products. With some media depending as much, if not more, on advertising revenue in proportion to sales revenue, advertisers assume a position of considerable economic importance and potential editorial influence. Moreover, through time, this corporate patronage becomes instilled in the culture and outlooks of media organizations which commission and produce media products generally supportive of business and elite interests.
- Filter 3: *The reliance of the media on information provided by government, business, and 'experts' funded and approved by these primary sources and agents of power*. Media routinely rely on government and corporate sources and this grants the latter privileged access to advance preferred views and values. This argument finds some support in ethnographic studies of newsroom practices (Schlesinger 1978; Tuchman 1978; Fishman 1980) and also in systematic studies of news access conducted by, for example, the early Glasgow University Media Group (GUMG). Elite media access comes about, according to Herman and Chomsky, because of the high prestige, credibility and presumed 'objective' knowledge associated with these sources, and these also help journalists to proclaim their own independence warding off possible criticisms about their news 'objectivity' (see also Tuchman 1972). Costs of media production are also effectively subsidized by powerful institutions of government and corporations who provide source material to the media free of charge: 'only the corporate sector has the resources to produce public information and propaganda on the scale of the Pentagon' (Herman and Chomsky 1988: 21).
- Filter 4: ' *"Flak" as a means of disciplining the media*'. 'Flak' refers to the negative

responses to media statements or programme content by politicians or publics organized by vested interests and this can exercise a chilling effect on media and journalists long after the initial criticism. 'The ability to produce flak', say Herman and Chomsky, 'is directly related to power' (1988: 26), and this can work both directly (phone calls from the White House, for example), or indirectly (by influencing various constituencies of interest who organize boycotts, or by setting up right-wing monitoring or think-tank operations). The government invariably is a major producer of flak targeting the media and seeking to curb any deviations from its preferred line.

- Filter 5: *'Anticommunism as a national religion and control mechanism'*. At the time of writing *Manufacturing Consent*, Herman and Chomsky observed how a deep-seated and seemingly irrational hatred of communism was embedded in much of US political culture and wider civil society. 'Communism', seen as antithetical to private property and threatening ruling class status and wealth, was used to mobilize populations against 'the enemy' and, because it was 'fuzzy', could easily be deployed against anyone who was seen to support non-capitalist states and/or radical agendas. Today, notwithstanding the collapse of the Soviet Union and other East European communist states, the sanctity and value of private property are arguably as engrained in national cultures as ever (Herman 2000). Post-9/11, however, many have perceived a new enemy on the scene and this has similarly been put to work in the media to mobilize fears and public opinion in support of the US's declared war on terror (Zelizer and Allan 2002; Altheide 2003; Harvey 2003).

Together, then, these five filters 'fix the premises of discourse and interpretation, and the definition of what is newsworthy' and 'they explain the basis and operations of what amount to propaganda campaigns' (Herman and Chomsky 1988: 2). The propaganda model was used to explain how the US media reported 'worthy' and 'unworthy victims' in Latin America and wars in Indochina in ways that could only bolster the US government's stated views and policies, no matter their bloody consequences for innocents abroad.

The propaganda model provides a formidable critique of the media's involvement in processes of 'manufacturing consent' and encapsulates, as we have heard, many of the critical arguments deployed by other theoretical approaches within this paradigm. But how adequate is it for a comprehensive understanding and explanation of mediatized conflicts in today's societies?

Some critical reflections

There is something unnerving about the 'propaganda model', not because it is entirely without foundation but because it is seemingly all-encompassing, ideologically functional and apparently unopposed. The alleged synergy of interests and outlooks between state, corporate interests and media operations permits little sense of the historical dynamics, contests of interest and even contradictions, both economic and political, which exist within and between different centres of power and how these can change through time. Both state and media are depicted in monolithic and relatively ahistorical terms, with the logic of capitalism and elite power seemingly cementing together their respective fates for all time. Is it possible, we may want to ask, that there is more movement, differentiation and contention within and between state, media and corporations than is suggested?

Given the study's social theorization of US society and media in terms of capitalism and market forces, the propaganda model tends to marginalize other forms of conflict and challenge. Issues of 'race', ethnicity, gender and sexual politics, for example, or the environment and countless single-issue campaigns, all pose challenges to political and corporate power and some have made significant advances in mainstream media across recent years as we shall see. Diverse struggles and their forms of mediatization cannot, it seems, always be adequately explained, or explained away, by the generalizing claims of the propaganda model (Cottle 2003a, 2003b).

Though studies of journalism production and professional practices can lend support to the propaganda model's claims about media dependency on dominant sources and corporate and government public relations, these same studies have also demonstrated a more complex and often decidedly less cosy relationship between media and powerful sources. The latter do not always secure privileged access across all fields of contention, and they can also find themselves dislodged from authorial dominance as major issues and public crises unfold through time and exert their own determinacy. In other words, there is often more complexity and contingency in the interactions, in the play of power, between sources and media and how these unfold through time than the propaganda model predicts (Schlesinger 1990; Thompson 1995; Robinson 2002; Cottle 2004a). Journalism codes and norms of professionalism may also condition interactions with the powerful and do so in ways that are not always beneficial to the powerful source (Soloski 1989; Hallin 1994).

The propaganda model, as well as paying relatively little attention to the professional world of media production, also pays scant attention to the complexities of media representation. It is as if the meanings and messages of the media are self-evident and require little if any interpretation or detailed analysis. Researchers today, however, have become increasingly sensitized to the social constructionist, rhetorical and performative nature of language, images and texts and how representations are implicated in actively producing meanings for understanding 'reality'. Arguably, then, we need to pay more attention to the nature and forms of media visuals, talk and text and how these are organized into narratives and discourses that construct meanings, not simply reflect them, if we want to better understand the nature of media propaganda. Once we begin to enquire a little more closely into media forms and texts, however, we often find that media messages are often less ideologically pure and closed than is assumed. 'Meaning', as one media theorist observed, 'is protean and equivocal;

it is difficult to grasp and pin down' (Dahlgren 1988: 291) and this, in turn, raises further questions about audiences and reception.

The title of Herman and Chomsky's book is *Manufacturing Consent*, but how and in what sense do they know that the media do indeed 'manufacture consent'? People obey or seemingly 'consent' both within their everyday lives and in systems of economic and political power for a variety of reasons and motivations including: tradition, apathy, pragmatic acquiescence and instrumental acceptance as well as, following Marx, 'the dull compulsion of the economic' (Abercrombie et al. 1980; Held 1987). Ideology theorized as 'social cement', in other words, is often overrated as an explanation for system maintenance. We cannot simply assume that media propaganda, even if documented, necessarily succeeds ideologically, or, even if it does, that this constitutes the principal explanation for popular compliance. Studies of media audiences quickly reveal that there is more cultural translation, context dependency and active sense making going on in processes of media reception than generalizing claims about 'manufacturing consent' appear to envisage, or investigate.

In the years following the publication of *Manufacturing Consent* the media landscape has also been transformed by new technologies and delivery systems, many of them digital and interactive, and many of them containing new opportunities for political manipulation and economic commoditization (Herman 2000). They also, however, present new spaces and opportunities for political organization and engagement (Bennett 2003; Hassan 2004; van de Donk et al. 2004). The propaganda model, as we have heard, works with an elite-dominated, top-down, few-to-the-many, model of communication but does it still equally apply in the context of a more horizontal and interactive, many-to-many, network of globally dispersed and interconnected communications? Before we can confidently talk about media domination and systemic closure in today's media environment we have to examine new media forms and consider to what extent these may circumvent or simply ignore national borders, and dominant political cultures, and impact the ecology of communications more generally.

This leads to one last observation. This is the curious evacuation of the political at the heart of the propaganda model. It is as if propaganda were not really needed because there is so little evidence of struggle, conflict and contention surrounding the operations and performance of the media. This, as already intimated in Chapter 1, doesn't sit easily with the views of many contemporary social theorists who see and theorize multiple fault lines, fissures and fractures in the world today driving new social and political agendas and cultural outlooks and identities. The five filters outlined earlier are apparently so effective, so overpowering, that the force-field of politics and power has become effectively stifled. When we move to consider a range of mediatized conflicts, however, we shall find that there is often more contention and more complexity in play than the manufacturing consent thesis seems capable of predicting or theoretically accommodating.

In summary, the propaganda model appears to short-circuit the complexities and dynamics of conflict-driven representations unfolding through time, as well as the strategic struggles informing media production and the cultural mediations inflecting their reception. Is the propaganda model, and the manufacturing consent paradigm more generally, thereby rendered theoretically redundant? Most definitely not. Notwithstanding the problems and issues raised earlier, the critical thrust of the manufacturing consent paradigm propels researchers to focus on the structural advantages of governmental power and corporate interests and how these can manipulate public agendas and, possibly, mobilize public opinion in respect of deep-seated issues and concerns such as war, terrorism and foreign policy. The manufacturing consent paradigm, for all its tendencies towards generalization, economic reductionism and ideological functionalism, provides a necessary means for engaging with important levers of economic and political power and how media performance is often subservient to these.

The media contest paradigm

Recent developments in the field of study have contributed renewed impetus to consider the democratic possibilities, as well as democratic foreclosures, enacted by media today. These include the decline of Marxist theorization with its privileging of class analysis and today's increased recognition of the complexities of the social landscape; evidence of contest and contention *within* media representations as well as the strategic interventions informing their production; occasional successful media campaigns by 'challenger' groups, such as environmental activists; and the changing media ecology including new interactive communication technologies and communicative possibilities. All have contributed to the unsettling of earlier theoretical certainties. Though arguably no less concerned about the mechanisms and inequalities of power than those working within the manufacturing consent paradigm, theorists working within the 'media contest' paradigm see the media in more dynamic, oppositional and politically contingent ways. Here the media are typically approached as sites of powered struggle and unequal contestation, rather than as a foregone ideological conclusion or as a mouthpiece for dominant interests.

Notions of media as 'public sphere' (Habermas 1974, 1989, 1996) – a communicative space in which ideas and information, discourses and opinions find public representation and elaboration and thereby help constitute civil societies – chime closely with the media contest paradigm and in fact the two often overlap considerably (Elliott 1986; Garnham 1986; Curran 1991; Frazer 1992; Hallin 1994; Dahlgren 1995; Husband 2000). We shall explore important ideas and debates surrounding the media approached as public sphere later. Other infusions into the 'media contest' paradigm include empirical analyses of media production and the complex interactions, and sometimes uncertain outcomes, between media sources and media in different fields of contention – findings that will also be returned to later.

Studies attending to media reporting in periods of state disunity and elite dissensus around policy issues and the opportunity that these conditions produce for more engaged media commentary and criticism, can also be positioned under this overarching 'media contest' paradigm (for example, Hallin 1986; Bennett 1990; Butler 1995; Wolfsfeld 1997; Robinson 2001; Entman 2004), even if exponents of the manufacturing consent paradigm may prefer to see these as aberrations only proving the rule. Numerous studies of media representations of conflict and how, particularly, accessed voices and participants fare within the parameters and possibilities of different media forms also feed into the media contest paradigm with its heightened sensitivity to the play of mediatized power (Livingstone and Lunt 1994; Elliott et al. 1996; Clayman and Heritage 2002; Cottle 2002).

Here we examine the exemplary work of the Israeli scholar, Gadi Wolfsfeld, and particularly his major work, *Media and Political Conflict: News from the Middle East* (1997). This outlines a 'political contest model' and helps to theoretically and empirically ground many of the characteristic features of the media contest paradigm. Wolfsfeld defines political contest and conflicts broadly:

> The competition over the news media is a major element in modern political conflicts. The Pro-Choice and Pro-Life movements in America, the Serbians and the Muslims in Bosnia, Amnesty International, Russia, Chechnya, Al-Qaida, and the American government all compete for media attention as a means to achieve political influence. Each antagonist attempts to promote its own frames of the conflict to the news media in an attempt to mobilize political support for its cause. If we can understand the rules of combat and the factors that lead to success and failure in the arena, we will be one-step closer to understanding the role the news media plays in such conflicts.
>
> The focus . . . will be on the role of the news media in *unequal political contests*. These include all public confrontations between a government and at least one other antagonist in which the state (or one state) has a significantly superior amount of coercive resources at its disposal . . . many conflicts fall under this category: protests, terrorist acts, riots, rebellions, revolutions, and all-out wars between powerful countries and weaker ones.
>
> (1997: 2; 2003: 81)

Wolfsfeld builds his political contest model on five major arguments, implicitly challenging the more blanket assertions of the manufacturing consent approach above, and aims to put politics and struggle back into the theoretical mix of media control and performance. 'Competition over the news media', can best be seen he argues, as 'part of a larger and more significant contest among political antagonists for political control' (1997: 2). His five major arguments can be briefly summarized:

- *'The political process is more likely to have an influence on the news media than the news media are on the political process'*. Here the media are contextualized in relation to the wider political context: (a) the media are more inclined to react to events happening elsewhere than to initiate them; (b) political antagonists will seek to use the media depending on how their political goals and the political context of their struggles change through time; and (c) political decisions can have a major influence on the ownership and control of the media. Avoiding media centrism and economic reductionism, Wolfsfeld's schema accents the political within media contests while incorporating a strong sense of the unequal state of power that conditions them across time.

- ' "*The authorities' " level of control over the political environment is one of the key variables that determine the role of the news media in political conflicts*'. The conduct of political struggle and control over media representations are seen to be related and can therefore change through time. When authorities dominate the struggle outside the media sphere, so they will find it easier to control the media environment but when they begin to lose control to challenger groups this grants the media an increased array of perspectives and voices, and challenger groups may now be able to promote their own media frames.

- '*The role of the news media in political conflicts varies over time and circumstance*'. This important claim implicitly challenges a priori theoretical views about media and the operations of political and economic power conceived in relatively settled or static terms. The role of the news media in conflicts, according to Wolfsfeld (1997), varies according to: 'the political context of the conflict, the resources, skills, and political power of the players involved, the relationship between the press and each antagonist, the state of public opinion, the ability of the journalists to gain access to the conflict events, and last but certainly not least what is happening in the field'. Thus, not only does the role of the news media vary across different conflicts, it can also change within the course of a particular conflict.

- '*Those who hope to understand variations in the role of the news media must look at the competition among antagonists along two dimensions: one structural and the other cultural*'. Here Wolfsfeld makes the important observation that antagonists compete both over *access* to the news media and *media frames*. While the former prompts *structural* analysis of the interactions and dependencies between media sources and the media, the latter invites *cultural* analysis of how norms, beliefs and routines influence the construction of media frames or the guiding interpretative frameworks organizing news representations. This second dimension reminds us that 'political contests are also struggles over meaning in which success within the news media can lead to higher levels of political support'.

- '*While authorities have tremendous advantages over challengers in the quantity and quality of media coverage they receive, many challengers can overcome these obstacles and use the news media as a tool for political influence*'. Qualifying the story of gloom and doom proposed in some versions of the manufacturing consent paradigm Wolfsfeld encourages us to consider how challenger groups and interests can nonetheless manage to secure media access and promote frames supportive of their particular aims and agendas. External events and political blunders of the powerful, for example, present opportunities for challengers and here media may draw on culturally pre-existent anti-authority frames (see also Thompson 1995; Kitzinger 2004).

Together, then, these five arguments propose that mediatized conflicts are neither constant nor linear. They are often composed of unequally weighted sides, have different determinants and present different opportunities and all these can change through struggle and time. Wolfsfeld paints a helpful metaphor to encapsulate his political contest model and the media's 'multi-purpose arenas':

> The competition between authorities and challengers over the news media is as fascinating and unpredictable as politics itself. In some ways the central arena resembles the modern sports facility that can be converted into several structures, each designed for a different type of event. Sometimes the arena is used for lavish spectacles in which officials show off their most colourful costumes and weapons. At other times it is a place for fierce contests in which challengers and authorities square off in brutal combat. And at yet other times it becomes a theatre in the round putting on tragic morality plays about the plight of the oppressed and the need for social change. The goal of this model is to better explain the political, social, and situational factors that dictate how and when the arena is transformed.
>
> (1997: 5)

Some critical reflections

The political contest model and the media contest paradigm more generally, provide an antidote to the bleak, seemingly unassailable, determinants of the manufacturing consent approach discussed earlier. Wolfsteld recognizes the structural imbalances of power and media opportunity and how these benefit government and other authorities in their information campaigns while also theorizing how challenger groups can make their voices heard and how media performance shifts through time and circumstance, and not always in support of dominant interests. In many respects this is a persuasive and scholarly approach. But what are its possible weaknesses and blind-spots?

Wolfsfeld's model deliberately aims to put 'the political' back into the theoretical frame but arguably does so at the expense of 'the economic'. In consequence he makes passing reference only to structures of media ownership, commercial imperatives and the general commoditization of culture. Though we may want to question an explanatory approach that relies on a heavy economic determinism for the reasons alluded to earlier, we may nonetheless expect to see some theorization of how market and commercial forces penetrate and condition the operations of the media. For example, how media genres developed to appeal to target audiences and consumers shape media frames and condition struggles for media access.

The theoretical habitus of the manufacturing consent paradigm is intellectually indebted to earlier positions of critical theory that continue to imbue it with a sense of historical teleology and condemnatory moralism in respect of capitalism and its global expansionism. These theoretical motifs often provide the backdrop, and often the foreground, of the analyses of contemporary media performance. Wolfsfeld's study, in comparison, pitches its theoretical sights in more analytically focused, empirically comparative and inductive ways. While his accenting of 'the political' helps avoid the twin traps of historical teleology and economic reductionism, his selected political contests do not appear to be theorized as part of the longer-term historical struggles or the (globally) powered geometry that infuse them. In the context of the struggles in the Middle East, the focus of his study, such oversights may be considered a political shortcoming.

Wolfsfeld's insistence that we approach media conflicts sensitized to both structural and cultural dimensions is nonetheless welcome, and helps to bridge the disciplinary divides that too often unhelpfully structure social science and humanity-based approaches to media analysis. Today we need to better integrate sociological analyses of the strategic power enacted by 'authorities' and 'challengers' in their bid to access and control the media with culturalist readings of media texts and performances, signs and symbols, and how these condition and frame media representations. Wolfsfeld's own studies, however, tend to rely for the most part on quantitative forms of content analysis and are confined to press reporting. As such they have not made use of available textual and visual methodologies. Significant silences also pertain in respect of empirical engagement with audiences and readers and how they make sense of the messages and meanings circulated by the media.

Arguably, a deeper engagement with contemporary positions of cultural theory, and not just in terms of how media texts and representations 'mean' or signify, but also how they can become resources for identity formation, is also required. How mediatized conflicts enter into the world of the everyday and the interactions and outlooks of communities in conflict, promises to take us deeper into how media representations circulate, are made sense of and become embedded in conflicted societies. For these deeper, culturalist and anthropological insights we have to look elsewhere. We also need to enquire into how new media technologies may be reconfiguring the play of mediatized power – both strategic and symbolic – in the Middle East and elsewhere.

Finally we may also want to add an important caveat to the political contest model and its claim that political action taking place outside the media influences the media more than vice versa. On occasion, as we shall see later, the media can in fact become the principal mover of mediatized events and mediatized public crises, performatively sponsoring and/or moving them forward in campaigning or championing mode. Such media phenomena need to be granted their due in a more comprehensive approach to mediatized conflicts and be thoroughly researched, theorized and explained.

Wolfsfeld's model, notwithstanding these criticisms, provides a sociologically informed and politically focused model that contributes significantly to the 'media contest' paradigm. It exemplifies, in an exemplary way, how many researchers studying mediatized conflict have moved to a less theoretically closed, more politically contingent and dynamic understanding of media and conflict and thereby helps to explain how struggles for media access and framing can sometimes play out in unpredictable ways, challenging authorities and centres of dominance.

The media culture paradigm

Our third paradigm contributes to the theoretical structuration of the study of mediatized conflicts by centring on questions of culture and cultural mediation. This paradigm, like the media contest paradigm, challenges the seemingly inescapable logics of the manufacturing consent paradigm but does so by enquiring into the complexities of popular culture and how media culture seemingly permeates everyday life and identities. Here processes of identity formation and the consumption of media texts and meanings by audiences assume focal interest – whether in respect of cultural readings of media texts or the contexts of media use and reception. While acknowledging the concentrations of economic and symbolic power located within the cultural industries, their increasing global dominance and relation to centres of western and US political hegemony, approaches within this paradigm also observe the multiple resistances, pleasures and competing discourses that play out on the contested media landscape. Differentiating it from the media contest paradigm, however, the media culture paradigm is based fundamentally on the explication of 'culture' as the medium of social representation and engagement rather than, say, the sociological terrain of media production and the source-media interactions or the powered strategizing of conflict protagonists.

The media culture paradigm develops out of the seminal period of cultural studies theorizing. Earlier this had creatively, and eclectically, reworked neo-Marxist theorization (Antonio Gramsci, Raymond Williams, E.P. Thompson, Lousi Althusser) with variants of European structuralism (Ferdinand de Saussure, Roland Barthes, Levi Strauss) to theorize how processes of ideology and, following the ideas of the Italian Marxist Antonio Gramsci, how struggles for hegemony, are played out on the terrain of popular culture. Necessarily this entailed a more encompassing interest in how different subject positions – youth, gender, ethnicity, national identity as well as class – became publicly represented and contested within the media sphere (Hall 1982; Turner 1996). Questions of 'representation' and media thereby became positioned centre-stage in cultural studies theorizing. Following the influential analyses of Stuart Hall and his colleagues at the Centre of Contemporary Cultural Studies at Birmingham in the UK (Hall et al. 1980), the intellectual stable of ideas associated with cultural studies theorizing has continued to expand, regionalize and factionalize with new infusions from, and border disputes erupting between, varieties of feminism, post-structuralism and post-colonial theory.

An eloquent practitioner of contemporary cultural studies theorizing, whose work has direct bearing for an understanding of mediatized conflicts, is Douglas Kellner and it is his recent work that serves as our exemplar of the media culture paradigm. Kellner is a prolific writer, having produced numerous books and articles over the years, but at the heart of his recent books *Media Culture: Cultural Studies, Identity and Politics Between the Modern and the Postmodern* (1995) and *Media Spectacle* (2003) are his central views on media approached in terms of media culture and media spectacles. Kellner opens *Media Culture* with the following:

> A media culture has emerged in which images, sounds, and spectacles help pro-
> duce the fabric of everyday life, dominating leisure time, sharing political views
> and social behaviour, and providing the materials out of which people forge their
> very identities. Radio, television, film, and the other media products of the culture
> industries provide the models of what it means to be male or female, successful or
> a failure, powerful or powerless. Media culture also provides the materials out of
> which many people construct their sense of class, of ethnicity and race, of nation-
> ality, of sexuality, of 'us' and 'them'. Media culture helps shape the prevalent
> view of the world and deepest values: it defines what is good or bad, positive or
> negative, moral or evil.
>
> (1995: 1)

Here we meet an approach, then, which sees media as part and parcel of everyday life and as inextricably fused with late modern forms of existence. Questions of identity, of who we feel and think we are, and how we define and position ourselves in relation to others, become an integral dimension of mediated culture. It is noteworthy, there-fore, that Kellner accents questions of identity at the very outset of his book. Clearly there is more going on in this formulation than the representation of issues narrowly conceived. Mediated images and ideas are capable of summoning deep-seated values, moral commitments and sense of collectivity – claims that have particular bearing on how mediatized conflict can summon publics and support. Kellner also wants to open up a theoretical space for understanding cultural contests:

> I argue that media culture is a contested terrain across which key social groups
> and competing political ideologies struggle for dominance and that individuals
> live these struggles through the images, discourses, myths, and spectacles of media
> culture.
>
> (1995: 2)

The themes of resistance and contestation inflect Kellner's theorization of media cul-ture as well as his identification of media spectacles which have become, he argues, a defining and central component of contemporary life:

> Social and political conflicts are increasingly played out on the screens of media
> culture, which display spectacles such as sensational murder cases, terrorist

bombings, celebrity and political sex scandals, and the explosive violence of everyday life. Media culture not only takes up always-expanding amounts of time and energy, but also provides ever more material for fantasy, dreaming, modelling thought and behaviour and identities.

(2003: 1)

This theorization of wider conflicts expressed through increasingly prevalent media spectacles signals a further dimension of mediatized conflict, and one that has tended to be overlooked in our two previous paradigms. Also underdeveloped in our two previous paradigms is the changing nature of communications and the possibilities for waging struggle opened up by new media. Kellner explicitly seeks to theoretically redress this lacuna:

> The changes in the current conjuncture are arguably as thoroughgoing and dramatic as the shift from the stage of market and the competitive and *laissez-faire* capitalism theorized by Marx to the stage of state-monopoly capitalism critically analyzed by the Frankfurt school in the 1930s. Currently, we are entering a new form of *technocapitalism* marked by a synthesis of capital and technology and the information and entertainment industries, all of which is producing an 'infotainment society' and spectacle culture.
>
> (2003: 11)

In order to grapple with the pervasive and penetrative nature of media culture Kellner proposes a 'multiperspectival cultural studies' that 'draws on a wide range of textual and critical strategies to interpret, criticize and deconstruct the artifact under scrutiny' (1995: 98). 'Culture', for Kellner, does not reside exclusively in the text, however, but is sociohistorically situated, often contested, and is expressed in and through media forms.

In summary, Kellner's theorization of media culture and media spectacles, situated within a broader and developing cultural studies framework, provides a further optic on mediatized conflicts. Something of the Frankfurt School's totalizing pessimism register in his views on today's 'technocapitalism' and commoditized 'spectacle culture', but so too do themes of identity, contestation and resistance. These as well as globalization and new media technologies all become worked into the theoretical mix. This, then, presents as an engaged and critical theoretical approach to the media, and one that also has relevance for the interrogation of mediatized conflict. But what are its limitations?

Some critical reflections

Kellner's theorizing of contemporary media culture and spectacles grants media a central presence within contemporary societies. Media culture, as we have heard, becomes insinuated into the life worlds of everyday existence and identities as well as the conduct and powered play of diverse struggles. Media culture, in effect, appears to be everywhere, colonizing both self and society. But how useful is this theoretical valorization of 'the cultural' when applied in the study of mediatized conflict? I want to develop this criticism in a number of related respects.

This generalizing view of 'media culture' and, increasingly, 'media spectacles' gives the impression that these features of late-modern societies become not only prevalent but all enveloping in respect of identities and social relations. We may want to object, however, that 'media culture', in so far as this constitutes a discernible object of enquiry, draws upon the social formation that exists outside of, or apart from, the media sphere – no matter the advanced state of media colonization in contemporary societies. A focus on media culture, then, can all too easily slide into a form of media centrism or even media determinism and occludes from view the complex of social relations, powered discourses and organizational and collective arrangements that impact on mediatized conflicts – sometimes from afar – and how these play out across time.

What appears to be missing from this media culture, media-centric, view is a closer engagement with the production contexts, social dynamics and wider trajectories of conflicts which inform and even, on occasion, alter the course of media phenomena, and which do so from outside the media sphere. To be fair to Kellner he acknowledges the importance of political economy, studies of news organizations and strategic propaganda campaigns by state and other interests and has even integrated findings from these approaches into his own studies (see Kellner (1992) and (1995: 199–228)). But these, it has to be said, appear to be grafted on rather than fully theorized and empirically integrated in his 'multiperspectival cultural studies' approach. The latter remains first and last an optic for 'reading' media culture and spectacle. Some successful media strategies, as noted earlier, may not even register within media culture at all given the effectiveness of source strategies of 'enclosure' – of keeping images and information out of the media (Ericson et al. 1989). The media contest paradigm, with its sociologically detailed, politically dynamic and empirically engaged analysis of the media provides a necessary corrective to this underdeveloped aspect of Kellner's contribution and the media culture paradigm more generally.

Kellner situates media culture in respect of the underlying trajectories of globalizing technocapitalism, but his concern to identify and illuminate the contested nature of popular culture, its resistances and progressive possibilities produces an unresolved and uneasy theoretical tension and explanatory gap between the two.

Media spectacles, Kellner observes, are an increasingly prevalent characteristic of contemporary media culture but if we want to better understand their differing trajectories and impacts, not only do we need to attend to the struggles that inform them but we also need to work harder to analytically distinguish between them and their effects, both hegemonic and disruptive. Here we need to strive for increased analytical and explanatory precision rather than collapsing differences and diversity of mediated phenomena into a totalizing view of contemporary 'media culture' and 'media spectacle' (Cottle 2006).

Kellner's work theoretically reintroduces the audience but his empirical engagement with actual audiences, as with both the previous exemplars, remains empirically underdeveloped. Audiences tend to be recovered via readings of the appeals and positioning of media texts and therefore have, at best, a phantom existence through the discussion of media culture and spectacle. Empirical studies of actual audiences and processes of cultural negotiation and appropriation, as well as possible resistance, now need to figure much more prominently within studies of mediatized conflict, and especially so in the media culture paradigm where so much theoretical store is placed on questions of media and identity.

One last observation concerns the tendency within cultural studies theorizing *writ large* to plunder media texts for evidence of contending discourses and the signs of resistance. Too often this political commitment to recover the oppositions embedded within media texts overlooks the possibility that not everything can always be traced back to the operations of power, however we may conceptualize this (Schudson 2000). The conventions and settled forms of media genres, for example, illuminate various ways in which mediatized conflicts are publicly constrained or elaborated (Cottle and Rai 2006), though these may not always best be conceived as expressive of the wider play of cultural power and its contending discourses.

These criticisms dent Kellner's theoretical edifice but they do not render it a write-off. His recent work, in fact, represents an eloquent, wide-ranging and in many ways penetrating effort to both theorize and research contemporary media culture, drawing upon the critical tradition of media scholarship while simultaneously reconfiguring and augmenting this to address contemporary times. We shall return to ideas of media culture and media spectacle in the chapters that follow.

Chapter summary

This chapter has reviewed and critically engaged with three exemplary theoretical approaches, each of which gives powerful vent to influential paradigms currently directing research into mediatized conflicts. Notwithstanding their respective blind spots and deficiencies, each provides sensitizing concepts and theoretical frameworks of use for a more encompassing, multidimensional and dynamic approach to the study of contemporary mediatized conflict. Each also provides a different vantage point from which to view, conceptualize and interrogate the media's possible contribution to a 'public sphere' of engaged social intercourse and interaction (see Figure 2.1).

The manufacturing consent paradigm, and its exposition in Herman and Chomsky's (1988) propaganda model, powerfully underlines the industrialized and capitalist nature of contemporary media and the formidable economic structures and political controls that 'filter' media content in the interests of corporate and elite political power. Seen through this lens the media rarely contribute to an arena of democratic engagement and public deliberation but to a distorted realm of communication in which propaganda and dominant views and values are disseminated largely unopposed.

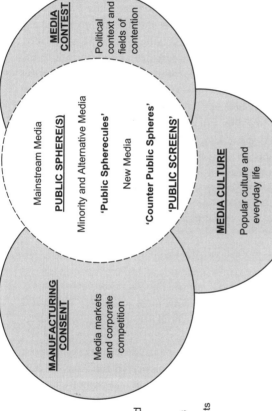

Key Concepts:
Strategic and Symbolic Communication
Access, Frames, Political Dynamics

Guiding Theory:
Sociology of Organizations, News and News Sources, Political Communications

Analytical Focus:
Strategic communications and media intervention

Essential View:
Media as multi-purpose arenas in which strategic and symbolic conflicts and contention are waged

Epistemology:
Analytical Empiricism

MEDIA CONTEST

Political context and fields of contention

Mainstream Media

PUBLIC SPHERE(S)

Minority and Alternative Media

'Public Spherecules'

New Media

'Counter Public Spheres'

'PUBLIC SCREENS'

MEDIA CULTURE

Popular culture and everyday life

Analytical Focus:
The play of cultural power and public constitution of identities

Essential View:
Media culture as pervasive, meaningful and contested, and constitutive of identities

Epistemology:
Hermeneutic/Interpretivist

Key Concepts:
Popular culture and everyday life, media spectacle and entertainment, discourse, identity, techno-culture

Guiding Theory:
Cultural Studies
Post-structuralism

MANUFACTURING CONSENT

Media markets and corporate competition

Key Concepts:
Cultural Industries
Dominance/Hegemony
Ideology/Legitimation

Guiding Theory:
Critical Theory/
Neo-Marxism
Political Economy

Analytical Focus:
Economic determinants and instrumental media power

Essential View:
Media as cultural industries manufacturing consent in support of dominant interests

Epistemology:
Critical Realism

Figure 2.1 Paradigms and the public sphere(s)

Generally informing the manufacturing consent paradigm is a methodological stance of *critical realism* explicating the structures and dynamics of power that lie behind the phenomenal forms of media output (Murdock and Golding 1984; McChesney 2003). For sharper illumination of how these general forces become mediated, negotiated and opposed at the level of social organization, professional practice and cultural mediation, we need more analytically refined foci.

The media contest paradigm generally contributes grounded and closely engaged levels of analysis, opening up to view a more contingent and politically contested view of media power and its operations. This perspective, often based on a method-ological approach of *analytical empiricism*, shines light on the complexities and strat-egies of media access, the dynamics of contention unfolding through time, and how struggles are framed in different media arenas. Political dynamics and the opportun-ities and risks of media participation all find increased salience in this paradigm, as do empirical ethnographies of news production, media–source interactions and theoriza-tion of media as 'public sphere(s)'. The latter becomes conceptualized as public arena(s) where strategic interests and symbolic contests are publicly waged, won and lost (see Figure 2.1). Gadi Wolfsfeld's 'political contest model', as we have heard, provides an exemplary instance of this approach.

And, finally, the media culture paradigm is struck by the incessant and all-pervasive glow of contemporary 'media culture' now deeply insinuated within popular culture, everyday life and identities. Here the dazzle and bright lights of media spectacles attract research interest and media culture is conceptualized as a terrain on which messages, meanings and identities are visualized and consumed and social struggles become culturally embodied and played out. This calls for a more *interpretivist* and *hermeneutic* methodological stance to media texts and cultural processes of meaning making. And here the media 'public sphere' is likely to be interrogated in respect of the genres and forms of popular culture and reconceived, and even renamed, as 'public screens', to signal a shift away from rationalist preconceptions about democratic debate and representation to one where spectacle and images are granted their cultural due (see Figure 2.1).

The fast-changing ecology of media communications also prompts theorists work-ing within each of these paradigms to engage with these developments, whether in respect of the proliferating outlets of mainstream media, the development of alterna-tive and minority media, or new interactive and digital media and networks including the Internet. Ideas of pluralized 'public spheres', 'counter public spheres' and even a multiplicity of politically fragmented and isolated 'public spherecules' (Gitlin 1998) have all been coined to try and help make sense of these developments, and these can also be mapped in respect of our three paradigms (see Figure 2.1). While the manu-facturing consent paradigm theorizes these new developments through a prism that focuses on continuing communication inequalities, digital divides and the marginaliza-tion of dissent, the media contest paradigm is disposed to examine their political efficacy and possible destabilizing and/or progressive impacts within the wider media ecology, and the media culture paradigm explores their cultural ramifications for identities of difference and new conceptions of the political. In such ways these paradigms continue to accommodate new developments and, notwithstanding identified weaknesses and blind spots, provide productive optics for a more multidimensional approach to contemporary mediatized conflicts.

Finally, it is worth noting that all three of our exemplary studies have engaged in comparative analysis of selected mediatized conflicts. None, in other words, has been so empirically neglectful or theoretically arrogant to develop their arguments and frameworks without also engaging with instances of media performance and output. This respect for evidence and argument, as well as for conceptual elaboration and theory building, also informs this book which now moves via a series of different mediatized conflicts to build a more multidimensional, dynamic and encompassing approach for the study of contemporary mediatized conflict.

Recommended reading

Allan, S. (2004a) *News Culture*. Maidenhead: Open University Press.

Cottle, S. (ed.) (2003a) *Media Organization and Production*. London: Sage.

Cottle, S. (ed.) (2003b) *News, Public Relations and Power*. London: Sage.

Herman, E. (2000) 'The Propaganda Model: A Retrospective', *Journalism Studies* 1(1): 101–12.

Herman, E. and Chomsky, N. (1988) *Manufacturing Consent: The Political Economy of the Mass Media*. New York: Pantheon.

Kellner, D. (1995) *Media Culture: Cultural Studies, Identity and Politics Between the Modern and Postmodern*. London: Routledge.

Kellner, D. (2003) *Media Spectacle*. London: Routledge.

Wolfsfeld, G. (1997) *Media and Political Conflict: News from the Middle East*. Cambridge: Cambridge University Press.

Wolfsfeld, G. (2003) 'The Political Contest Model', in S. Cottle (ed.) *News, Public Relations and Power*. London: Sage.

REPORTING DEMONSTRATIONS AND PROTEST: PUBLIC SPHERE(S), PUBLIC SCREENS

This first substantive case study of mediatized conflicts focuses on demonstrations and public protest. Historically these are means by which citizens can register their collective disagreement and dissent, build public support and legitimacy for their aims, and influence governments, policy formation and even societal change. In democratic societies they are an established mechanism by which citizens can express their civil rights and, in non-democratic societies, they are frequently used as part of the struggle for democracy and the extension of citizenship. This chapter sets out to examine how major demonstrations have been reported in western societies and explicates the theoretical frameworks guiding this research. We begin by consulting two 'classic' studies of demonstrations and protests – one conducted in the United Kingdom and one in the United States – and review their principal findings and key explanations for the 'political framing' and 'ideological closure' discerned in mainstream media reporting. These studies provide critical findings rehearsed in numerous studies ever since, to the point perhaps where they have become uncritically accepted as universal features of all media protest and demonstration reporting.

More recent research, however, opens up further levels of complexity and discerned political opportunity. These are found in the discursive contention and often spectacular forms of contemporary mediatized protests as well as considerations of geopolitics, dramaturgy and changing repertoires of protest. Attending to these dimensions of demonstration and protest introduces more politically contingent, historically dynamic and tactically evolving interactions between protestors and media and these help to explain how some demonstrations and protests can in fact buck the media trends documented in earlier studies and secure sympathetic media coverage to advance their strategic and political aims.

Current approaches to media conceptualized in terms of 'public sphere', or 'public screens', touched on in the previous chapter, also invite a more discursively contested view of media performance and encourage us to rethink ideas of media spectacle in more politically productive terms. Here we consider studies of the latest wave of global activism and transnational mediatized protests from Seattle in 1999 and beyond. Contrasting these more recent studies with earlier 'classic' findings provides an ideal opportunity to reflect on both continuities and discontinuities in the nature and theorization of mediatized demonstration and protest. The discussion concludes by considering the part played by the Internet in today's changing media ecology and its possible synergy with the politics and organizational forms, loosely affiliated identities and globally dispersed interests that have come together in the latest wave of transnational protests and demonstrations.

Media and demonstrations: civil rights and civil wrongs

Two classic research studies conducted in the field of media and communications research are based on detailed analysis of a major demonstration in London in 1968 and the 1960s student movement in the US, both protesting against American involvement in the Vietnam War. The first, originally published as *Demonstrations and Communication: A Case Study* by James Halloran et al. (1970) also formed the basis of a summary article, 'Political Deviance: The Press Presentation of a Militant Mass Demonstration' published by Graham Murdock (1981), and was based on detailed and systematic analysis of press and broadcasting coverage, participant observation and a limited audience research study. The second, *The Whole World Is Watching: Mass Media in the Making and Unmaking of the New Left* by Todd Gitlin (1980/2003) examines in depth and over time the role of the US media in the changing politics and fortunes of the student movement, 'Students for a Democratic Society' (SDS). Findings from both these seminal studies have set the frame of analysis for later studies and the theorization of mediatized conflicts more generally. They repay careful reading.

Halloran et al. recount how a major mass demonstration against the Vietnam War was organized by a coalition of student groups, trade unions, religious, peace and anti-war groups in London on 27 October 1968. Interestingly, prior to the march, the press speculated on anticipated violence and trouble, setting the frame for the demonstration that would follow. *The Times*, for example, ran a front-page story headlined 'Militant Plot Feared in London' and described how detectives had discovered 'militant extremists' who planned to use the march as a cover for attacks on the police and public buildings. This 'inferential framework', based on the media's selective interpretation of the political events of May 1968 in Paris and the challenge to de Gaulle's government by a coalition of social forces, set the frame for subsequent reporting. According to Graham Murdock this 'definition of the event', this expectation of violence, 'served to concentrate attention on the form of actions to the neglect of underlying causes' and, moreover, 'the implicit equation of militancy with violence bypassed the counter definitions of these terms offered by the participants' and in this way 'the march was emptied of its radical political content' (1981: 210). This conclusion was derived from a close analysis of the media's reporting, preceding, during and immediately after the London demonstration.

On the day, the march was in fact relatively peaceful. An estimated 70,000 people marched along the agreed route through central London to a rally in Hyde Park. A breakaway march to Grosvenor Square sought to register their protest outside the American Embassy and to do so by burning a US flag. Three thousand went to Grosvenor Square where approximately 50, supported by a further 200 pushing from behind, attempted to break through a police cordon that had been positioned around the American Embassy. Scuffles broke out and a police officer was kicked by a demonstrator as he fell to the ground. This picture was prominently placed on their front pages by all but one of the British national daily newspapers and served to symbolize the press's 'definition of the situation' as one of violence and extremism. Most newspapers, for example, focused on the events at Grosvenor Square under such headlines as: 'Police Win Battle of Grosvenor Square as 6,000 Are Repelled (*The Times*), 'Fringe Fanatics Foiled at Big Demonstration – What the Bobbies Faced' (*Daily Express*) and 'The Day the Police Were Wonderful' (*Daily Mirror*). In this way, then, the politics of collective violence at the heart of the demonstration – the violence of one nation state against another – became 'emptied out' and was replaced by a picture of the situation defined by interpersonal violence and 'militant extremism'. Graham Murdock concludes that:

> the image of the 27 October Demonstration coincided with, and reinforced, the more general definition of the political situation evolved by the political élite and that in this way the press played an indispensable role in the process of managing conflict and dissent, and legitimating the present distribution of power and wealth within British capitalism.
>
> (1981: 222–3)

He also stresses that 'despite difference of emphasis and presentation, the same basic news image of the event was shared by all the Fleet Street dailies. It cut right across the conventional, "quality/popular", "Right/Left" distinctions. It was also shared by both television networks' (1981: 213). Murdock explains this ideological convergence not as the result of collusion or conspiracy between the press and politicians, 'but as the logical outcome of the present organization of news gathering and processing and the assumptions upon which it rests' (1981: 223). More specifically he discusses a number of mutually reinforcing production-based determinants, which can here be briefly summarized:

1. *The 24-hour production cycle and consequent 'event orientation' of news.* This 24-hour daily cycle of news produces an 'event orientation' news where 'certain aspects of a situation pass the news threshold while others remain more or less permanently below it' (1981: 213–14). A coup or assassination attempt in

a developing country, for example, is far more likely to be reported than a continuing guerrilla war. This event orientation also tends to displace from public view underlying conditions and causes. 'The coverage of the demonstration, for example, focused almost entirely on incidents of violence and on the person-alities involved, and bypassed completely any consideration of the demonstrators' political perspective' (1981: 214).

2. *The commercial imperative to attract readers.* The commercial and competitive nature of the news marketplace results in news being presented in ways that make it instantly intelligible and meaningful. In the case of the demonstration this led to the press referencing the mass political protests of May 1968 in Paris and the Chicago riots in the US as a 'relevant' context. Moreover, 'the presentation of events in terms of the theatrical and spectacular follows logically from journalists' conceptions of what attracts their readers' (1981: 215). Mass demonstrations, however, often play into the hands of the media because 'by choosing to work through the medium of public spectacle, demonstrations invariably open themselves to the possibility that they will be appropriated as entertainment' (1981: 216). This 'entertainment' tendency becomes exacerbated in a marketplace where newspapers play to the middle ground to maximize sales and revenue.

3. *News 'objectivity' and its commercial synergy.* Journalistic notions of objectivity underpin the event orientation of news and the search for the widest possible audi-ence/readership. By focusing on events, rather than their political interpretations, newspapers can claim to be simply 'reporting events', avoid being seen as overly partisan and thereby appeal to a wide readership.

4. *Media competition and ideological convergence.* In a context of marketplace com-petition newspapers will borrow and rehearse stories printed elsewhere to save costs and avoid being 'scooped'. In consequence, says Murdock, they tend to rely on stories originated elsewhere and which may not have been fully investigated and this produces an ideological convergence in news coverage.

5. *Political elite access and the centring of political consensus.* Political elites and their views tend to find privileged media access, not dissenting voices and views. This is produced by the general orientation of the press towards the political establish-ment, the established structure of news and its pursuit of conflict, drama and personalization – all found within the world of politics – as well as the value of political elites to underwrite journalist claims to objectivity. Murdock provides the example of how, a few days before the major demonstration, the *Guardian* news-paper carried a report by a prospective Conservative candidate who claimed to have information that some students were learning techniques of insurrection and sabo-tage and comments that 'the fact that a political figure with high credibility had made this accusation, enabled the paper to print a highly newsworthy story without having to take responsibility for its substantive accuracy' (1981: 219).

6. *Journalist socialization.* Journalists learn the professional craft and professional norms of reporting on the job and their successful deployment determines career

prospects. As one reporter, quoted by Murdock, explains: 'No journalist I have met writes what he (sic) knows will be cut. What would be the point? If he has a story which he knows will cause controversy back at the news desk he will water it down to make it acceptable (Eamonn McCann, cited in Murdock 1981: 221).

Together, then, these six interrelated features of news production forge a powerful, and seemingly iron-caste, explanation for why 'the basic definition of the situation' framing news reporting 'largely coincides with the definition provided by the legitimated power holders' (1981: 208). These findings and conclusions found further support and elaboration in a similarly influential study conducted on the other side of the Atlantic.

Todd Gitlin's study, *The Whole World is Watching* (1980/2003), analyses the media's changing relationship with, and representations of, the New Left in America. He charts how the emergent 1960s student movement – 'Students for a Democratic Society' (SDS) – was at first largely ignored by the news media: the 'SDS did not perform photogenically; it did not mobilize large numbers of people; it did not undertake flamboyant actions. It was not, in a word, newsworthy' (1980/2003: 26). Following the Berkeley Free Speech movement the media produced occasional sympathetic media coverage, but it was not until the major SDS March on Washington in April 1965 and a succession of student antiwar protests that the movement became 'big news' and encountered an onslaught of media criticism. 'The amplification was already selective', argues Gitlin, 'but it now emphasized certain themes and scanted others. Deprecatory themes began to emerge, then to recur and reverberate' (1980/2003: 27). These framing devices included:

- *trivialization* (making light of movement language, dress, age, style, and goals);
- *polarization* (emphasizing *counter*demonstrations, and balancing the antiwar movement against ultra-Right and neo-Nazi groups as equivalent 'extremists');
- *emphasis on internal dissension*;
- *marginalization* (showing demonstrators to be deviant or unrepresentative);
- *disparagement by numbers* (under-counting);
- *disparagement of the movement's effectiveness.*

(1980/2003: 27)

Later that same year, and as parts of the antiwar movement turned to more militant tactics, further themes featured in the media's repertoire of framings. These included:

- *reliance on statements by government officials and other authorities*;
- *emphasis on the presence of Communists*;
- *emphasis on the carrying of 'Viet Cong' flags*;
- *emphasis on violence and demonstrations*;
- *delegitimizing use of quotation marks* around terms like 'peace march';
- *considerable attention to rightwing opposition to the movement* especially from the administration and other politicians.

(1980/2003: 27–8)

By such representational means, argues Gitlin, 'the impression was conveyed that extremism was rampant and the New Left was dangerous for the public good' (1980/ 2003: 29). Through time and growing media exposure the movement grew but also became changed by the 'adversary symbiosis' nature of this relationship. Sections of the student movement and its leadership became tactically dependent on the media for exposure of their activities, causing rifts and factions within the movement, and individual leaders in the media spotlight came to personify the movement in public and acquired personal celebrity status. Crucially the movement lost control of its ability to certify and control its own leaders: 'Celebrity as a political resource for the movement, as a means toward political ends, lapsed into a personal resource to be invested, horded, and fought over – or abandoned' (1980/2003: 146). He concludes:

> The important point is that the movement paid a high price for the publicity it claimed and needed. It entered into an unequal contest with the media: although it affected coverage, the movement was always the petitioner; the movement was more vulnerable, the media more determining.
>
> (1980/2003: 128)

Gitlin, like the authors of the UK anti-Vietnam War demonstration study, also provides a complex of reinforcing factors and processes that explain this hegemonic framing. He summarizes these as follows:

> Some of this framing can be attributed to traditional assumptions in news treatment: *news* concerns the event, not the underlying condition; the *person*, not the group; *conflict*, not consensus; the fact that '*advances the story*', not the one that explains it. Some of this treatment descends from norms for the coverage of deviance in general: the archetypal news story is a crime story, and an opposition movement is ordinarily, routinely, and unthinkingly treated as a sort of crime. Some of the treatment follows from organizational and technical features of news coverage – which in turn are not ideologically neutral. Editors assign reporters to beats where news is routinely framed by officials; the stories then absorb the officials' definition of the situation. And editors and reporters also adapt and reproduce the dominant ideological assumptions prevailing in the wider society. All these policies are anchored in organizational policy, in recruitment and promotion: that is to say, in the internal structure of institutional power and decision. And when all these sources are taken into account, some of the framing will still not be explained unequivocally; some must be understood as the product of specifically political transactions, cases of editorial judgement and the interventions of political elites.
>
> (1980/2003: 28)

These two studies of British and American demonstration and dissent can rightly be regarded as classics in the field of mass communications research, and for good reasons. Both are based on in-depth analysis and respect for empirical evidence and elaborate conceptual and theoretical frameworks that help to illuminate important dynamics and forms of mediatized protests. They both also produce remarkably similar, non-reductionist, explanations for the dominant framing enacted by the media; in each case these are grounded in an understanding of news organization and news processes as well as the influence exerted by surrounding commercial and political forces. Importantly, both studies also move to develop a more dynamic and interactional view of the media's relation to protest and protestors and how its representations enter into the public definition of events.

Gitlin's study, as we have heard, talks of an 'adversary symbiosis' and Halloran and his team also addressed how the media's 'inferential framework' of expectations entered into the public 'definition of the situation' influencing the behaviour and actions of the police, other media, the wider public and possibly the demonstrators themselves. Media representations, in other words, cannot be seen to be politically innocent or outside the action. Rather, they became infused in the action itself and the responses that followed, often entrenching expectations, polarizing social groups and precipitating certain forms of behaviour. On occasion, the media's preliminary 'definition of the situation' may even become a *self-fulfilling prophesy*. Media expectations of violence can all too easily lead, for example, to law enforcement agencies 'tooling up', and groups labelled as deviant consolidating as they prepare for anticipated trouble (Murdock 1984).

David Waddington (1992) usefully depicts the interactional nature of much media reporting of public disorder situations (Figure 3.1) and does so based on a review of different disorder situations including riots, football hooliganism, mass picketing and the Troubles in Northern Ireland. His model encapsulates many of the recurring findings from these studies and helps to illuminate how media representations can contribute to cycles of action and response, exacerbating the likelihood of conflict and perpetuating public misunderstanding.

This interactional model usefully encapsulates many of the media's representational frames and features identified by researchers, and highlights how the media are often contributing to the very events and actions that they representationally condemn but find so newsworthy. A considerable body of evidence suggests that these depicted findings are in fact recurring features across diverse disorder situations. Waddington asserts, for example, that 'the role of the media in public disorder has been found to be consistent across different historical periods, geographical locations and types of disorder', and, notwithstanding differences of mediums and media outlets, 'analyses of media coverage of disorder have consistently found more similarities than differences in media coverage' (1992: 175). But can we still generalize in similar terms on the basis of more recent findings? Are there other dynamics and levels of complexity that also need to be taken into account? Do the media always, invariably and necessarily impose 'definitions of the situation' on protests and dissent which coincide with the views of dominant interests? The remainder of this chapter explores these questions further.

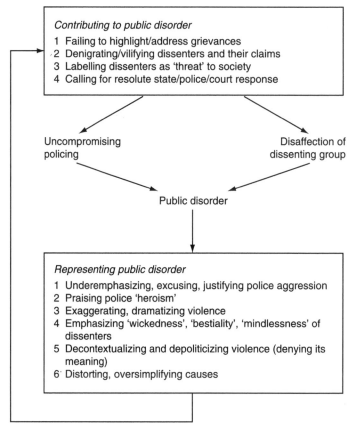

Figure 3.1 The media's relationship to public disorder
© Reproduced with permission from Waddington, D. (1992) *Contemporary Issues in Public Disorder*, p. 176. London: Routledge.

Geopolitics, dramaturgy and repertoires of protest

Three further levels of complexity – political, cultural and strategic – also need to be opened up for consideration in respect of the media's relationship to, and representations of, demonstration and protest before we can generalize on the basis of earlier studies and their critical findings. Arguably it is time to take a new look at different situations of mediatized protests and demonstrations, better contextualize and historicize their specificity and explore how politics, cultural symbolism and strategy can all play a part in shaping and inflecting media representations.

Geopolitics

The studies consulted earlier have focused for the most part on demonstrations and protests reported in western liberal democracies. If we broaden our frame of reference to include the reporting of protests and demonstrations in different political contexts as well as in respect of comparative international news reporting we can considerably sharpen our view of how geopolitical interests can shape and inflect the reporting of protests and demonstrations around the world, sometimes in the most decisive of ways. Yew-Jin Fang's study of the *People's Daily* in the Peoples Republic of China (PRC), for example, methodically reveals how this government-controlled newspaper reported protests and demonstrations very differently when referring to countries which the PRC regarded as politically hostile (e.g. South Africa and Israel) in comparison to those countries with which it had cordial relations (e.g. Chile, Venezuela, Argentina, Nepal and Algeria) (Fang 1994). Fang's systematic analysis of a large corpus of newspaper reports attended to key lexical terms and the syntactic structures embedded within the descriptions of events. Her results prove fascinating reading. Attending to the labels used by the *People's Daily* to describe the events reported in different countries produces Table 3.1.

The term *douzheng* ('struggle'), explains Fang, in the political contest of the PRC, has a strong positive connotation. This term was found in articles which portrayed events in South Africa and Israel, but no examples were found in reports concerning

Table 3.1 Instances of labels given to the events reported

	Hostile countries	Non-hostile countries	Total
douzheng ('struggle')	9 (6.0)	0 (0)	9
jihui ('mass rally')	10 (6.6)	0 (0)	10
Shiwei, shiwei youxing ('demonstration', 'march')	93 (61.6)	9 (16.1)	102
kangyi ('protest')	18 (11.9)	13 (23.2)	31
chongtu ('clash')	19 (12.6)	12 (21.4)	31
baoluan, saoluan ('riot')	2 (1.3)	22 (39.3)	24
Total	151 (100.0)	56 (100.0)	207

Note: The percentages in parentheses represent the proportion of each label in relation to all the labels for that column. For example, the term 'struggle' accounted for 6 per cent of the total number of labels used for situations of unrest in hostile countries.
Source: Reproduced with permission from Fang, Y.-J. (1994) 'Riots and Demonstrations in the Chinese Press', *Discourse and Society* 5(4): 472 © Sage Publications.

the 'non-hostile' countries. The term implies legitimacy and also encourages a show of solidarity for the demonstrators, especially when used in such headlines about Apartheid South Africa as: 'Cruel Suppression Arouses More Intense Resistance: The Struggle of the Black Masses in South Africa Intensifies'. Similarly, the unrest in South Africa and the Palestinians in the Israel-occupied territories is rarely described as *baoluan* or *saoluan* ('riots') with their generally negative connotations of illegitimacy, disorder and mayhem. Lexical terms, then, connote a semantic field of meanings and these can, and according to Fang's findings are, routinely and systematically deployed in ways that reflect the geopolitical alignments of the PRC government. Fang's study also considers how the syntactic structures organizing sentences in the *People's Daily*'s reporting also carry ideological charge, again oriented to the PRC government's international political relationships. The syntactic structures used in the description of police action against the demonstrators/'rioters' or the consequences of the events, reveal subtle ways of describing such actions. One way to avoid mentioning the police and their causation of death and injury is to use intransitive verbs, for example: 'Thirty people died' or 'Thirty people sustained injuries'. In the news reports about demonstrations and protests in non-hostile countries, rather than identifying those who caused the deaths or injuries, people are simply described as having died or sustained injuries: 'At least 12 people have died, and 61 sustained injuries . . . in the clash'. In contrast, transitive sentences often require the agent of the action to be identified: 'The police killed thirty people', 'Thirty people were killed by the police'. Again, systematic investigation of transitive and intransitive sentences in the reporting of demonstrations and protests in countries hostile and non-hostile to the PRC reveals striking patterns in the linguistic structures used and which correlate to the informing political and semantic field (Table 3.2).

Fang's work, then, powerfully demonstrates how 'demonstrations', 'protests' and 'riots' are lexical terms deeply impregnated with meanings; how media label and define an event, or group of people, positions them within a semantic field of meanings and

Table 3.2 Instances of transitive and intransitive sentences when referring to police action

	Hostile countries	Non-hostile countries	Total
Intransitive	23 (22.5)	23 (82.1)	46
Transitive	79 (77.5)	5 (17.9)	84
Total	102 (100.0)	28 (100.0)	130

Note: The percentages in parentheses represent the proportion of each sentence type in relation to all the sentence structures for that particular column.
Source: Reproduced with permission from Fang, Y.-J. (1994) 'Riots and Demonstrations in the Chinese Press', *Discourse and Society* 5(4): 475 © Sage Publications.

these meanings can have political charge and consequences. This finding should not be presumed to be confined to the news reporting of Communist China, as a similar systematic analysis of the lexical terms deployed by the UK media in respect of Britain's inner city 'riots', 'disorders', 'disturbances', 'rebellions' or 'uprisings' clearly documents (Cottle 1993a: 161–98). Fang's study also illustrates how demonstrations and protests in different countries can in fact receive very different news treatment by news organizations and how this depends, in the case of the PRC, on the government's political alignments and allegiances in respect of other states. The study, therefore, powerfully reintroduces 'the political' into the explanatory mix and suggests that not everything can be accounted for with reference to the routines of news production.

Dramaturgy

A different study also encourages us to introduce a deeper conceptualization of 'the cultural' into our deliberations, again opening up the possibility that not all demonstrations and protests are destined to receive unfavourable or negative media attention. Doug McAdam (2000) makes the case, for example, that the American Civil Rights Movement, headed by Martin Luther King in the 1960s, successfully won public support and exerted pressure on the US government to concede to their civil rights demands on the basis of a skilful political strategy and deliberate 'dramaturgical' framing. He asks how we can account for King's media staying power and why he and the Southern Christian Leadership proved so successful in attracting favourable media attention (2000: 124).

Martin Luther King and the SCLC leadership deliberately courted the media spotlight and staged actions that they were confident would provoke racists and authorities into committing acts of violence. And, as we have already heard, violence, confrontation and disruption are newsworthy. But this does not account, says McAdam, for the generally sympathetic treatment that King and his followers managed to secure within the mainstream US media. Here we need to consider the content or 'ideational framing' of King's intervention and how this spoke simultaneously to different 'publics' as well as its dramatic and culturally resonate appeal or 'dramaturgy'. McAdam's analysis is best heard in his own words. First, ideational framing:

> in accounting for King's success in attracting sympathetic media coverage, much of the credit must go to the substantive content of his thought. Quite simply, no black leader had ever sounded like King before. In his unique blending of familiar Christian themes, conventional democratic theory, and the philosophy of non-violence, King brought an unusually compelling yet accessible frame to the struggle. First and foremost, there was a deep 'resonance' (Snow et al. 1986) to King's thought. Specifically, in employing Christian themes and conventional democratic theory, King succeeded in grounding the movement in two of the

ideational bedrocks of American culture. Second, the theme of Christian forgiveness that runs throughout King's thought was deeply reassuring to white America burdened (as it still is) by guilt and a near phobic fear of black anger and violence. . . . Third, King's invocation of Gandhian philosophy added an exotic intellectual patina to his thought that many in the northern media (and northern intellectuals in general) found appealing. Finally, while singling out this or that theme in King's thought, it should be noted that the very variety of themes granted those in the media (and the general public) multiple points of ideological contact with the movement. Thus, secular liberals might be unmoved by King's reading of Christian theology but resonate with his application of democratic theory and so on.

(2000: 126–7)

Now dramaturgy:

King and his SCLC lieutenants' genius as 'master framers' . . . extended beyond the ideational content of their formal pronouncements.

Arguably the best example of SCLC's penchant for staging compelling and resonate dramas is their 1963 campaign in Birmingham. In April of that year, the SCLC launched a citywide campaign of civil disobedience aimed at desegregating Birmingham's public facilities: but why among all southern cities was Birmingham targeted? The answer bespeaks the SCLC's strategic and dramaturgic genius. As a major chronicler of the events in Birmingham notes, 'King's Birmingham innovation was pre-eminently strategic. Its essence was . . . the selection of a target city which had as its Commissioner of Public Safety "Bull" Connor, a notorious racist and hothead who could be depended on not to respond non-violently' (Hubbard 1968, 5). . . . After several days of uncharacteristic restraint, Connor trained fire hoses and unleashed attack dogs on peaceful demonstrators. The resulting scenes of demonstrators being slammed into storefronts by the force of the hoses and attacked by snarling dogs were picked up and broadcast nationwide on the nightly news. Photographs of the same events appeared in newspapers and magazines throughout the nation and the world. The former Soviet Union used the pictures as anti-American propaganda at home and abroad. Thus, the media's coverage of the events in Birmingham succeeded in generating enormous sympathy for the demonstrators and putting increased pressure on a reluctant federal government to intervene on behalf of the movement.

In short, by successfully courting violence while restraining violence in his followers, King and the SCLC were able to frame the events in Birmingham as highly dramatic confrontations between 'good' movement and 'evil' system. Moreover, the movement's dominant religious ideology granted this interpretation all the more credibility and resonance. These were no longer demonstrators; rather they were peaceful, Christian petitioners being martyred by an evil, oppressive system. The stark highly dramatic nature of this ritualized confrontation between good and evil proved irresistible to the media and, in turn, to the American public.

(2000: 127–8)

McAdam, following his analysis of the civil rights movement, as we have heard, argues that it was above all the 'compelling dramaturgy' of King's tactics that galvanized different publics – segregationists, supporters, wider public and federal government – into action and which unleashed irresistible dynamics of reform. This was a difficult balancing act to pull off, he suggests, but its success granted Martin Luther King and the US civil rights movement tremendous political leverage.

Repertoires of protest

McAdam's historical recovery of the dramaturgic framing of the civil rights movement in America also points to the importance of the collective form of protest and how, in this instance, it served well the movement's strategic purposes. Protests, historically, can take very different forms, whether delegations and demonstrations, sit-ins and spectacular stunts, acts of calculated civil disobedience to diverse forms of direct action. Sean Scalmer (2002) has usefully traced in the context of Australia, for example, how today's spectacular 'dissent events' often creatively innovate on the basis of preceding and constantly evolving forms of protest – findings that also apply to other national contexts and indeed these changing repertoires of protest often migrate from one national setting to another:

> The petition and the delegation were increasingly supplanted by the march and the demonstration; the march and the demonstration were rapidly complemented by the 'invasion' and the 'occupation'. The available forms of contention multiplied. In a moment of sustained interaction, tension and improvisation, new clusters of political performance became available. By the early 1970s, staging had become the dominant repertoire of collective action. A great variety of Australians had learnt to 'stage contest' and to 'perform disruption'. Tools of direct democracy were now in wide circulation . . . it is precisely the capacity to shock, to disrupt and to confront which makes the 'performance of staging' such a powerful resource. It is this capacity, indeed, which allowed new performances to feed widespread political mobilization, and thereby to nurture the movements for women's liberation, Aboriginal rights, gay liberation, and protection of the environment.

(2002: 74–5)

Changing repertoires of protest, often deliberately designed and performed to attract the media spotlight, are increasingly based on a growing media awareness and reflexivity in respect of the media's past representations and their tendency to frame demonstrations, protests and dissent through an ideologically inflected lens and one known to be attracted to spectacle and theatre as well as conflict, controversy and deviance. No wonder, perhaps, that 'dissent events' and spectacular stunts so often feature in the repertoires of contemporary protests. This dynamic interplay between media and protestors also bears thinking about in the context of shifting media interests and the news media's capacity to become energized by novel or spectacular stunts and to quickly move on to other news stories when faced with constant repetitions of the same. The endless game of protestor–media 'catch-up' generates creative innovations in the evolving forms or repertoires or protest and, in this respect, exerts its own degree of determinacy upon the public displays of symbolic power.

There may, however, be deeper social processes at work in the contemporary repertoire of protests other than the felt need to produce media spectacles, stage photogenic stunts and perform colourful pageantries or 'dissent events'. We shall return to considerations of the possible elective affinity between new media technologies and new political forms of organization later. But first we need to revisit, and possibly re-evaluate, ideas of media 'spectacle' in the context of debates centring on recent protests approached through the conceptual prism of the 'public sphere' – or 'public screens'.

Global activism and media: public sphere(s) or public screens?

In recent years, following the translation into English of Jürgen Habermas's *The Structural Transformation of the Public Sphere* (1989), media theorists and researchers have increasingly approached media performance and representation armed with ideas of how the media can and should bring into being a 'public sphere'. That is, constitute an accessible public space for the exchange and dissemination of ideas facilitating democratic discussion and opinion formation and underpinned by ideas of the 'collective good'. Notions of the public sphere also chime with the increasingly contested nature of civil societies addressed by contemporary social theory and variously inform, as we have heard, three overarching paradigms in the field of media and communications research (see Chapter 2 and Figure 2.1). Famously, Habermas defined the 'public sphere' as follows:

> By the 'public sphere' we mean first of all a realm of our social life in which something approaching public opinion can be formed. Access is guaranteed to all citizens . . . Citizens behave as a public body when they confer in an unrestricted fashion – that is, with the guarantee of freedom to express and publish their opinions – about matters of general interest. In a large public body this kind of communication requires specific means for transmitting information and influencing those who receive it. Today newspapers and magazines, radio and television are the media of the public sphere.

> (1974: 49)

As we might expect, given the conflicted nature of political theory as well as contending notions of 'democracy', 'citizenship' and 'matters of general interest', Habermas's formulation of the public sphere has not gone unchallenged. Criticisms and suggested revisions of the concept range across the historical, empirical, the conceptual and the theoretical (Elliott 1986; Garnham 1986; Curran 1991; Frazer 1992; Peters 1993; Hallin 1994; Livingstone and Lunt 1994; Dahlgren 1995; Thompson 1995; Gitlin 1998; McGuigan 2000; McKee 2005). Most scholars today nonetheless accept that the concept of the 'public sphere' (or similar: 'public spheres', 'alternative' or 'counter public spheres', 'public sphericules') has utility as both critical benchmark and normative ideal for the interrogation of contemporary media performance and output.

Two academic camps have generally taken up opposing positions on the concept of the 'public sphere', and these have become played out in various studies of the media and its representations of conflict. One group, based on Enlightenment premises, argues for the necessity of rational, consensual debate in which universal reason and deliberation are able to prevail while the other moves towards post-Enlightenment premises and reconceptualizes the concept of public sphere(s) in more relativist and culturally expressive ways where differences can be publicly recognized but where consensus may neither be attainable nor necessarily deemed socially a good thing. While the first camp tends to approach the media 'public sphere' armed with ideas of critical rationalism and its capability to marshal 'public knowledge' and deliberate and discuss substantive 'issues'; the latter, informed by cultural studies and post-modern perspectives, theorizes how media disseminate meanings in 'popular culture' and everyday life and how these sustain 'identities' of difference. While usefully opening up to analysis differing communicative modes embedded within media representations – cognitive and affective, rational and expressive, argumentative and aesthetic, propositional and symbolic, dialogic and disseminatory – when championed at the expense of their communicative twin these same categories all too often deny the possibility of a more integrated understanding of the multidimensional nature and communicative complexities of today's media communications (Corner 1995; Dahlgren 1995; Cottle and Rai 2006; see also Chapter 9). But how do these ideas and arguments relate to the mediatization of contemporary demonstrations and protests?

At the turn of the 20th century and into the first decade of the 21st global activists took to the streets to protest against neo-liberal globalization, disrupting meetings of the World Trade Organization, International Monetary Fund and World Economic Forum in such major cities as Seattle, London, Prague, Genoa, Cancun and Melbourne. These mass protests made use of dramatic images and spectacular forms of action designed to attract mainstream media interest, and they also made good use of new media technologies – video-cams, mobile phones and above all the Internet. These communication technologies, as we shall hear, facilitated and seemed particularly well-suited to the political aims and organizational aspirations of the demonstrators. But first we need to revisit and possibly rethink ideas of spectacle.

Our classic studies of demonstration and protest pointed to the inherent risks that demonstrators run when captivating the media spotlight through the deliberate use of public spectacles and how this can lead to the media 'emptying out' the political arguments at the heart of the demonstration and demonstrators' aims. Recent studies, based on the latest forms of protest, have challenged this theorization as unduly pessimistic. Geoffrey Craig in his analysis of the three-day protest against the 2000 World Economic Forum (WEF) held in Melbourne, for example, argues that the visual and dramatic nature of the violent protests that ensued was both necessary and effective 'given that contemporary political practice is, to a large extent, governed by the management of visibility' (2002: 43). Observing how demonstrators were often portrayed in a negative light and how television screens became filled with images of violent clashes between police and demonstrators outside the WEF venue, he nonetheless invites us to reappraise the political value of this and other spectacular forms of contemporary mediatized protests. Images of the protestors' blockade and the violence that followed, contributed to:

> raising the consciousness of the public and increasing pressure on the interests of global capital. In this sense, the blockade of the Forum was not the primary objective. . . . Spectacles, then, can be regarded as focal points that visualize issues and events, and generate public discourse. . . . In this sense, the spectacle of the WEF protestors was not an irrational, empty gesture but an appropriate and effective communicative strategy in a mediated society. They have got our attention and they have got us talking.
>
> (2002: 51)

Craig's analysis, then, posits spectacle as a potent means for generating public discourse and discussion. Others, however, have gone much further in their evaluation of the political value of spectacle.

In their article, 'From Public Sphere to Public Screen: Democracy, Activism and the "Violence" of Seattle', Kevin M. DeLuca and Jennifer Peeples (2002) argue that the mediatized World Trade Organization protests in Seattle in 1999 provide the opportunity to map a new international citizens' movement and its tactical use of new and established communication technologies. Like Craig, they also seek to reconceptualize exactly how this movement communicates and in so doing coin the idea of the 'public screen', deliberately contrasted to Habermas's original conception of the 'public sphere':

> In comparison to the rationality, embodied conversations, consensus, and civility of the public sphere, the public screen highlights dissemination, images, hypermediacy, spectacular publicity, cacophony, distraction, and dissent. We have focused on the image event as one practice of the public screen because it highlights the public screen as an alternative venue for participatory politics and public opinion formation that offers a striking contrast to the public sphere.
>
> (2002: 145)

This analysis, seemingly, relocates the 'political' to the 'image event' itself rather than to the wider deliberative engagements prompted by such mediatized spectacles. Even so it seems image events are not entirely without thought: 'We must consider image events, then, as visual philosophical-rhetorical fragments, mind bombs that expand the universe of thinkable thoughts' (2002: 144).

Whether this positive valorization of media spectacles in terms of 'public screens' ultimately proves to be too one-sided in its enthusiastic displacement of 'public sphere' politics more rationally and deliberatively conceived, is something that has to be seriously pondered. While it certainly opens up a new, and I think necessary, vista on the mediatized spectacles of recent protests and one that seemingly challenges earlier studies as unduly pessimistic about the role of spectacle, drama and performance in contemporary public life, can we really afford to forego the necessity to engage with propositional arguments and discursive contention more traditionally conceived? Perhaps too it is worth remembering, in a context that alludes to images as 'mind bombs' and 'philosophical-rhetorical fragments' (DeLuca and Peeples 2002), that media visuals of demonstrations and protests are often highly partisan and semiotically aligned to editorial outlooks (Cottle 1998a: 205–13). How dissent and contention become publicly defined, elaborated and, importantly, argued about in the mediatized public sphere, as well as visualized and instantiated in hypermediated spectacle in alternative venues for participatory politics, is therefore crucial for understanding processes of public sense making and the communication of politics.

Interestingly, a very different view of the Seattle demonstrations and its mediatization is offered by Andrew Rojecki (2002). While this study also challenges blanket conclusions extrapolated from earlier studies as too pessimistic, it does so on the basis of a very different analysis and theorization of the Seattle protests. Rojecki examines reports of the Seattle protests in *USA Today,* CBS television broadcasts and influential newspapers, *The New York Times, Los Angeles Times* and *Washington Post.* He documents how an 'initial focus on surface features – costumes and stunts – quickly deepened to the underlying issues they symbolized' (2002: 159). Mainstream media did not, he concludes, 'mount an assault on the credibility or knowledgeability of its participants when their costumes, methods for gaining attention, or civil disobedience and mass arrests could easily have become the focus of coverage' (2002: 162–3). In fact:

> the range of views in the news and in commentaries was as wide as that expressed by the protestors themselves, creating a critical field that encompassed a heretofore unimaginable combination of conservative elites, traditional reformers, and neo-Marxist protestors.
>
> (2002: 166)

His explanation for this new media access and radical pluralism is threefold, and comprises: (1) the erosion of state sovereignty over political economy in times of economic globalization; (2) the elimination of the Soviet system as a rhetorical resource for movement critics; and (3) new information technologies altering movement structures. Together these three conditions, argues Rojecki, destabilized the former field of the political elite consensus and opened up new representational possibilities in the media. Elite dissensus, at both national and international levels, was an outcome of the economic processes of globalization which produced disruptive and differential impacts on national-based interest groups. The end of the cold war also presented crucial rhetorical advantages for the anti-globalization movement. The 'elimination of the Soviet Union as a long-standing symbol of repression and the economic system it championed', says Rojecki, 'deprives conservative opponents of a dependable ideologically-based platform for launching their attacks on dissident movements' (2002: 156). His analysis, like that of DeLuca and Peeples, also identifies the Internet as a third major benefit for the protestors. The Internet 'offers under-resourced interest groups tools that provide extraordinary leverage for mobilization and organization' (2002: 157). In the Seattle demonstrations, the Direct Action Network coalition used websites, listservs, and e-mail to coordinate activities, mobilize membership and provide expertise on a variety of issues. But the importance of the Internet extends beyond its technical capacity to overcome obstacles of time and space for those increasing numbers of people positioned on the right side of the digital divide. Importantly, it also seemed to fit the politics and organizational forms of the movement itself. Rojecki explains:

> The anti-globalization movement can form a looser coalition of more fragmented but related interests. The result is a greater resilience and a decidedly flatter structure . . . One could see a style of decision-making characteristic of this new kind of movement . . . because the loose coalition making up this movement is less dependent on a single defensive issue for withstanding an ideologically charged field of resistance, it is more resilient, less likely to falter.
>
> (2002: 158–9)

According to this account, therefore, the Internet appears to offer an organizational capacity and synergy that is particularly well suited to activists, and the new wave of transnational protests and activism (see also Castells 1997, 2001; Bennett 2003, 2004; Wall 2003; van de Donk et al. 2004; Porta and Tarrow 2005). As cyber-protest researchers have suggested: 'It seems that the fluid, non-hierarchical structure of the Internet and that of the international protest coalition prove to be a good match and that it is no coincidence that both can be labelled as a "network of networks" ' (van Aelst and Walgrave 2004: 121). Lance Bennett develops this point further:

> When networks are not decisively controlled by particular organizational centers, they embody the Internet's potential as a relatively open public sphere in which the ideas and plans of protest can be exchanged with relative ease, speed and global scope – all without having to depend on mass media channels for information or (at least, to some extent) for recognition.
>
> (Bennett 2003: 20)

The Internet while certainly no panacea for the inequalities of strategic and symbolic power mobilized in and through the mass media evidently contains a socially activated potential to unsettle, and possibly on occasion disrupt, the vertical flows of institutionally controlled 'top-down' communications and does so by inserting a horizontal communicative network into the wider communications environment. This can be depicted in the following topographical representation of the complexities of the contemporary 'media sphere' (Figure 3.2). Different aspects of this conceptualization will be returned to and elaborated further in the chapters that follow.

How the different flows and networks of the contemporary media sphere intermingle and reciprocally influence each other will, inevitably, become a key area for future research. This new media ecology arguably contains more political opportunities for dissenting voices and views than in the past and these are being communicated

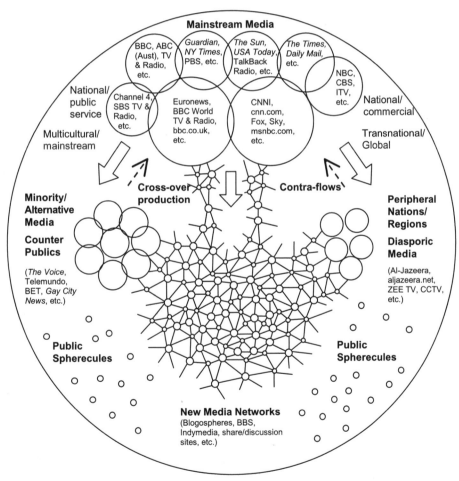

Figure 3.2 Media sphere (public sphere(s) and public screens)

through complex networks linking alternative and mainstream media and communication flows:

> impressive numbers of activists have followed the trail of world power into the relatively uncharted international arenas and found creative ways to communicate their concerns and to contest the power of corporations and transnational economic arrangements. In the process, many specific messages about corporate abuses, sweatshop labour, genetically modified organisms, rainforest destruction, and the rise of small resistance movements, from East Timor to southern Mexico, have made it into the mass media on their own terms.
>
> (Bennett 2003: 18–19)

New media technologies, then, add new communicative ingredients into the media ecology mix as well as the possibilities for new forms of politics and mediatized protests. Though unlikely to displace traditional repertoires of protest conducted in other venues or the necessity for coverage in more mainstream media, the capacity of new technologies to support and sustain dispersed coalitions of protestors and new forms of political organization was dramatically evidenced in the events of Seattle, and since. We shall return to considerations of new communication technologies and their possible destabilizing, or reconfiguring, impact on diverse fields of conflict and contention in many of the chapters that follow (see especially Chapters 5, 6 and 8).

Chapter summary

This chapter has served to illuminate what's at stake as well as some of the complexities shaping mediatized conflicts. Early studies of demonstrations and protests documented how the media label and frame conflicts and how these 'definitions of the situation' served hegemonic interests. These representational outcomes are theorized in relation to a complex of organizational practices, commercial logics and prevailing cultural outlooks. Importantly, these studies argued that media representations do not only have important consequences on how conflicts are perceived more widely but also on the actions and reactions of protestors and representatives of the state. In such ways media representations can enter into public life, sometimes exerting powerful impacts and becoming actively involved in conflict processes. This interactional and developmental feature of mediatized conflicts is developed further in studies of exceptional media phenomena discussed in the next chapter.

We have also heard, however, that the field of contention animating protests and demonstrations can occasionally win more sympathetic media portrayal. Where once 'ideological closure' and 'manufacturing of consent' were seen, 'discursive contest' and 'dramaturgy' are found to open up new contingencies and political openings. Here geopolitical interests, strategic use of dramaturgy as well as evolving repertoires of protest all point to historically changing fields of mediatized contention. Current debates centring on the media as public sphere, or public screens, have also helped to address the spectacular forms and performative nature of many contemporary protests, sensitizing researchers to their often spectacular and imagistic nature and challenging analyses that confine their critical sights to language-based accounts of media framing.

In contrast to earlier studies, however, it is noticeable that 'public screen' studies of mediatized protest are conspicuously silent about the role of production dynamics as well as strategic claims making and struggles over definition that are often at the centre of protests and demonstrations. This is unfortunate. Focusing exclusively on the spectacular and visual all too easily loses sight of the sociological and powered nature of strategic and discursive struggles enacted within and through such mediatized displays, and which may be animating many of them in the first place. Demonstrations and protests, by definition and demographic enactment, are invariably a means to an end, not the end themselves and therefore we need to understand how communicative aims have been realized or derailed in the encounter with media and other claims makers. The politics of spectacle does not subsist in spectacle alone.

Finally, the rise of the Internet and its intervention within wider media ecologies, as well as its social and political appropriation by loose coalitions of dispersed and diffuse interests and identities, further fuel dynamics of change unsettling established flows of 'top-down' communication and facilitating new political forms of organization and expression (see Figure 3.2). These substantive findings, representing new departures in the field of mediatized conflict research, are discussed further in the following chapters.

Recommended reading

Bennett, L. (2003) 'New Media Power: The Internet and Global Activism', pp. 17–38 in N. Couldry and J. Curran (eds) *Contesting Media Power: Alternative Media in a Networked World*. Oxford: Rowan and Littlefield.

DeLuca, K.M. and Peeples, J. (2002) 'From Public Sphere to Public Screen: Democracy, Activism and the "Violence" of Seattle', *Critical Studies in Media Communication* 19(2): 125–51.

Gitlin, T. (1980/2003) *The Whole World Is Watching: Mass Media in the Making and Unmaking of the New Left*. Berkeley, CA: University of California Press.

Murdock, G. (1981) 'Political Deviance: The Press Presentation of a Militant Mass Demonstration', pp. 206–25 in S. Cohen and J. Young (eds) *The Manufacture of News – Deviance, Social Problems and the Mass Media*. London: Constable.

Rojecki, A. (2002) 'Modernism, State Sovereignty and Dissent: Media and the New Post-Cold War Movements', *Critical Studies in Media and Communication* 19(2): 152–71.

Scalmer, S. (2002) *Dissent Events: Protest, the Media and the Political Gimmick in Australia*. Kensington: University of New South Wales Press.

4 | FROM MORAL PANICS TO MEDIATIZED PUBLIC CRISES: MOVING STORIES OF 'RACE' AND RACISM

Every now and then exceptional, high-profile, media phenomena breach normal media conventions, disturb routines of news reporting and culturally reverberate throughout society. For a time these mediatized events dominate news agendas, generate considerable public interest and unleash palpable emotions. Occasionally they can also prove capable of releasing powerful forces of affirmation and renewal and even transformation and change. These exceptional mediatized phenomena assume different forms but all seem capable of galvanizing identities and mobilizing 'publics' whether in defence of some state of affairs or in support of diverse projects of change. Clearly they demand serious investigation. They may be able to tell us much about how the media appeals to imagined communities and contributes to 'society in action'.[1]

This chapter identifies and discusses four types of exceptional media phenomena, each of which has the capacity to powerfully express wider contentions and collectivities and mobilize interests and identities – sometimes in politically disruptive ways. By examining 'moral panics', 'media events', 'mediated scandals' and 'mediated public crises', this chapter addresses how media can sometimes powerfully intervene in the life of societies and does so by summoning moral and collective forces. To understand the cultural charge of these exceptional phenomena we shall need to draw on a repertoire of culturalist and anthropological concepts and ideas – ritual, symbolism, affect and media performance, as well as more sociologically informed ideas of discursive contention, strategic communication and source power. The intellectual antecedents informing this discussion, then, can be traced back to Durkheim as well as to Marx with later theorists often drawing on both in their efforts to make sense of these expressive, ritualistic and sometimes disruptive forms of mediatized phenomena in contemporary societies. To help give concrete purchase to the discussion that follows, the chapter deliberately focuses principally on 'race' and racism and how these have become refracted in and through exceptional mediatized phenomena.

Media and 'race'

In societies marked by racism, segregated by 'race' or characterized by multiethnic identities, the meanings circulated by the media and consumed by audiences in particular historical times and social contexts can have profound consequences. This is because media representations, as we have already heard, do not simply 'reflect' society but can play an active part in constituting what the nature of that society is, of how its social relations are conducted, and in defining what its future may be. Historically, representations can reveal the dominant thinking about 'race' at a particular moment in time and how the prevailing culture legitimizes racist practices. Expressive of both history and culture, however, the meanings of media representations are not destined to legitimize dominant ideas of 'race' or symbolically naturalize racial inequalities; they can also become the site of contestation and contribute to necessary processes of change. Today's media, it seems, are capable of polluting the cultural pool of images and ideas about minority groups thereby reinforcing or reinscribing prejudicial views and racist practices, but they can also challenge past stereotypes, promote multicultural understanding and intercultural dialogue and culturally legislate against the essential inhumanity of racism (Cottle 2000a, 2004b). In such ways media representations can powerfully enter into the life of society, its politics of redistribution and recognition (see Chapter 9).

Many studies of representations of 'race' have been conducted in different countries over recent years and these have served to document how the media have generally portrayed images and ideas of ethnic minority groups and communities in problematic ways. Whether positioned in relation to social problems of deviance and crime, inner-city deprivation and poor housing, disorder and riots, health scares or immigration and asylum seeking, minorities are publicly presented in association with, and often positioned as the source of, social problems (see, for example: Butterworth 1967; Kerner 1968; Hartmann and Husband 1974; Miles 1984; Murdock 1984; van Dijk 1991; Jakubowicz 1994; Bullimore 1999; Philo and Beattie 1999; Article 19 2003). These general findings are important but they can inadvertently overlook longer-term dynamics of change (see, for example: Wilson and Gutierrez 1995; Ross 1996; Law 2002; Malik 2002), the discursive contention that is often embedded within media representations (Hansen and Murdock 1985; Fiske 1994a; Mercer 1994; Hall 1997; Hunt 1997; Jacobs 2000), as well as the inroads of multicultural agendas and sensibilities on the practices and contexts of media production (Seymour-Ure 1974; Braham 1982; Cottle 1993a, 1997; see also Figure 3.2).

New departures in the field of mediatized conflict, therefore, have variously sought to map and theorize the changing representations and cultural politics of 'race' and how this is played out in the contemporary field of the media. This includes a number of media scholars who have turned their sights on high-profile media phenomena with a racial focus. In many respects these studies develop on earlier models of moral panics, the first of our exceptional mediatized phenomena.

Moral panics

Stanley Cohen opened his classic study of 'moral panics' with these memorable words:

> Societies appear to be subject, every now and then, to periods of moral panic. A condition, episode, person or group of persons emerges to become defined as a threat to societal values and interests; its nature is presented in a stylised and stereotypical fashion by the mass media; the moral barricades are manned by editors, bishops, politicians and other right thinking people; socially accredited experts pronounce their diagnoses and solutions; ways of coping are evolved or (more often) resorted to; the condition then disappears, submerges or deteriorates and becomes more visible. . . . Sometimes the panic passes over and is forgotten, except in folklore and collective memory; at other times it has more serious and long-lasting repercussions and might produce such changes as those in legal and social policy or even in the way society conceives itself.
>
> (1972: 9)

The theory of moral panics, fundamentally, is premised on Durkheimian ideas of 'society in action', and developed to account for how collective fears and anxieties become amplified and sensationalized in the media and often focused on a symbolic other, a folk devil. This ultimately serves processes of societal control through the collective policing of moral boundaries and, typically, institutionalized law and order responses. In many respects this is classic Durkheimian sociology of deviance. Moral panics become the vehicle for the reassertion of consensual societal values in opposition to the media's depicted threat. Moral panic theory, notwithstanding a number of criticisms discussed later, continues to provide a useful model for understanding the complex dynamics of media–society interactions and how the media can periodically contribute to the reanimation or construction of collective solidarities, especially when set against a backdrop of historical and social change (Critcher 2003).

When focused in respect of the divisive and politically charged terrain of 'race', moral panics can unleash potentially explosive and consequential effects – reinforcing and unleashing racist ideas and practices. Stuart Hall et al. (1978) provided a detailed case study of just such a moral panic in their detailed case study, *Policing the Crisis: Mugging, the State and Law and Order* of the UK, which focused on the media 'mugging' scare of the 1970s. Deliberately integrating Cohen's 'interactionist' model of moral panics within a neo-Marxist theorization of the British state and its crisis of legitimacy in a period of rapid change, this moral panic, they argued, served to ideologically manufacture consent and legitimize the state's increasingly authoritarian response to the growing problems of law and order engendered by historical and economic change. It did so by powerfully condensing potent themes of crime, youth and 'race':

> When things threaten to disintegrate, the Folk Devil not only becomes the bearer of all our social anxieties, but we turn against him the full wrath of our indignation.

> The 'mugger' was such a 'Folk Devil' . . . young, black, bred in, or arising from the 'breakdown of the social order' in the city; threatening the traditional peace of the streets, the security of movement of the ordinary respectable citizen; motivated by naked greed . . .
>
> (1978: 161)

The mugging moral panic, then, activated racist sentiments and fears and set them loose within a field of social crisis and increasing state authoritarianism.

Policing the Crisis, at over 400 pages, elaborated a complex and theoretically sophisticated critique of the British state and the role of the media and moral panics in sustaining hegemonic power. It was not without weaknesses however. Criticisms include: (a) its underdeveloped analysis of the exact mechanisms linking media and state and the production of a moral panic ideologically consonant with the state's interests; (b) the relatively undifferentiated view of both media (see Figure 3.2) and state informing the study's analysis; and (c) the idea of moral panics as necessarily elite driven and as ideologically functional for dominant interests. In today's globally dynamic and increasingly mediated societies we may also want to suggest that (d) notions of a uniform societal control culture begin to creak under evident cultural heterogeneity and social differentiation; and, moreover (e) that 'folk devils' now often 'fight back' in both mainstream and alternative media (McRobbie 1994); (f) ideas of moral panics as relatively discreet phenomena can also been questioned in a mediated world where cultural discourses intermingle and become overlaid and infused with each other (Watney 1987) – though to be fair, Hall et al. (1978: 226) recognized this in their particular study with its mapping of different societal conflicts and how these ideologically merged and transgressed society's various thresholds of acceptable behaviour. Simon Watney also challenges moral panic theory for its epistemological slippage between a 'discursive' and 'objectivist' understanding of moral panics when seeking to measure their distortion from the 'real', while also entertaining a discursive construction of social problems and phenomena.

More recently still, Sheldon Ungar (2001) maintains in an important article entitled 'Moral Panics versus the Risk Society' that today's risks are environmental not moral, that these risks stem from authorities not 'folk devils' and that these provoke open contests between claims makers which are not amenable to easy legislation. We shall have more to say about the 'risk society', environment and the media later (see Chapter 7), but here we can note that risk society is no less infused with moral claims and appeals and, as argued by Sean Hier (2003) in a countering article, 'Risk and Panic in Late Modernity', processes of globalization and the fragmentation of contemporary identities possibly encourage the demonization of outsiders and the development of new moral panics rather than leading to their displacement (see Chapter 9).

Notwithstanding criticisms and refinements of moral panic theory over the years (Goode and Ben-Yehuda 1994; McRobbie 1994; Media International Australia 1997; Thompson 1998; Ungar 2001; Critcher 2003; Hier 2003; Kitzinger 2004), the concept, I believe, continues to have purchase on today's media and its periodic reporting of various issues and public anxieties. We only need, for example, to reflect on how sections of the mass media in diverse countries in Europe, Australia and elsewhere have recently sought to amplify public fears and anxieties around issues of immigration and asylum seekers, often racializing these groups as 'Others' in the process, to see how moral panics can find fertile soil on which to grow (see Jacka and Green 2003).

Media events

Exceptional media phenomena focused in respect of issues and anxieties about 'race' are not confined to the peculiar dynamics of moral panics. Scholars have also attended to a different class of conflictual media phenomena, such as the mediatized O.J. Simpson case, the Los Angeles Police Department's beating of Rodney King, the Los Angeles 'riots' that followed the acquittal of the LAPD officers involved in the King case, as well as the Dan Quayle–Murphy Brown debate and Mike Tyson trial (see Fiske 1994a, 1994b; Hunt 1999; Jacobs 2000). All these tapped into and brought to the surface deep-seated and conflictual undercurrents of 'race' in America. Such phenomena, termed by John Fiske as 'media events', are 'sites of maximum visibility and maximum turbulence' (1994b: 7). The contention at their centre and brought into public visibility and discussion by the media can prove challenging and disruptive as well as the means by which hegemony reasserts itself. Darnell Hunt, for example, in his study of the O.J. Simpson case dubbed by some as the murder trial of the century, identifies the underlying contention at the heart of this major televised event as follows:

> The Simpson case is most assuredly about more than just the murders and the trial outcomes. . . . ceremonial elements indeed pervaded the case and the public's reaction to it. But the case also tapped into enduring societal conflicts, into the struggles between counter-hegemonic projects for change and hegemonic projects for maintenance of the status quo. And much to the chagrin of authorities, 'reconciliation' was not always the outcome celebrated.
>
> (Hunt 1999: 43)

Hunt identifies four discreet 'projects' and discourses that informed and also served to make sense of and proscribe in relation to the trial of the black celebrity and former sports icon. O.J. Simpson, it will be recalled, first fled the police, was then arrested and accused and was finally tried and then acquitted of the brutal murder of his wife and her friend, and for the most part all this was dramatically captured on camera for enthralled television audiences.

> underlying the unprecedented levels of public fascination with the case, underlying even the media's ability to exploit the tragedy for profits, rests an enduring ideological contest between competing social interests. These interests ultimately drive

what I call the 'Celebrity Defendant,' 'Domestic Violence,' 'Black "Other," ' and ' "Just-Us" system' projects. Throughout the case, these four projects continually jockeyed for position on the media's limited agenda.

(1999: 50)

Like Hunt, John Fiske also places cultural struggles over meaning at the heart of conflicted media events focused on 'race' and racism, and argues that it is this which grants them their electrifying charge and potentially explosive effects. He theorizes these as 'hyperreal' phenomena where the distinction between 'events' in the world and 'media events' becomes less certain, or important:

> The term *media event* is an indication that in a postmodern world we can no longer rely on a stable relationship or clear distinction between a 'real' event and its mediated representation. Consequently, we can no longer work with the idea that the 'real' is more important, significant, or even 'true' than the representation. A media event, then, is not a mere representation of what happened, but it has its own reality, which gathers up into itself the reality of the event that may or may not have preceded it.

(1994b: 2)

This position usefully reminds us of the way that, for most of us, the media remain the only means we have of accessing the events referenced as well as the way in which important aspects of such hypervisual media spectacles often originate within the media themselves. It also has the virtue of placing social antagonisms at the heart of 'media events' as well as their captivating, sometimes mesmerizing, fascination for audiences. However, when used in this way the term also fails to analytically discriminate between very different cases of 'media events', both consensual (Dayan and Katz 1992) and conflicted, and it also fails to address the longer-term dynamics propelling mediatized phenomena forward to different levels of intensity through time.

These same criticisms can also be put to recent work on 'media spectacles' by Douglas Kellner (2003). Building on Guy Debord's (1983) 'society as spectacle' thesis, Kellner maintains, as we heard in Chapter 2, that media spectacle is becoming one of the organizing principles of the economy, polity, society and everyday life. Kellner's work has the distinct virtue of grounding 'media spectacle' in relation to contemporary forces of globalization, technological revolution and the restructuring of capitalism. Notwithstanding his own criticisms of Debord's work for providing a 'rather generalized and abstract notion of spectacle', however, his inclusion of such wildly different media spectacles as major sports events, celebrities, musical extravaganzas, political scandals, 'Terror War' and TV series such as 'The X-Files', 'Buffy, The Vampire Slayer' and 'Big Brother', as well as major Hollywood blockbusters and the release of the children's novel 'Harry Potter', all leads, it has to be said, to a rather similar, totalizing impression. Discussions of 'media spectacle' too often suffer from a lack of analytical precision and tend towards a presumed explanatory self-sufficiency located at the level of the cultural. *Hypervisualization* as much as routine media visualization, we may want to argue, remains no less indebted to the world of contending interests and social forces condensed in the moment of production and, contrary to Debord view of 'society as spectacle', nor should we underestimate the continuing communicative capacity of words, talk and print-based media to engage audiences.

Whether approached as essentially consensual (Dayan and Katz), conflicted (Hunt, Fiske), or spectacular (Kellner) the discussion of 'media events' too easily grants to the media phenomenon self-sufficiency and the concept appears to be inherently ill-equipped to pursue developmental features of media representations over the longer term. For a stronger grasp of the temporal, narrative and social dynamics propelling exceptional media phenomena forward – including those focusing on issues and identities of 'race' – we need to consult two further identifiable classes of exceptional media performance: media scandals and mediatized public crises.

Media scandals

Media scandals typically depend on revelations and claims that are then followed up by further disclosures and/or counterclaims and which often build to a climax and occasion some form of socially or morally approved sanction. In this respect, they can analytically be positioned as a sub-class of Fiske and Hunt's classification of conflictual 'media events', though the term 'media events' can quickly become a misnomer for certain mediatized phenomena, such as media scandals, that play out in the media over a considerable period of time. James Lull and Stephen Hinerman usefully define media scandals as follows:

> Scandal serves as a term to delineate a breach in moral conduct and authority. *A media scandal occurs when private acts that disgrace or offend the idealized, dominant morality of a social community are made public and narrativized by the media, producing a range of effects from ideological and cultural retrenchment to disruption and change.*
>
> (1997: 3, emphasis in original; see also Tiffen 1999)

Interestingly, Lull and Hinerman make no prescriptions about the exact effects of media scandal since these may be variously integrative or disruptive, hegemonic or transformative. Media scandals according to the same authors can also be classified as types according to whether they involve (a) prominent individuals in public institutions, (b) stars and celebrities, or (c) ordinary people who have engaged in transgressive, sometimes heinous, acts and behaviour (Lull and Hinerman, 1997: 19–25). High-profile mediatized scandals, including the O.J. Simpson and Mike Tyson trials and the video recording of the LAPD beating of Rodney King, among others, exhibit these elements of mediatized scandal and do so charged by the additional element of 'race'. They have a powerful dynamic and narrative quality also:

Mediated scandals are not only stretched out in time: they also display a sequential structure in the sense that one phase of the scandal is typically followed by another, although this sequential pattern is by no means rigid or fixed . . . if one is situated in the midst of a mediated scandal and watching (or participating in) its development in real time, it is extremely difficult to predict how it will unfold.

(Thompson 2000: 72–3)

Here, then, the theorization of media scandals begins to periodize the movement of these exceptional media phenomena through time, and invites an appreciation of the contingencies of outcome dependent on how these symbolic struggles are waged, won or lost in each of its various phases.

Mediatized public crises

Our last category of exceptional mediatized phenomena, 'mediatized public crises', refers to a wider class of disruptive media performances than political scandals (Alexander and Jacobs 1998). These are propelled by dynamics moving sequentially through time and can reverberate out across society as well as penetrate to the normally subterranean beliefs and myths of civil society. They often exhibit elements of mediatized ritual (Cottle 2006) and can involve aspects of shame and public degradation (J. Carey, 1998). As such, they have the capacity to challenge political authorities and hierarchical systems of power and potentially even unleash consequential and transformative effects (Elliott 1980; Wagner-Pacifici 1986; Alexander 1988; Ettema 1990; Alexander and Jacobs 1998; Jacobs 2000; Cottle 2004a).

Ideas of 'social drama' developed by the anthropologist Victor Turner (1974, 1982) have proved particularly relevant in this context:

In previous studies I have used the notion of a social drama as a device for describing and analysing episodes that manifest social conflict. At its simplest, the drama consists of a four-stage model, proceeding from breach of some social relationship regarded as crucial in the relevant social group, which provides not only its setting but many of its goals, through a phase of rapidly mounting crisis in the direction of the group's major dichotomous cleavage, to the application of legal or ritual means of redress or reconciliation between the conflicting parties which compose the action set. The final stage is either the public and symbolic expression of reconciliation or else of irremediable schism.

(1974: 78–9)

Turner's schema of 'social dramas' helps to this day to capture the potentially transformative impacts of mediatized public crises and how these can depend on symbolic and ritual elements, as well as the play of strategic and institutionalized power.

Here the work of Jeffrey Alexander and Ronald Jacobs provides the most sophisticated theorization of 'mediatized public crises' to date, incorporating a sense of narrative progression, the contested and symbolic nature of public crises, as well as the contingencies and opportunities for change that these can unleash. Mediatized public crises, they argue,

> tend to increase the distance between the indicative and the subjunctive, thereby giving to civil society its greatest power for social change. In these situations, the media create public narratives that emphasise not only the tragic distance between is and ought but the possibility of historically overcoming it. Such narratives prescribe struggles to make 'real' institutional relationships more consistent with the normative standards of the utopian civil society discourse.
>
> (1998: 28)

Unlike established views of ritual as necessarily binding the collectivity and working in the service of dominant hegemonic interests this view of mediatized public crisis directs research attention to the contested and disruptive nature of these phenomena. Conflict, contest and contention, then, are at their hub and once the mediatized wheel of public crises begins to gather momentum through time, both their trajectory and eventual destination cannot always be known or predicted in advance. Mediatized public crises turn on the spokes of ritual, symbolism, emotion and affects as well as narrative and performance lending them dynamism and cultural power. To help establish these various theoretical claims as well as illuminate their analytical and explanatory purchase on a particular case, the remainder of this chapter now reports on a recent 'mediatized public crisis' in the contested field of British 'race' and racism.

Media and the racist murder of Stephen Lawrence: a case study

The Institute of Race Relations (2002a) documents 124 racially motivated killings in England and Wales in the period 1970–2003. In 2000, 53,090 racist incidents alone were recorded by the police in England and Wales, including 7887 common assaults and aggravated woundings – a figure that we reliably know from the British Crime Survey is an under-representation (Commission for Racial Equality 1999; Institute of Race Relations 2002b). This collective stain of British racism and violence rarely finds, however, public exposure and concerted response (Cottle 2000a, 2004b). The case of Stephen Lawrence, an 18-year-old black student stabbed to death in southeast London in April 1993, proved to be very different.

Institutionally the case unfolded within the criminal justice system and involved two police inquiries, two police reviews, the Crown Prosecution Service (CPS), committal and trial proceedings, a private prosecution, a coroner's public inquest and a public inquiry authorized by the new Labour Home Secretary four years after the murder. This, in turn, resulted in Sir William Macpherson's Report that found police incompetence and institutional racism to blame for the five prime suspects' evasion from the law and the injustice experienced by the Lawrences (Macpherson 1999). A raft of wide-ranging, and consequential, legislative reforms followed aimed at, *inter alia*, changing policing practices, increasing ethnic minority recruitment and instituting social reforms designed to tackle 'institutional racism' (now publicly acknowledged and defined for the first time) within police services as well as over 44,000 separate public institutions throughout British society.

The Stephen Lawrence *case*, then, unfolded within the arenas and processes of the criminal justice system; but the public *story* of 'Stephen Lawrence' was principally played out within the nation's media (and some international media too). To be publicly seen and, importantly, 'felt' as a mounting crisis releasing consequential effects, the Stephen Lawrence case had to be placed within a narrative framework that could establish its significance and meaning. While the campaign for justice for Stephen Lawrence by his parents and their supporters undoubtedly won some media exposure (Cathcart 2000), this work of public meaning construction – both cognitive and affective – was principally enacted by the media. It was here that the symbolic and moral charge of the case became *generalized* outwards and *canalized* to different publics in society.

Breach

The public story of the Stephen Lawrence case developed unevenly and over a considerable period of time before it enveloped the nation as a moment of social reflexivity and critique. Initially the murder in April 1993 was ignored by large sections of the British news media and those that reported it did so on inside pages. Nelson Mandela's visit two weeks after the murder and his words of support for the Lawrence family helped attract some media interest and Doreen Lawrence, Stephen's mother, used the opportunity to publicly criticize the police and their handling of the investigation. At this point, the Stephen Lawrence case also attracted some news interest through community marches and demonstrations protesting against the rising tide of racist violence in areas of south-east London (where at least three other racist murders had recently been committed). But it was not until the 'bombshell' decision announced by the CPS not to prosecute the prime suspects that a 'breach', in Turner's sense, opened up that paved the way for a period of mounting crisis.

Mounting crisis

The CPS decision not to prosecute the five prime suspects on grounds of 'insufficient evidence' on 30 July 1993, crystallized the family's growing lack of confidence in the criminal justice system and, in the context of growing community calls for action against the rising tide of racist violence, signalled a public 'breach' of trust in the authorities charged with the responsibility of investigating and prosecuting racist murder. The Stephen Lawrence case now moved into a protracted phase of 'mounting crisis' that ran until 15 March 1998, the day before the opening of the Public Inquiry. Across this period, the Stephen Lawrence story was kept in the public eye on a mundane basis through a succession of news updates and his name also began to be referenced in reports of other racist attacks and murders. The name 'Stephen Lawrence', at first a 'sign' of the murder of a particular black teenager in south-east London, thereby began to transform into a symbol that could act as a common focal point holding together diverse events and issues within the troubled field of 'race' and racism. None but the most rabidly racist could deny the inhumanity and injustice of his murder. But there were other features that also made 'Stephen Lawrence' a universal symbol of racial injustice within white British society.

Young, gifted and black – Stephen was studying for his exams to become an architect – he did not conform to the usual media stereotypes of black youths as criminal, disaffected or otherwise troublesome, and his parents seemingly matched the middle-England ideal profile of hard-working, God-fearing and self-improving first-generation immigrants content to make their own way in British society. The sign of 'Stephen Lawrence', then, spoke to different discourses within the field of British 'race' relations and registered with emotive force and political urgency the essential inhumanity of his murder. Additional symbolic charge was also generated by two key moments of failed institutional redress: the private prosecution mounted by the Lawrences and their legal team followed by the coroner's public inquest into Stephen Lawrence's death. Each was characterized by moments of high tension and ritual drama and each, through its performative mediatization, flooded the Stephen Lawrence story with emotional affect and moral charge.

Stephen Lawrence's murder, as we have heard, at first received limited press reporting. Now, three years later with the opening of the private prosecution on 19 April 1996, it was prominently replayed in terms that emphasized its racist brutality: 'Hacked to Death Just for Being Black' (*The Sun*), 'Race Hate Led to Boy's Knife Killing' (*Daily Mirror*), 'Black Student Killed "Out of Racist Hatred" ' (*The Independent*). Under the headline 'Black Teenager "Murdered" by Race-hate Gang', *The Times* described Stephen's last hours and included eye-witness statements and graphic accounts of the attack. Press reporting, then, was now giving full vent to the racist nature of the attack and its appalling violence.

When the case collapsed on 25 April 1996, after the judge ruled that both Duwayne Brooks's testimony (who had been with Stephen Lawrence when he was attacked) and the video evidence of the prime suspects acting out racist attacks were inadmissible, the media reported the anger that attended this latest 'breach' of justice: 'It's Just Not Fair' (*The Sun*), 'So Who Did Kill Stephen? Father of Race Murder Victim Demands Justice' (*Daily Mirror*). The mainstream press also followed up on the collapse of the prosecution and many provided lengthy transcripts of the covert police video that, again, underlined the extreme racism of the prime suspects:

Depth of Hatred Revealed in Covert Video

Neil Acourt brandished a knife, waved it around and thrust it into the wall or furniture uttering vile racist abuse.

'I reckon that every nigger should be chopped up mate and they should be left with nothing but fucking stumps.'

(The Independent 26 April 1996)

Touched by the understandable grief and sentiments of the Lawrences and repulsed by the suspects' grotesque display of verbal racism, the British press collectively became emboldened in its support for the Lawrences. The coroner's public inquest was reported in detail. Police blunders were publicly revealed for the first time and various police claims were challenged by the Lawrences' legal team. The refusal by the five accused to answer questions in the witness box also produced universal press condemnation. In its mediatization, the ritual drama and affect of the inquest was publicly elaborated and commented on by both the press and broadcasting institutions and by the time the inquest reached its final, unprecedented, verdict the story was guaranteed to receive extensive coverage. The *Guardian* led with the story on its front page: 'Unlawfully Killed in an Unprovoked Racist Attack by Five White Youths' (14 February 1997). The mainstream British press followed up on the verdict with detailed commentaries and analysis reflecting on the failure of the criminal justice system to deliver justice to the Lawrence family.

The *Daily Mail* went further in a stunning performative intervention. On 14 February, under the headline 'Murderers' blazoned across its front page, it reproduced pictures of the five prime suspects sub-titled 'The Mail Accuses These Men of Killing. If We Are Wrong, Let Them Sue Us', and did so in the knowledge that none of the suspects would want to risk self-incrimination in a libel case. The paper's action, praised in many quarters, was not motivated by a coincidence of views with those of the Lawrences, however, but indignation at the way in which the process of criminal justice had seemingly been thwarted by, to use their terms, five 'moronic thugs' and how this threatened to 'damage race relations and the reputation of British justice' (14 February 1997).

Through the public mediatization of the coroner's inquest, and the earlier private prosecution, then, the Lawrence story signalled issues of 'race' and racism as well as injustice at the heart of its public telling. Press advocacy and the media's elaboration of emotions and feelings generated by the case powerfully moved the story into a subjunctive register and this had been enacted by both 'quality' broadsheets and 'popular' tabloids. The Stephen Lawrence story had thereby entered into a moral realm in which symbolism and ritual would play an increasingly important part in determining how it discharged its political effects.

Redress

According to Turner it is in the redressive phase 'that both pragmatic techniques and symbolic action reach their fullest expression', for it is here that society is 'at its most "self-conscious" '. Redress often exhibits 'liminal features, its being "betwixt and between" ' and may be conducted through the 'idiom of judicial process, or in the metaphorical and symbolic idiom of a ritual process' (1974: 41). With each successive failure of the criminal justice system and with each new report of continuing racist attacks and murders in London and elsewhere in Britain, the sign of Stephen Lawrence accumulated further symbolic power. The phase of judicial and symbolic redress began on 17 March 1998, the opening day of the government instigated public inquiry, included the release of the Macpherson Report on 24 February 1999, and continued across the first wave of political responses and public discussion in March of that year. It mirrors Turner's discussion remarkably.

The inquiry opened with a minute's silence in memory of Stephen Lawrence, before rehearsing, to use Turner's terms, 'a distanced replication and critique of the events leading up to and composing the "crisis" ' (1974: 41). This began with detailed scrutiny and criticism of the botched police investigations: 'Inquiry Told of Lawrence Case Blunders' (*The Independent* 25 March 1998), 'Cops Waited Two Weeks to Quiz Murder Suspects' (*The Sun* 25 March 1998), 'Amazing Trail of Blunders by Police: Inquiry Opens with Catalogue of Errors' (*Daily Mail* 25 March 1998). But it was the highly charged testimonies and emotional scenes of the inquiry itself as much as the disclosure of previously hidden details which sustained the sense of 'communitas' now infused in its public mediatization.

On the second day of the inquiry Doreen Lawrence testified: 'Mum's Hell at Murder of Stephen' (*The Sun* 26 March 1998), 'The Anger and Anguish of Mrs Lawrence' (The *Guardian* 26 March 1998). The following day this emotional intensity was deepened even further with the heart-rending testimony, publicly aired for the first time, of a couple who had cared for Stephen Lawrence as he lay dying: 'You Are Loved, Woman Passer-by Whispered as Stephen Slipped Away' (*Daily Mail* 27 March 1998). The intensity of this emotional discharge was not dependent only on spoken testimonies at the inquiry, however, but inhered in the media's performative enactment of them. Consider, for example, the following crafted extract from the front page of *The Independent*:

> **Passing Before Their Eyes, One by One, Were the Racist Thugs They Believed Killed Their Son**
>
> IF HE felt the slightest twinge of self-consciousness, he did not show it. Jamie Acourt swaggered into the room, glanced at the massed ranks of hostile faces and settled down in the witness box, adjusting the lapels of his freshly pressed suite.
>
> Twenty feet away, Neville and Doreen Lawrence gazed steadily at this young man, with his slicked back dark hair and insolent demeanour. Acourt slouched back in his chair, unfazed by the attention . . .
>
> (30 June 1998)

Expectation of public drama also informed the participation of the Metropolitan Police at the inquiry, building to a climax as public apologies were belatedly offered by senior representatives of the Met, declined by the Lawrences, and as calls for Sir Paul Condon's resignation began to be heard. This was now essentially a moral drama being played out on the media stage and in which public accountability, humility and shame were seemingly demanded and, periodically, offered up as a means of demonstrating public contrition – and slowing the flow of public opprobrium being directed at the institution of the police. By the time Sir Paul Condon was required to take the stand, public expectancy was palpable. The *Guardian* displayed this dramatic event on its front page: 'Lawrence Family Spurns Met Chief's Personal Apology over Racist Murder: When Sorry Is Not Enough' (2 October 1998).

Alongside and contributing to the daily mediatized enactment of the public inquiry, the press also produced an upsurge in background stories, features, opinion pieces and editorials both contributing to and expressing wider processes of cultural reflection. This produced such headlines as: 'Shame on the Racists in Our Police Ranks' (*The Times* 9 August 1998), 'Forgotten Victims of Race Hate: The Murder of Stephen Lawrence Was Not an Isolated Incident. Nor Was the Bungled Police Response to His Death' (The *Observer* 7 February 1999), 'Straw Demands More Black Cops' (*The Sun* 10 February 1999) 'Why Racists Flourish in an Anti-racist Force' (*The Independent* 24 February 1999).

The press also focused on itself and other media in an upsurge of media reflexive pieces. Liberal broadsheets, for example, reflected on the symbolic status acquired by Stephen Lawrence in the media and compared this historically to other 'watershed' cases, thereby extending and deepening both its historical and political reach: 'Lawrence Becomes Black Icon' (*The Independent* 20 December 1998), 'Icon for a Sceptical Age' (The *Observer* 10 January 1999), 'Tragedies That Shaped Perceptions' (The *Guardian* 26 February 1999). Such media reflexivity grew across the mounting crisis and redress phases, but assumed its most prominent aspect following the release of the Macpherson inquiry Report on 24 February 1999.

The release of the Macpherson Report, six years after the murder, represented the pinnacle moment of symbolic redress. Here the political centre of society came together to publicly demonstrate its support for the Lawrences, acknowledge a collective sense of shame and lend support to symbolic processes of redress. This all-party support was embodied in the statements by leading politicians in the House of Commons on 24 February 1999, statements that were broadcast live and in full by television as well as in abridged form later that same day, and then reported by the press the following day:

> Prime Minister, Tony Blair: Madam Speaker, I think it right today to praise Doreen and Neville Lawrence for their courage and dignity. We should confront honestly as a nation the racism that still exists within our society. We should find within ourselves as a nation the will to overcome it. The publication of today's

report on the killing of Stephen Lawrence is a very important moment in the life of our country; it is a moment to reflect, learn and to change. It will certainly lead to new laws, but more than that it will lead to new attitudes, a new era in race relations and a new more tolerant and inclusive Britain.

(BBC2 *Westminster* 24 February 1999)

Following the official release of the Macpherson Report on 24 February 1999, the media collectively performed a spectacular outpouring that dominated the media sphere on this day, and for many days and weeks thereafter. This was performed on front pages, in double-page spreads, supplementary pages and special reports, and all making full use of page layout, visual impact and championing headlines including: 'Stephen Lawrence's Legacy: Confronting Racist Britain' (The *Guardian*), 'A Family Tragedy, a Police Force Disgraced and a Nation Shamed' (*The Independent*), 'Judge's Damning Report on Race Murder Will Change Britain' and 'The Legacy of Stephen' (*Daily Mail*), 'Straw War on Racism' (*The Sun*) and 'Legacy Will Be Social Change' (*The Times*) (see Image 4.1a and b). Television also played its part in taking Stephen Lawrence into people's homes and did so with special-edition news programmes in the run-up to the Macpherson Report's public release as well as specially commissioned current affairs and documentary programmes, including a special edition of *Question Time*, the popular national discussion programme hosted by Sir David Dimbleby (BBC1 25 February 1999) (see Image 4.2).

Britain's mainstream media, then, collectively reported the response from the political centre of society as a moment of historical import. This 'cultural flooding' also signalled a liminal moment outside of routine time and party politics and thereby helped to promote a sense of national renewal and moral solidarity. While different newspapers, as we have seen, had sought to emphasize certain aspects of the case and not others, for a while at least they evidently felt obligated by a shared recognition of 'national shame' and the need for a moral commitment to change. This new public mood continued to be expressed by and also conditioned press performativity for some time thereafter.

Reintegration/Schism

Following the announcement by the Prime Minister and Home Secretary in the House of Commons on 24 February 1999, the Labour government embarked on turning Macpherson's 70 recommendations, and some of its own, into legislation and policy. This did not, however, preclude some sections of the media challenging the pace of reforms or the validity of the concept of 'institutional racism', or even refuting claims of widespread police racism. But the mainstream media nevertheless evidently felt obligated to a deeper collective sense of 'society' and as one now in need of repair after its bruising from the Stephen Lawrence case.

This was a necessary collective project if the social imaginary of British civil society

Image 4.1a *The Independent*, 25 February 1999
Source: © *The Independent.* Photo: David Rose.

Image 4.1b *Daily Mail*, 25 February 1999
Source: © *Daily Mail*. Photo: Kieran Doherty/Reuters/Picture Media.

Image 4.2 *Question Time*, BBC1, 25 February 1999

was once again to re-establish itself as a taken-for-granted, if mythical, place of even-handed justice and social inclusion protected by, rather than undermined by, the forces of law and order. As time moved on, however, the press began to reassert their editorial independence from the moral mood that they had helped to produce. Some newspapers now sought to slow if not derail the momentum of reform being directed at the forces of law and order, while others performatively stoked the engine of change. But for a time, the moral momentum of the Stephen Lawrence story had powerfully intervened in the life of society, polity and culture and it had contributed a powerful impetus to how civil society could and should be.

Ten years after the murder of Stephen Lawrence the media publicly enacted this commemoration and momentarily revitalized something of the subjunctive mood, the sense of communitas that had earlier invested the story with such transformative energy. Right-wing tabloids again bowed to the sacred aura that surrounded the name of 'Stephen Lawrence' and publicly acknowledged the far-reaching energies that this had previously stirred. *The Sun*, for example, reported the words of the Prime Minister and, in typical *Sun* style, sensationalized these in terms of a 'war against racism' and momentarily refrained from criticizing the 'post-Macpherson' reforms (23 April 2003). The liberal broadsheets, by contrast, sought to performatively enact the ten-year anniversary as a major event and thereby maximize the opportunity to raise issues and reflect on questions of 'race', racism and British identity. The black broadcaster, writer and later Chairman of the Commission for Racial Equality, Trevor Phillips, among many other commentaries in The *Observer*, reflected on what the Stephen Lawrence case had meant to Britain and British identity. Under the headline 'How Tragedy, Trial and Error Brought Us All Together' (The *Observer Review*, 6 April 2003), he invoked the legacy of Stephen Lawrence and put it to work once again in respect of the new wave of asylum seekers and migrants experiencing racism: 'One thing that we could learn from Stephen Lawrence's death is that we must not wait 50 years to create a legal framework that protects the new migrants . . .'.

More than ten years after the murder of Stephen Lawrence, then, sections of Britain's media continued to performatively invoke the subjunctive mood galvanized by the Stephen Lawrence case and sought to revivify and extend its catalytic force to continuing concerns of 'race', racism and identity in British society.

Chapter summary

This chapter has deliberately confined its analytical sights on an exceptional class of media phenomena and how these have variously refracted and publicly enacted the politics of 'race' and racism – often in dramatic, ritualized and performative ways. The discussion has thereby begun to open up the expressive and symbolic dimensions of media representations as well as their cultural charge and power when focused in respect of society's deep-seated conflicts and contentions. Four sub-classes of exceptional media phenomena – moral panics, media events, media scandals and mediatized public crises – have all been discerned as potent vehicles for the discharge of collective identities and sentiments, ideas and discourses about 'race' and racism. Symbolism, story, drama and performance have invariably informed these mediatized phenomena granting them cultural power as they elicit and express wider solidarities or 'publics' subjunctively oriented to how society should be. Strong elements of ritual reside at the heart of these mediatized phenomena and these, as we have seen, need not necessarily be presumed to be narrowly confined to securing consensus or the maintenance of hegemonic power. Some mediatized phenomena reverberate throughout civil society, destabilizing social relations and publicly 'lifting the lid' on normally concealed and contentious issues. They may even hold potentially transformative charge.

The mediatized case of Stephen Lawrence is a case in point. This mediatized public crisis, I argued, has served to expose the shameful racist secrets of white British society to public illumination and moral censure. The Stephen Lawrence case became a potent symbol and catalyst for change and it proved to be a litmus test of the extent to which British society was prepared to move beyond the anachronistic practices of the past, acknowledge institutional racism and embrace cultural diversity. Exceptionally, then, this case focused national attention on deep-seated issues of 'race', racism and British identity and it embroiled as it did so powerful institutions of state and elite public figures. Mediatized public crises, though little researched, can discharge powerful cultural effects and contribute to dynamics of reflexivity and change. The study of mediatized conflict, I conclude, needs to incorporate a stronger appreciation of how public dramas or mediatized rituals can tap into moral forces oriented to how society should or could be, and how exceptionally the media perform these into public dramas that culturally resonate and symbolically summon a sense of collective purpose and, sometimes, commitment to change.

Note

1. This chapter draws in parts on more extensive discussions of mediatized rituals (Cottle 2006) and the Stephen Lawrence case (Cottle 2004a, 2005a).

Recommended reading

Alexander, J.C. and Jacobs, R.N. (1998) 'Mass Communication, Ritual and Civil Society', pp. 23–41 in T. Liebes and J. Curran (eds) *Media, Ritual and Identity*. London: Routledge.

Cottle, S. (2004a) *The Racist Murder of Stephen Lawrence: Media Performance and Public Transformation*. Westport, CT: Praeger.

Cottle, S. (2006) 'Mediatized Rituals: Beyond Manufacturing Consent', *Media, Culture and Society* 28(3) (forthcoming).

Fiske, J. (1996) *Media Matters: Race and Gender in US Politics*. Minneapolis, MN: University of Minnesota Press.

Hall, S., Critcher, C., Jefferson, T., Clarke, J. and Roberts, B. (1978) *Policing the Crisis: Mugging, the State and Law and Order*. Basingstoke: Macmillan.

Hunt, D. (1999) *O.J. Simpson Facts and Fictions: News Rituals in the Construction of Reality*. Cambridge: Cambridge University Press.

Jacobs, R.N. (2000) *Race, Media and the Crisis of Civil Society: From Watts to Rodney King*. Cambridge: Cambridge University Press.

5 | WAR JOURNALISM: DISEMBODIED AND EMBEDDED

Wars are fought on different battlefields, different fronts. Across the 20th century and into the first decade of the 21st, governments and the military have sought to control the media in order to win the 'battle for hearts and minds' and conduct 'the propaganda war'. This is well known and documented and in a sense understandable. The stakes in war, it hardly needs to be said, are high: death, destruction, the regearing of national economies and politics and, in 'total wars', the existence of both state and established way of life can be under threat. Even when national survival is not in jeopardy, when democratically elected governments take their nations to war they run the risk of losing political legitimacy, especially as military casualties mount and body bags return to home shores. Under such circumstances governments are compelled to seek the mandate of public support, and they do so via the media. It is hardly surprising, then, that journalism comes under the greatest pressures in times of war. What is surprising, and demands serious scrutiny, are the lengths to which democratically elected governments will go in controlling the media and manipulating public opinion in support of their war aims.

Prior to the Crimea War (1854–6), the British army simply wrote its own campaign reports, if it bothered at all. William Howard Russell, the first war correspondent, writing for *The Times* of London and observing the military incompetence and wasted lives in the Crimea, wrote to his editor, 'Am I to tell these things, or hold my tongue?' (cited in Knightly 2003: 6). His dispatches sent back to London caused a flurry of public criticism and eventually contributed to the downfall of the government (though it has to be said, the editor at the time, John Delane, preferred to circulate some of these incendiary reports to government privately rather than have *The Times* incur possible government wrath). Over the next one and a half centuries, up to and including the US-led invasion of Iraq (2003), democratic governments such as the United States, the United Kingdom and Australia have deployed a combination of mechanisms to censor, control and manage the flow of information in times of war, and have done so in the context of rapidly changing communication technologies.

In World War I, Lord Kitchener, the Minister of War, declared that war correspondents found on the Western Front would be arrested and repeat offenders would be shot, before the military changed its mind and accommodated a select group, along with their new silent film cameras, in lavish castles ('chateaux warriors') well away from the scenes of human carnage (Knightley 2003; Taylor 2003). Reflecting on the grotesque blood-letting of industrialized trench warfare the Prime Minister, Lloyd George, summed up the government's position at the time: 'If people really knew, the war would be stopped tomorrow. But of course they don't know and can't know. The *correspondents don't write and the censorship would not pass the truth*' (cited in Knightley 2003: 116–17, emphasis added). In World War II, the patriotism of war correspondents was also relied upon and backed up by tight systems of censorship in the fields of combat: 'On D-Day 1944, censors accompanied 558 accredited print and radio correspondents on to the five Normandy beaches "checking that not one of them wrote or radioed despatches that would help the enemy or dismay people at home" ' (Taylor 2003: 71).

The Vietnam War, the first 'television war' and also the first major US military defeat on foreign soil of the 20th century, secured mythic standing as the most uncensored war in history and also as the war in which the media sapped morale and the political resolve to continue – the so-called 'Vietnam War syndrome'. According to Daniel Hallin, however, the near-absence of censorship did not mean the absence of restrictions on the flow of information which could damage public support for the war (1986: 133). Rather, the system of control that kept journalists 'in line' was the routines of journalism, the ideological assumptions journalists shared with officials and, in the case of television, the views of the American soldiers encountered in the field (1986: 134). Though the 'Vietnam War syndrome' is generally contested by academics, as we shall hear, there is no doubting its influence on military thinking and the controls imposed on subsequent media wars.

In the Falklands/Malvinas War (1982), the British government and military operated a 'pool system', restricting the numbers of journalists and their crews accompanying the British task force to the occupied islands to only 29 British nationals. All were assigned to a military 'minder' ('Public Affairs Officer'), had their copy 'cleared' by a censor (the word 'censored' in media reports was censored), and they remained dependent on military communication systems to despatch their reports (often delayed by up to two to three weeks) (GUMG 1985; Harris 1994; Carruthers 2000). The US imposed a total exclusion of all journalists when it invaded Grenada (1983), firing warning shots at journalists who attempted to reach the Caribbean island by speed boat (Knightley 2003). When invading Panama (1989) it followed the Falklands experience and permitted a small 'pool' only of journalists who operated under strict guidelines and were expected to share available information.

A two-tier 'pool system' was enacted in the Gulf War (1991), dubbed by some the

'CNN war' or 'video game war' because of the part played by the first global 24-hour news channel in its coverage, and the media's use of the Pentagon's military videos showing precision bombing and missile attacks. Only journalists from coalition nations – Britain, France, US – were allowed to take up the 200 places allocated to the Media Reporting Teams (MRTs) which, under close supervision of public relations officers, could visit the troops encamped in the desert. The American pool system did not permit independent satellite equipment and copy and pictures had to be approved by military minders before being submitted via Forward Transmission Units to the 1500 journalists ('hotel warriors') safely stationed in Riyadh who received daily, carefully orchestrated, military briefings timed to coincide with press and television deadlines. A few coalition reporters were allowed, however, to remain in Baghdad though often receiving flak from politicians and other media for so doing, especially when reporting on causalities – 'collateral damage' – inflicted by coalition bombs (Taylor 1992; Carruthers 2000). The pool system was also used in the US war against the Taliban in Afghanistan (2001). The US-led invasion of Iraq (2003) was covered by around 3000 journalists based in the region, and here the US military introduced the much discussed system of journalist 'embedding' or the assigning of journalists to military units that permitted them to witness first hand the military's progression of the war. This produced the return of grainy, often action-packed pictures via videophones and new uplink communications. We shall have more to say about 'embedding' later.

While censorship and controls are often justified on the grounds of enhancing the chances of military success and not jeopardizing the lives of combatants, in practice we know that carefully orchestrated military press briefings, the timely release of favourable information and images, and the propagation of half-truths and downright distortions, as well as covert and overt operations targeting journalists and their news organizations, are all designed to win the propaganda war. In war, as the title of Phillip Knightley's (2003) celebrated history of war correspondents states, truth is the first casualty. In an increasingly interconnected and politically interdependent world, the battle for hearts and minds can be conducted on different media fronts: the home and military fronts, the enemy's front, and sometimes equally as importantly the international front of potential allies, global political elites and brokers of world opinion such as the United Nations. Governments and military planners assiduously examine, as we have heard, past media wars and seek to develop more effective controls to be used in the next conflict.

We also know, however, that wars are quintessentially newsworthy. They resonate with deep-seated news values (Galtung and Ruge 1973), especially conflict, violence, deviance and drama and, in the case of visual media, provide a succession of spectacular scenes. Wars also provide the raw material for strong human interest stories where journalists can seek and find pathos and tragedy, heroism and camaraderie, acts of selflessness and personalized experiences of suffering. In war everyday realities are turned upside down and this departure from the familial, quotidian world arguably represents the archetypal 'deviance' story: captivating and reaffirming through disorder and destruction collective bonds and communal values. Wars can also be rendered into powerful narratives. The stories of war unfold through time, moving through discernible phases and generating feelings of dramatic tension, anxiety and possible catharsis before reaching final, destructive, dénouement. National feelings of communal identity, pride and patriotism, as well as historical parallels and past myths, are all summoned through the genre of war reporting and these generally seek to position 'Us' in opposition to 'Them', and do so in symbolically and rhetorically affective ways. Discourses of 'race' and racism often become insinuated into the arguments and legitimizations of war, perhaps necessarily so, taking 'the Other' outside the ontological world of humanity and moving them towards the killing zone. So too discourses of gender which are also likely to be worked into the representational mix as cultural myths and sentiments based around binary oppositions of familial roles and public duty, everyday domesticity and military endeavour, home sanctuary and battlefield danger are publicly symbolized and populated with images of warrior men, nurturing mothers and innocent children (Taylor 1991; Goldstein 2001; Lemish 2005; see also Images 5.1 and 5.2).

Media wars, then, resonate culturally and have commercial value for media businesses but they also position journalists and their professional claims concerning the public's right to know at odds with state and military efforts to curb and control the flow of information. While this tension exists in peace time too, it becomes exacerbated in war time often revealing the bases of power underlying state–media interactions more generally. Today this interaction is not only reflexively monitored and responded to by states and military planners, but by the media and publics. The academic literature on war reporting is extensive: shelves in second-hand bookshops groan under the weight of journalist memoirs; and war films depicting correspondents in heroic terms have become an established sub-genre in their own right. We shall have occasion to reflect on this cultural reflexivity on mediatized war in the discussion that follows.

The remainder of this chapter now steers a path through the voluminous research on war reporting, summarizing key findings, addressing major debates and signalling new research trajectories. First, principal mechanisms and explanations for the media's documented subservience to government war aims and propaganda are reviewed. Second, important theoretical models of media–state interactions in times of war, building on the 'manufacturing consent' paradigm but also developing a more politically dynamic and historically nuanced model, are outlined. Third, with the help of ethnographic studies of war correspondents we go culturally deeper into the phenomenology of war and how the professional myths of war correspondents contribute to patriotic war reporting, irrespective of external controls and censorship. Fourth, theoretical debates about globalization, specifically 'information warfare', '24/7 real-time reporting' and 'non-western media sources' and their impact on war reporting are consulted. Here we also consider the latest military tactic of 'embedding' used in the invasion of Iraq (2003) and consider the role played by media images of body horror in mobilizing

Image 5.1 'Women of Britain Say "Go" poster, World War I (Courtesy of Imperial War Museum, London)

Image 5.2 'Keep These Hands Off' poster, World War II (Courtesy of Library and Archives, Canada/Credit: Gordon K. Odell/C-090883)

opposition for war, a theme investigated in recent studies of audience reception and public beliefs.

Media at war: what's known

Study after study of the media at war concludes that national media generally fall in line behind their national governments. If the lead-up period to war is marked by at least some reporting of elite dissensus or wider opposition, this rapidly evaporates once hostilities have begun and support for home troops begins to rally (GUMG 1985; Reese 2004). To summarize a wealth of research study findings to date, this supportive media stance is textually encoded in: (a) the extent, prominence and increased visualization of war coverage; (b) the syntactic structures, lexical choices and images used to describe and symbolize key war events and protagonists; (c) the discursive accounts of the causes and consequences of the war; (d) the media's authority skew towards military and political sources and the latter's privileged forms of media entry; (e) the systematic under-representation of voices of opposition and dissent; and (f) the informing presuppositions and partisan alignments structuring and framing media discourses more generally (see Table 5.1).

Generally absent from war coverage are in-depth discussion of the home country's geopolitical interests, enacted government controls and censorship, and scenes of casualties, horror and decimated bodies (GUMG 1985; Taylor 1998; Boyd-Barrett 2004; Miller 2004). In contrast, discussion of military tactics, military gains and military professionalism (often by accessed retired military generals and other 'independent' experts), as well as discussion of the enemy's blunders, losses and ruthless nature, are all salient features in media wars as are government press conferences and, recently, pyrotechnic scenes of exploding ordinances relayed to music and the military's provision of video capturing laser-controlled missiles hitting their targets (GUMG 1985; Herman and Chomsky 1988; Morrison and Tumber 1988; Taylor 1992, 1998; Harris 1994; Miller 1994; Hallin 1997; Liebes 1997; Carruthers 2000; Knightley 2003; Allan and Zelizer 2004; Hoskins 2004; Tumber 2004; Tumber and Palmer 2004).

While the technical parameters and media forms of mainstream war coverage may change through time, the broad political alignment of media in support of state and military power appears to be generally constant. 'As *institution*', concludes Susan Carruthers in her history of war reporting, 'the media have generally served the military rather well' (2000: 272–3). How are we to explain this? Six principal explanations recur in the research literature.

First, as already encountered in discussion of Herman and Chomsky's propaganda model, a political economy approach identifies the operations of media markets and corporate behaviour as fundamental. Major US news networks, for example, are owned by global conglomerates most of which are entertainment businesses: CBS is owned by Viacom-Paramount; ABC by Disney; CNN by AOL-Times-Warner; and Fox

Table 5.1 Mad Dogs and Englishmen

Mad Dogs and Englishmen

We have	**They have**	**Our ships are . . .**	**Iraq ships are . . .**
Army, Navy and Air Force	A War machine	An armada	A navy
Reporting guidelines	Censorship		
Press briefings	Propaganda	**Israeli non-retaliation is**	**Iraqi non-retaliation is**
		An act of great statesmanship	Blundering/Cowardly
We	**They**		
Take out	Destroy	**The Belgains are . . .**	**The Belgians are also . . .**
Suppress	Destroy	Yellow	Two-faced
Eliminate	Kill		
Neutralise or decapitate	Kill	**Our missiles are . . .**	**Their missiles are . . .**
Decapitate	Kill	Like Luke Skywalker zapping	Ageing duds (*rhymes with Scuds*)
Dig in	Cower in their foxholes	Darth Vader	
We launch	**They launch**	**Our missiles cause . . .**	**Their missiles cause . . .**
First strikes	Sneak missile attacks	Collateral damage	Civilian casualties
Pre-emptively	Without provocation		
		We . . .	**They . . .**
Our men are . . .	**Their men are . . .**	Precision bomb	Fire wildly at anything in the skies
Boys	Troops		
Lads	Hordes	**Our PoWs are . . .**	**Their PoWs are . . .**
		Gallant boys	Overgrown schoolchildren
Our boys are . . .	**Theirs are . . .**		
Professional	Brainwashed	**George Bush is . . .**	**Saddam Hussein is . . .**
Lion-hearts	Paper tigers	At peace with himself	Demented
Cautious	Cowardly	Resolute	Defiant
Confident	Desperate	Statesmanlike	An evil tyrant
		Assured	A crackpot monster

Heroes	Cornered	Our planes . . .
Dare-devils	Cannon fodder	Suffer a high rate of attrition
Young knights of the skies	Bastards of Baghdad	Fail to return from missions
Loyal	Blindly obedient	
Desert rats	Mad dogs	• All the expressions above have been used by the British press in the past week
Resolute	Ruthless	
Brave	Fanatical	
Our boys are motivated by	**Their boys are motivated by**	**Their planes . . .**
An old fashioned sense of duty	Fear of Saddam	Are shot out of the sky
		Are Zapped
Our boys	**Their boys**	
Fly into the jaws of hell	Cower in concrete bunkers	

Source: The *Guardian*, 23 January 1991 p. 21 (© Guardian Newspapers Limited 1991).

by News Corporation (See Figure 3.2 on p. 51). This 'incorporation', say its critics, can only lead to the increasing predominance of entertainment values over traditional news values as corporations pursue audiences, ratings and revenue (Thussu 2003). Oliver Boyd-Barrett also demonstrates in his broad political economy approach to the US invasion of Iraq how a strong coincidence exists between the cultural semiotics of the 'war genre' and the commercial interests of media corporations:

> Classic warfare is the epitome of a 'good story', high in tension and drama, with complex main plots and sub-plots played out within traditional binary opposi-tions of aggressor and victim, winner and loser. While expensive to cover, warfare is commercially rewarding for the media, since its threat and unfolding ignite insatiable audience appetites for news. Advertisers may initially fear the risk of juxtaposing products with unsavoury and unsettling issues, but they soon benefit from higher audience numbers and from the potential for linking merchandise with the semiotics of patriotism.
>
> (2004: 26)

Studies of TV ratings in the same conflict including 24/7 news channels such as CNN and Fox in particular, bear out the claim that audiences increasingly turn to the media and news shows in times of war, and that new channels like Fox have capitalized on this through patriotic cheerleading. They also capitalize on Hollywood-style entertainment values when enthusiastically embracing, for example, the Pentagon's video of US Private Jessica Lynch being 'rescued' from an Iraqi hospital by the US military. 'Saving Private Jessica', it later transpired, involved no military opposition at the Iraqi hospital where she was receiving medical attention for injuries sustained when her vehicle crashed – and not, as originally claimed, from a shoot-out with the enemy. This didn't stop the media 'iconicising Lynch as the face of American heroism' and underlines the con-temporary marketization of war and the commodification of its symbolic forms (Brown 2003: 63).

The second powerful explanation is the media's routine reliance on authority sources or 'primary definers' (Hall et al. 1978), which is theorized as an outcome of the media's normal routinization of daily news production and the journalists' efforts to underwrite claims to objectivity and impartiality. In times of war this structural orien-tation to the centres and institutions of power becomes pronounced. As the Director of News and Current Affairs at the BBC explained to the Glasgow University Media Group following the Falklands conflict: 'The BBC's journalists do indeed find it natural to ask "an important person" – a senior civil servant or government minister, for instance – for they are the people whose decisions largely determine how things will run in our democracy'. To which the GUMG commented, 'If such exhaustive consult-ation limits other opinions, then the media are also helping to determine how things will run in our democracy' (GUMG 1985: 2–3). This authority skew institutionally emasculates journalism when it becomes, for example, reliant on partial and delib-erately vague military press briefings that contribute to, rather than aim to clear, the 'fog of war'. All wars invariably reveal, after the event if not during, major distortions, misinformation and campaigns to deceive. The 2003 invasion of Iraq by the US and its allies was no exception. This war was widely and publicly legitimized in the media on grounds of Iraq's alleged connection with Al-Qaeda (America's number one target in its post-9/11 'global war against terror'), Saddam Hussein's stockpiling of weapons of mass destruction (WMD) and the dictator's human rights record – the first two claims have subsequently proved impossible to verify.

The third explanation is censorship. This is imposed on the media through a variety of legal and governmental means such as the Official Secrets Act, libel laws and, in the UK, 'D-notices' (now renamed 'Defence Advisory Notices') that are forwarded by the Defence, Press and Broadcasting Advisory Committee to prominent editors. These claim to give 'recipients sufficient guidance on subjects in which considerations of national security could be involved, to enable an editor to decide whether to publish, spike or seek advice from the Secretary' (http://www.dnotice.org.uk/notices.htm).

The historically reflexive and powerful controls imposed by the military on journalists in the field of war from the Crimea War (1854–56) to the US and coalition invasion of Iraq (2003), already described earlier, provide the fourth plank of explanation. The media's dependence on military access, military transport systems, military minders, military briefings, military communication systems and military protection in the military-controlled theatre of war all powerfully contribute to the military's ability to manage and contain the flow and content of journalism reporting. When combined with legal and governmental strictures (and flak) enacted on the home front this invariably makes for a highly effective curb on media reporting.

The fifth explanation refers to nationalism and patriotism and how journalists can often be relied upon to 'get on side' and become caught up within the rising tide of national sentiment and patriotic fervour. We shall return later to sociological investigations of this cultural phenomenon and its possible bases in the peculiar phenomenology of war. Here we can simply note that patriotism and nationalism, both everyday and banal, publicly staged and triumphalist, find easy vent in wartime. A senior UK ITN journalist reflecting on imagined ideas of the Nation in the Falklands war (even though public and political opinion were divided at the time) illustrates how such ideas can influence reporting in war time:

> We're a national news service. We reflect the Nation and the mood of the Nation. The Nation trusts us. We reciprocate that trust by giving people the truth including the bad things, unless that would undermine morale; then we wouldn't put that on.
> (GUMG 1985: 18)

Patriotism, like its blood cousin nationalism, tends to be historically selective and culturally eclectic. It often draws on past events already encrusted in myth and reworks these to add collective resonance and symbolism to current circumstances, the latter granting licence to their public elaboration. Just one example will have to suffice here, though all media wars can be culturally inflected in similar ways.

When discussing Australia's media war in the invasion of Iraq in 2003, Michael Bromley discerns how the Australian myth of the 'digger', became resurrected. The term 'digger' originated in reference to the tough and hardy pastoralists wrestling an existence from the unforgiving Australian bush in the 19th century but then became reinscribed in the conceptualization of ordinary Australian citizen-soldiers in World War I and the doomed military campaigns carried out by the Anzacs (Australian and New Zealand Army Corps) in Gallipoli in Turkey. This myth remains to this day a potent source of ideas and feelings for possible activation and appropriation:

> Since the 1990s politicians have contested the right to lay claim to the Australian legend with its working-class roots in egalitarianism, mateship, the fair go and practical improvisation embedded in the ANZAC myth. In April 2003, trying to counteract opposition to Australia's participation in the invasion of Iraq, Howard again appealed to this collective memory. . . .
>
> . . . the importance of the Australian military effort lay not in its meagre material presence but in its symbolic aura, and the ways in which journalism and the media could be relied on to invoke and evoke in response the myth of the 'digger' as a potentially universal rallying point for Australians.
>
> (2004: 238)

As we can see, the Australian myth of the 'diggers', invoked in commemorations each year on Anzac Day, was politically appropriated by Australia's Prime Minister John Howard as he sought to mine seams of patriotism in support of his government's commitment to the US-led war against the Iraqi regime.

Professional journalist views on 'taste and decency' forms a sixth explanation. Again, studies of war reporting point to countless instances of the media self-censoring images of the human carnage caused by war, especially when inflicted on non-combatants by the media's 'own side'. Scenes of the US bombing in the 1991 Gulf War of the al-Amiriya bunker in Baghdad that incinerated over 400 sheltering civilians, many women and children, were heavily censored by the western media. The alleged role of images of warfare in affecting public morale and the political resolve to fight wars also resides at the heart of the Vietnam War syndrome – discussed below.

Theorizing beyond the Vietnam syndrome – and back again?

The Vietnam War syndrome, as we have heard, has played a major role in military thinking and the subsequent controls placed on journalists in war ever since. While televised images of military casualties, both 'Ours' and 'Theirs', in Vietnam certainly found some media exposure, some powerfully assuming iconic status and searing into people's consciousness (for example, the self-immolation of Buddhist monks protesting against the war; the shooting of a Vietcong suspect by General Nguyen Loan; or the picture of a fleeing naked Vietnamese girl terribly burned by a US napalm attack on her village) (Cumings 1992: plate 6)), contrary to military thinking this does not constitute evidence that the media undermined the US war effort or, more implausibly, 'lost' the Vietnam War. Daniel Hallin (1986, 1994) rebuts the 'oppositional media' thesis head-on in his detailed examination of media performance throughout the Vietnam War. In so doing, he elaborates a politically responsive model of media–state relations that moves beyond the ahistorical formulations often found under the manufacturing consent paradigm, exemplified in Herman and Chomsky's propaganda model, and which has relevance for understanding media–state relations and policy formation more generally.

Hallin conceptualizes the journalist's professional world in terms of three overlapping spheres, each of which involves the application of different journalistic standards. At the core is the 'sphere of consensus': the region of 'motherhood and apple pie' comprising objects and events that are generally accepted by society as non-controversial (1986: 116–18). Here journalists do not ordinarily feel obligated to present opposing views and may even act as advocates or ceremonial protectors of consensus values. This is surrounded by the 'sphere of legitimate controversy' where notions of journalist objectivity and balance reign supreme, exemplified in reporting of electoral contests and legislative debates, with parameters generally defined by the political party system. Beyond the sphere of legitimate controversy lies the 'sphere of deviance'. Here political actors and views not deemed worthy of being heard by journalists and the political mainstream of society are found. Claims to journalist neutrality once again melt away in the sphere of deviance and the media may 'play the role of exposing, condemning, or excluding from the public agenda those who violate or challenge consensus values' (Hallin 1994: 54).

Deploying this model, Hallin notes how media reporting of Vietnam in fact changed across time following unfolding events on the ground and how these registered inside the US political establishment. The 1968 Tet offensive by the Vietcong, though repulsed by the US military, shocked political elites and proved to be a key moment in the war and in changing the tide of political support:

> In short, then, the case of Vietnam suggests that whether the media tend to be supporting or critical of government policies depends on the degree of consensus those policies enjoy, particularly within the political establishment. . . . News content may not mirror the facts, but the media, as institutions, do reflect the prevailing pattern of political debate: when consensus is strong, they tend to stay within the limits of the political discussion it defines; when it begins to break down, coverage becomes increasingly critical and diverse in the viewpoints it represents, and increasingly difficult for officials to control.
>
> (1994: 55)

Hallin's rebuttal of the oppositional media thesis opens up a more politically contingent model of state–media interactions (see also Bennett 1990; Butler 1995, Wolfsfeld 1997; Entman 2004) and fractures claims of media ideological closure and the state's dominance of media agendas advanced by exponents of the manufacturing consent paradigm.

Piers Robinson (2002) usefully develops this argument further when seeking to understand exactly how and when the media may not only respond to elite consensus or dissensus, as elaborated in Hallin's model, but also take the initiative and independently intervene in the policy-making process. Again referring to the Vietnam War, Robinson argues that, 'media coverage, having passively reflected elite consensus prior to 1968, became an active participant in elite debate by adopting the side of those opposed to the war and, in the presence of executive policy uncertainty, influencing key policy-makers to move to withdrawal' (2001: 538). In other words, Robinson is maintaining that under particular conditions when the executive itself, and not just surrounding elites, is conflicted about policy, or when no policy is in place to deal with newsworthy events, the media may independently seek to shape policy (see Table 5.2). He concludes, 'the importance of the media regarding political outcomes is far greater than allowed for by existing manufacturing consent theory' (2001: 541).

While this position does not seek to reinstate the 'Vietnam syndrome' or suggest that media images of war and human suffering can in themselves alter policy (the *CNN effect*), when critically framed by the media in relation to a wider policy vacuum or conflicted executive policy arena, so they may come to exert an influence on shaping government policy. This more sophisticated understanding of media–state interactions allows, under exceptional conditions, for media influence on state policy and reverses the manufacturing consent paradigm's expectation of state influence on media. As

Table 5.2 The policy–media interaction model and theories of media–state relations

Level of elite consensus	Media–state relationship	Role of the media
Elite consensus	Media operates within 'sphere of consensus' (Hallin)	Media 'manufactures consent' for official policy
Elite dissensus	Media operates within 'sphere of legitimate controversy' (Hallin)	Media reflects elite dissensus as predicted by Hallin and Bennett
Elite dissensus *plus* policy uncertainty within government and critically framed coverage	Media takes sides in political debate and becomes an active participant	Media functions to influence direction of government policy

Source: Reproduced with permission from Robinson, P. (2001) 'Theorizing the Influence of Media on World Politics', *European Journal of Communication* 16(4): 536 © Sage Publications.

such, it helps to open up to empirical analysis the complexities that may, on occasion, characterize media–state interactions in respect of foreign policy and other conflicted arenas.

Going culturally deeper: the phenomenology of war and professional myths

Ethnographic studies of war correspondents have also prised open further levels of complexity in respect of the media's relationship to war. Going culturally deeper into the war environment inhabited by war correspondents and exploring their cultural milieu and professional myths, researchers have recovered further possible explanations for the nature of war reporting. David Morrison, based on one of the most insightful studies to date of war correspondents (Morrison and Tumber 1988), has written, for example, on the phenomenological shift that war correspondents have to make as they move from the non-violent norms and expectations of everyday civilian life to the organized violence and militarized killing of the war zone:

> For the civilian, whose world is based on the premise of non-violence, the violence that occurs in war means not simply moving from one world to another, but of arranging the new reality in such a way that it sits incorporated into existing constructions of reality. The journalist covering war at close quarters moves into a new world where existing civil attitudes, values, perception of treatment toward others cannot exist unmodified.
>
> (1994a: 315)

While some correspondents, according to Morrison, may steadfastly decline the invitation to see the world through the military's perspective on organized death and produce humanistic 'howls of protest', others through time and force of circumstance incrementally come to accept their new situation and take on the military's social construction of reality (see also Glover 2001). Much will depend on the exact nature of their war immersion and also the extent to which they can periodically access settings or networks that remain distanced from the theatre of war. In the Falkland's conflict, for example, the small group of journalists who accompanied the British armada to the islands in the South Atlantic became fully enmeshed into the military world. Over the course of the campaign, the journalists got to know their military subjects well, training with them, sharing their days and recreation time and getting to know some of them as friends. Their very lives depended on them:

> In effect what was happening to the journalists was that their professional need to cover a story in a detached way was slowly being swamped by the very real, human need to belong, to be safe. The comradeship and closeness demonstrated by the troops, which the journalists so admired, were not just the random product that

an occupational association throws up, but the response of having to work closely together . . .

(Morrison and Tumber 1988: 99)

This enmeshing proved consequential for their war reporting. Incrementally the journalist began to identify with the military perspective and point of view, and this could help to account for why some may have turned a blind eye to circulating claims about British military misdeeds and possible atrocities:

> The journalists not only merely observed their subjects, but lived their lives and shared their experiences, and these experiences were of such emotional intensity that the form of prose which journalists use to take the reader into that experience – the 'I was there' form – provided not only a window for the reader, but also a door for partiality irrespective of any desire to remain the detached professional outsider.
>
> (1988: 95–6)

Not all war correspondents of course live in such close proximity to their military subjects. Many will continue to inhabit their own professional cultural milieu and socialize with other correspondents when reporting on wars in distant places. Here ethnographies have recovered further cultural depths of relevance for understanding the nature of war reporting. Marc Pedelty's study of the Salvadoran Foreign Press Corps Association (SPECA) at the end of the El Salvador civil war in 1992 is a case in point. Like Morrison and Tumber's study, Pedelty explores the correspondents' special relationship to the violence and terror of war, and maintains:

> War correspondents have a unique relationship to terror . . . a hybrid condition that combines both voyeurism and direct participation. For these 'participant observers' violence is not a matter of values. . . . They need terror to realise themselves in both a professional and spiritual sense to achieve and maintain their cultural identity as 'war correspondents'.
>
> (1995: 2)

Pedelty's correspondents, then, are said to have both a professional and personal investment in the mythical 'war correspondent' most recently popularized in such films as *Salvador* and *Under Fire* both about Salvador, as well as such others as *The Killing Fields* and *The Year of Living Dangerously*. This is no simple internalization of cinematic myths, however, but is analysed as rooted in the daily routines, thwarted ambitions, constraints and frustrations of war correspondents' professional practices and everyday lives. He observes how many of the US correspondents, especially those who rarely ventured outside of San Salvador, ran little personal risk of danger or violence, and yet accounts of danger and violence figured prominently in their self-image as revealed in their stories to each other:

> Yet that fantasy counts for something. These and other social rituals make the fantastic myths of war correspondence seem real, or at least realizable, by

separating identity from practice. The war correspondents' cultural identity is formed and reconstructed mainly within the free play of ritual and popular culture, as separated from the contradictory and destabilizing circumstances of daily work.

(1995: 146)

Whereas Pedelty's interpretation is rooted in an appreciation of the war journalists' sub-culture as an active response to their professional and organizational circumstances, Morrison in his study of the experiences of journalists reporting the Falklands war takes cognizance of the wider (and incremental) unsettling of civilian norms in militarized conditions. Both may well have validity though each, I would contend, is likely to hold differently in different theatres of war and in respect of the particular conditions that they throw up.

Pedelty's 'parachute' correspondents flew in and out of El Salvador without fully understanding the conflict and were particularly vulnerable to elite source manipulation; many of them we are told rarely ventured outside the security of the capital Salvador. But this is not the situation faced by all correspondents. Increasingly rising numbers of inexperienced freelancers seeking to establish a foothold in an increasingly 'casualized' media industry take themselves to the heart of conflict zones, and many have paid the ultimate price for their professional aspirations. But not all can be presumed to be following an invariant mythic script of 'war correspondent' (McLaughlin 2002; Leith 2004). At the time of writing, the Committee for the Protection of Journalists (CPJ) records 56 journalists killed worldwide in 2004, most of them in Iraq; 246 have been murdered and a further 67 killed in cross-fire during the period 1995–2004 (CPJ 2005).

Globalization and the changing theatre of war

The field of war reporting has changed as the nature of warfare itself has changed and both are influenced by, and contribute to, wider processes of globalization. Globalization, argues Frank Webster, means that nation states become increasingly 'porous' (2003: 59). Media communications now flow across borders; news reporting can take place in real-time 24 hours a day, seven days a week and this, inevitably, makes it increasingly difficult for states to control and contain the tides of information washing around global shores (see Figure 3.2 on p. 51). Global marketplaces, trade and capital flows are also no longer tied to nation states as they once were and this gives rise, according to Anthony Giddens, to 'states without enemies', that is, nation states who no longer seek international dominance through interstate wars fought over territory. The Stockholm International Peace Research Institute (SIPRI) seems to lend support to this view when documenting that in 2004 all 19 major conflicts in the world – those causing over 1000 battle-related deaths in any one year – were classified as intrastate (not interstate) conflicts, though it cautions that 'in a globalized world, intra-state conflicts are becoming increasingly international in nature and in effects' (SIPRI 2005). Today's intrastate conflicts, often so called 'degenerate' (Shaw 2003: 23–5) or 'uncivil wars' (Keane 2004: 109–24), tend to be prosecuted with extreme brutality on civilian populations and are conducted for the most part in the South under conditions of globally exacerbated inequality. Such conflicts and globalizing conditions also give rise to 'enemies without states': new fundamentalisms pitched against the dominant world order and striking out beyond national borders (see also Urry 2003: 131–2).

Some researchers have also sought to draw a clear distinction between 'industrial war' and 'information war' (Webster 2003; see also Castells 2001: 158–63 on 'non-linear war'). Industrial warfare, generally associated with wars from 1914 to the 1970s, suggests Webster, was conducted by nation states, involved disputes over territory and mobilized either whole or significant numbers of populations either as combatants or workers organized in a national, planned and industrialized war effort. Information war, in contrast, doesn't require mass mobilization but increasingly involves 'knowledge warriors' hooked into computerized communication, surveillance and guided weaponry systems that 'fuse information with firepower' and can do so with devastating results. Information warfare produces a 'post-heroic' military where overwhelming force and/or remotely delivered firepower can deliver 'instant wars' lasting only days and weeks rather than months and years. In information war, civilian populations can be remote from the war, but their dependence on media and information if anything becomes more pronounced. This is because the legitimacy of democratized states relies on public support as does the military's continuing capacity to wage war:

> precisely because Information Warfare is typically waged in the name of democracy itself, then public approval is critical to its conduct. A corollary is that, while today the public are no longer mobilized to fight wars as combatants, they are mobilized as spectators of war – and the character of this mobilization is of utmost consequence.
>
> (Webster 2003: 64)

This need for 'perception management' though greater today than ever, has in fact become 'extraordinarily difficult to achieve in today's complex and variegated information environment' (2003: 64), and the state and military's capacity to successfully win the battle for hearts and minds in industrial war, has been eroded and destabilized in information war (see also Dillon 2002, and Figure 3.2). If correct, this argument clearly qualifies some of the principal research findings on war reporting recounted above. It has not gone unchallenged however.

John Downey and Graham Murdock (2003) take issue with current military discourse about the so called 'revolution in military affairs' (RMA) thought to be brought about by new communication technologies, as well as the idea of a decisive rupture or break between 'industrial war' and 'information war'. Contemporary warfare is theorized not principally in relation to its communication and hi-tech dimensions but in respect of the geopolitics of US Empire and the asymmetries of globalized guerrilla warfare that this is said to have produced. They note, historically, how

> the strategic importance of the telegraph system was firmly established by the outbreak of world war one. This led to the cutting off of the German cables linking Germany to the US within hours of the expiry of the British ultimatum in 1914, as the first maneuver in the battle to win American support (Taylor, 1995: 177). By the time World War Two started, the kind of complex distanciated command and control systems associated with the arrival of Information Warfare were fully operational, permitting the rise of *Blitzkreig* – rapid, coordinated air and land attack – as a form of war.
>
> (2003: 74)

In other words, command, control and communications systems, so central to notions of information war have been central to military strategy and tactics for some considerable time. They also argue that the military's claims concerning precision guided ordinance minimizing 'collateral damage' are widely exaggerated and 'frictions' within and between existing communication and surveillance systems also undermines claims about their efficacy. Most critically, perhaps, they argue that focusing on the high-tech nature of modern weaponry as well as communication systems displaces that which needs to be placed centre stage in current academic and public debate: the geopolitics of power and its relation to the globalization of asymmetric warfare including the use of low-tech weapons against civilian populations:

> The 9/11 attacks were the most significant manifestations to date of the globalized guerrilla war that has emerged over the last decade. They herald a counter revolution in military affairs in which low-tech weaponry has demonstrated its capacity to by-pass current weapons systems and communication networks.
>
> (2003: 83)

Clearly, Downey and Murdock are right to question ideas of 'information war' (Webster 2003), 'network-centric warfare' (Dillon 2002) and the so called 'revolution in military affairs' in so far as each becomes spellbound by technology and succumbs to technologically determinist thinking while failing to theorize the geopolitical interests and asymmetries of power driving and structuring contemporary conflicts. We can also agree that notions of a rupture between 'old war' and 'new war', however specified, as with most 'breaks' in history, are unlikely to be quite so clear-cut in reality. Even so, the role of new communications systems and technologies in (a) the military conduct of war; (b) governmental legitimization of war; (c) media war reporting; and (d) the public contention and mobilization of dissent to war remain important foci of analytical interest and research, even though these also need to be theorized in relation to wider transformations of politics, power and global dynamics of change. We shall return to debates about mediatized terror and terrorism in Chapter 8. Here we briefly raise three further developments in the world of globalizing journalism and how each impacts on war reporting.

24/7 Real-time reporting

The advent of 24/7, real-time, news as Webster noted above, has changed the nature of news broadcasting in times of war, though again it is a matter of some debate about how exactly. Daya Thussu (2000, 2003) is in no doubt that this development can be regarded as the latest extension of western and US global news dominance. The advent of 24/7 real-time news channels – CNN, BBC World, Fox – as well as regional and national 24/7 news services, he argues, remain highly dependent on western news agencies. For the most part they also mimic US news styles and agendas and, in their 'infotainment' treatment of conflicts and virtual wars, produce 'live TV and bloodless deaths' (Thussu 2003). Live reporting of conflicts has become one of the characteristic features of 24/7 news and, in an increasingly crowded and competitive news market-place produces a tendency to sacrifice depth for immediacy, analysis for speculation, and considered news packages for live, often uninformed, commentary. In wartime, pressures of continuous live reporting render journalists even more vulnerable to spin and propaganda and to the fog of war. Use of computerized graphics, satellite imagery, military supplied video of 'precision strikes' and 'chat show' experts all reinforce the infotainment presentation of 24/7 satellite news services: 'As a result of this homogenisation of coverage of conflicts – bloodless and largely devoid of any real sense of death and destruction – the audience can be desensitised to the tragedy and horror of war' (2003: 124).

Live coverage can also produce its own dramatic effects as many viewers witnessed in the first Gulf War. Here, for example, an NBC reporter excitedly responds to a siren warning of an incoming Scud attack just as he was about to go live to air from Saudi Arabia:

> Get us up on audio. Please, get us up. Hello, New York? This is Saudi Arabia. This is not a drill. Hello, New York? [Holding up gas mask] This is Saudi Arabia. This is Saudi Arabia. This is not a drill. New York? OK, let's go. We're firing Patriots. We've got flares and we've got sirens. Let's go – focus! [Explosion in distance; Kent ducks] There goes a Patriot, let's go!
>
> (cited in Taylor 1992: 69)

This piece of live action earned the reporter concerned nicknames of 'Scud Stud' and the 'Satellite Dish' from his colleagues, and granted him, for a while at least, minor celebrity status. To what extent such coverage is enlightening as well as captivating is, of course, debatable.

Andrew Hoskins (2004) also attends to the distinctive forms of television's war coverage in his study of how recent forms of television news contributed to the production of 'new memory', that is, mediatized social memory through circulated images of war, repeated 'flashframes' and the 24/7 fetish of liveness. He argues that television effectively obliterated from public view the reality and horror of war while substituting spectacle and the thin immediacy of 'reality-TV' viewing:

> the Iraq War involved the prioritizing of image-dissemination over news gathering and time over content. Effective analysis and understanding were substituted with the self-evidency of immediate images as the thresholds for what was included as news was lowered. Commentator prompts reveal the utter emptiness of much of the live coverage, with 'let's listen in' or 'let's watch and see what's going down' directing audiences to adopt reality TV modes of consumption.
>
> (2004: 76)

The media in this commercialized environment of produced spectacle increasingly focus on the correspondents themselves who now become the subject of the story as much as its narrator. In 2003 the apogee of this process was literally embedded in the invasion of Iraq where 'the "up close and personal" mass embedding of correspondents dominated news output and obscured critical discourse on the war' (2004: 73).

Embedding

The latest military tactic of embedding journalists with military units in the invasion of Iraq coincides with the rise of 'reality TV' as well as the insatiable content needs and characteristic temporal aesthetic of 'live' 24/7 news programmes. Most commentators argue strongly that this latest form of military control could only lead to 'embeds' effectively getting 'in-bed' with the military and losing the necessary distinction between warrior and correspondent (Keeble 2004: 50). Consider the following dramatic exchange between CNN anchor Aaron Brown and embedded reporter Walter Rogers, a case in point:

> *Rodgers*: The pictures you're seeing are absolutely phenomenal. These are live pictures of the Seventh Cavalry racing across the desert in Southern Iraq . . . If you ride inside that tank; it is like riding in the bowels of the dragon. They roar. They screech. You can see them slowing now. We've got to be careful not to get in front of them . . .
> *Brown*: Wow, look at that shot.
> *Rodgers*: . . . is truly historic television and journalism.
>
> (CNN 20 March 2003)

While it is true that embedded journalists certainly had a partial and selective view of the Iraq war and because of their proximity to selected action were likely to play up the dramatic and spectacular, the general claim that the 600 US and 128 British embeds became the conduit for military dictated propaganda is not entirely borne out by research evidence. Justin Lewis and Rod Brookes (2004), based on a systematic analysis of the British reporting of the Iraq War, note how embedded British reporters were

(a) less likely than other forms of reportage to imply the existence of WMD and (b) provided more balanced, less celebratory, accounts of the Iraqi people's reactions to US/UK military action. Without the embeds, they suggest, 'broadcasters would have been much more dependent upon information from military briefings, and far less able to provide independent testimony of what was occurring' (2004: 289). They conclude:

> The Pentagon's embed strategy was ingenious because it *increased* rather than *limited* access to information. By giving broadcasters access to highly newsworthy action footage from the front line, they were encouraging a focus on the actions of US and British troops, who would be seen fighting a short and successful war. The story was all about winning and losing, rather than a consideration of context in which the war was fought.
>
> (2004: 298–9)

In such circumstances crude forms of military censorship could become increasingly irrelevant because they become largely redundant given the media's own proclivity towards the dramatic, visual and immediate, a finding which also resonates with findings about the media's self-censorship in respect of images of death and damaged bodies.

Audiences and body horror

Here a common shibboleth needs to be dispatched on the basis of recent research findings. This is the compassionate but naïve view that if images of the reality of warfare, of death and destroyed bodies, could find sufficient public exposure people would be less inclined to rally behind a cheerleading media and governments would lose the popular mandate for war. This common presumption is largely mistaken. It is certainly the case that western media have contributed to a powerful 'system of representations which marginalizes the presence of the body in war, fetishizes machines, and personalizes international conflicts while depersonalizing the people who die in them' (Gusterton, cited in Taylor 1998: 163). And we also know that the western media routinely self-censor 'red meat' images of body horror on grounds of 'taste and decency' (though interestingly, to different degrees in different countries and cultures) (Petley 2003). However, it does not automatically follow that showing images of body horror will produce anti-war sentiments or undermine the stomach for war. As Susan Sontag has commented in *Regarding the Pain of Others* (2003), images of mutilated bodies can be used 'to vivify the condemnation of war, and may bring home, for a spell, a portion of its reality to those who have no experience of war at all', but these images of 'atrocity may give rise to opposing responses. A call for peace. A cry for revenge. Or simply the bemused awareness . . . that terrible things happen' (2003: 11–13). Empirical research tends to bear out Sontag's reflections.

As part of a larger study of the first Gulf War, Morrison (1992) examined how audiences responded to media images, focusing on the terrible scenes – both broadcast and censored – of the bombed al-Amiriya shelter in Baghdad. Ten discussion groups, split by age, class, gender and national geography were conducted as well as a survey of over 1000 adults interviewed at home. The research revealed that, though upset by the scenes, they did not for the most part alter people's resolve towards the war. The first Gulf War in 1991 was widely seen as a 'just war' by many of the British public (85% according to Morrison's own findings), and this steeled people's reactions to the human suffering that the war produced, though rarely seen (Taylor 1998). Morrison comments, 'If justice is the shield for sensibilities, the viewers themselves wish to be protected from the absolute horrors of war' and he found 'no one in the group discussions who wished for the cindered body shots relayed by the agency, WTN, to be broadcast. Viewers considered that they were too horrific to screen' (1994b: 23).

If a similar study were repeated in respect of the US invasion of Iraq in 2003, given the lack of consensus surrounding this war which began without United Nations support as well as the increased circulation of images of violence via the Internet and other means (see Chapter 8), it is possible that public responses may have been different. Even so, Morrison's findings point to an underlying complexity in respect of mediated scenes of horror and one which does not support an anti-war thesis based on calls for unrestricted public exposure to scenes of war.

While research studies such as these challenge ideas of a simple causality between images of human suffering and audience response or the generation of particular audience beliefs, this does not necessarily lead to the conclusion that such images should not be publicly circulated. In fact, there are strong grounds to say that such scenes, no matter how upsetting, should be seen because they can bear witness and potentially contribute to a politics of shame. John Taylor puts the case eloquently for what's at stake in the public display of images of body horror and why 'civility' should never be allowed to censor their circulation:

> But civility sits uneasily with war – unless it is known to be describing official histories, censored reports and popular victories. How would the Holocaust be remembered if it existed only in 'civil' representations – those which were most discreet? What would it mean for knowledge if the images ceased to circulate, or were never seen in the first place? What would it mean for civility if representations of war crimes were always polite? If prurience is ugly, what then is discretion in the face of barbarism?
>
> (1998: 195–6)

Recent studies by members of the Glasgow University Media Group offer further insights into the possible roles performed by media images in people's understanding of wars and conflicts (Philo 2002; Philo and Berry 2004). In a study examining audience responses to television's news portrayal of the *intifada* in Israel, the researchers conducted 14 focus groups comprising 100 people selected on the basis of income, age and gender and administered a questionnaire to 743 young people. They also conducted a news editing exercise where focus groups were given a set of 16 photographs taken from

TV news coverage of the *intifada* and invited to use these to prepare a news story. By these methods the researchers aimed to reveal if the participants were able to reproduce the news language and explanations of the conflict provided by television news. Focus group members were invited to reflect on the impact of television news on their thinking and how certain scenes impacted their feelings. One focus group member, for example, commented on the lack of context and background in much news reporting of the Israeli–Palestinian conflict as well as the role of emotive images in his thinking:

> One of the problems with most of the news is that you get the atrocity, the horror but it's the background that is the key bit . . . I'm pretty ignorant of it really and that's the more important, more interesting, important stuff, the background, the origins rather than the latest [action] . . .
>
> When that boy and his dad were shot by Israeli soldiers, unfortunately the British TV cut the pictures, but even so it's still fairly shocking and that re-energized, reawakened my interest. Just because that brought it home to me as a parent. If I was in that situation with my son . . . that did make me realize just what it must be like. (Middle-class male group, London)
>
> (cited in Philo and Berry 2004: 215)

These, and many other statements like them, lend support to Greg Philo and Mike Berry's overall conclusions about the impoverished basis of television news for understanding the nature of the Israeli–Palestinian conflict and how news images of human suffering first need to be contextualized before they can be made sense of by audiences. Visual images of the Palestinians as the underdog, for example, do not necessarily produce a sympathetic response: 'A key factor is how such imagery is contextualized through explanations of cause and how these affect understanding of the legitimacy and rationale of the two sides' (2004: 238). A principal conclusion is that the lack of historical background needed to understand the Palestinian actions in the occupied territories results in news presentations which construct a view of Palestinians as 'starting' the trouble and Israelis as 'retaliating'. Israelis are thereby generally depicted as simply defending themselves against acts of terrorism. This partial media construction they conclude influences people's beliefs and common misunderstanding of the nature of the conflict.

We cannot conclude this discussion of mediatized body horror, however, without also referencing new dynamics in the international and global flows of news (see Figure 3.2 on p. 51). Though often censored by the mainstream media, images of war casualties and other scenes of war horror are becoming more readily available through alternative media sources such as the Internet as well as news contra-flows produced by non-western media such as the middle-eastern TV news satellite services Al-Arabiya and the Qatar-based pan-Arabic satellite television channel Al-Jazeera. Set up in 1996 with financial backing from the Emir of Qatar following the demise of the London-based BBC and Saudi Arabian Arabic television network, Al-Jazeera has revolutionized broadcasting in Arab countries. In the West, however, it has become known for its reporting and regional perspectives on the world post-9/11 and particularly its circulation of video messages from Osama Bin Laden, scenes of Iraqi civilian casualties and US military dead and injured and US prisoners of war. Predictably it has incurred considerable 'flak' from the US government as well as other media (a theme addressed further in Chapter 8).

There are also grounds to suggest that a more deadly form of flak has also been delivered by the US military when targeting journalists perceived as hostile or paying insufficient care to those operating outside of military controls (Gopsill 2004; Hoskins 2004: 72). The Al-Jazeera Baghdad bureau was shelled by an American missile on 8 April 2003, killing one of its reporters and this occurred despite the news organization having informed the Pentagon about its exact location. The Al-Jazeera office in Kabul in the Afghanistan war in 2001 was also bombed, deliberately, by an American missile. Like the messenger of old it seems, bringing unfavourable news to the Emperor is fraught with risk. Al-Jazeera symbolizes both the promise and need for a considerably augmented exchange of global views and voices, images and ideas, discourses and dialogue from different vantage points around the globe (El-Nawawy and Iskandar 2003; Miladi 2003; Azran 2004; Iskander and El-Nawawy 2004). It also symbolizes something of the cultural distance and dissonance as well as organized systems of constraint and control that globalizing infusions into the mainstream of western media inevitably produce and confront, especially in the context of war. Depending on how these contradictory forces and emergent flows play out in the future so we may be able to speak of a possible global public sphere:

> As a globalized public sphere becomes more complex and interconnected, it will become important to theorize the implications for public support for military conflict ... As these debates over military conflict become globalized and denationalized, beyond the scope of any single community, there remains the hope that these policies can be debated clearly through a more multilateral cultural lens.
>
> (Reese 2004: 263)

Chapter summary

This chapter has reviewed the key explanations and findings from the voluminous research literature focused on media at war. We have noted how the historically evolving and reflexive interplay between military and media continues to produce new forms of military control, constraint and censorship. We have also observed, however, something of the cultural complexities embedded in both the phenomenology of war and professional sub-cultures of war correspondents and how these inform professional practices and identities. The changing nature of warfare in globalizing times also opens up further developments in the field of study. Crude censorship, the manipulation of messages and propaganda, continues to inform all media wars, and is probably destined always to do so, just as military controls will continue to be refined and sharpened in the context of changing media technologies. Not that tension and contradiction must always characterize the relationship between military and media. The latest military controls enacted through journalist embedding demonstrates a clear affinity with the media's increasing predispositions to entertainment and infotainment based in the competitive world of 24/7, live broadcasting and gives dramatic shape but often superficial form to war reporting today. Embeds today and tomorrow are destined to confuse the roles of military warrior and war correspondent, injecting adrenalin rather than analysis into their dispatches from the front. (It is doubtful whether the military will ever permit embeds in a theatre of war that is deemed to be anything other than a likely military success.)

When images of the human costs and consequences of war manage to squeeze through the formidable military controls and self-enacted professional censorship, they are unlikely in themselves to alter public views or support for military actions. They nonetheless remain a necessary component of war coverage, potentially bearing witness to the suffering frequently caused in our name and which should never be rendered invisible on moral grounds of civility, taste or decency. New contenders within the international marketplace of circulating images and ideas have joined the mainstream western media and these are now beginning to challenge dominant media agendas and hold out the promise of an expanded cultural interchange in the future, notwithstanding the considerable obstacles and difficulties identified. Mediatized war, inevitably, will continue to be a battlefield in its own right, and one where journalists are expected by governments, military and publics to persue conflicting goals and demonstrate contradictory allegiances.

Recommended reading

Allan, S. and Zelizer, B. (eds) (2004) *Reporting War: Journalism in Wartime*. London: Routledge.

Carruthers, S. (2000) *The Media at War: Communication and Conflict in the 20th Century*. Basingstoke: Macmillan.

Hallin, D. (1986) *The 'Uncensored War': The Media and Vietnam*. Oxford: Oxford University Press.

Knightley, P. (2003) *The First Casualty – The War Correspondent as Hero, Propagandist and Myth Maker from the Crimea to Iraq*. London: André Deutsch.

Taylor, J. (1998) *Body Horror: Photojournalism, Catastrophe and War*. Manchester: Manchester University Press.

Thussu, D.K. and Freedman, D. (eds) (2003) *War and the Media*. London: Sage.

6 | PEACE JOURNALISM AND OTHER ALTERNATIVES: ON HOPES AND PRAYERS

The voluminous studies of war reporting, mapped in the previous chapter, parallel the media's fascination with war. A similar parallel also informs academic study of peace reporting – war's invisible twin. This mirrors, with few exceptions, the media's relative lack of interest in processes of non-violent conflict resolution and reconciliation. As a necessary counterpoint to the preceding discussion and as a way of getting a further fix on the nature and possibly changing dynamics of mediatized conflicts, this chapter explores the case made by advocates of 'peace journalism' and other 'corrective' journalisms, including 'development journalism', 'public journalism' and on-line 'alternative journalism'.

All these different journalisms can be dubbed 'corrective' in that they deliberately define and position themselves in opposition to established, traditional forms of journalism, challenging foundational news values, dominant agendas, privileged elite access and so called 'professional' journalist practices. Their declared mission, based on critiques of actually existing media, is to redress the perceived deficiencies and distortions of mainstream news representations and better align journalism, *inter alia*, to projects of social responsibility, economic development, political participation and cultural democracy. They promise, in other words, to harness journalism to normatively informed projects of change and thereby shift the media's role and responsibilities in respect of mediatized conflicts.

Given what we know about the news media, however, their institutions and practices, logics and determinants, can these more critically engaged forms of journalism really hope to dent the edifice of mainstream journalism and make a difference? And, if so, by whose mandate and on what political and normative grounds do they do so? Issues of theoretical coherence and conceptual validity as well as institutional determinacy, political agency and normative desirability all need to be scrutinized before we can accept their respective claims and aims at face value. The following, then, sets out to address the hopes and prayers of these alternative, corrective journalisms and appraises their politics and prospects for change. We begin by consulting ideas of peace journalism and studies of peace reporting, followed by discussion of development journalism, public journalism and finally on-line alternative journalism.

Peace journalism: muting the sound of guns?

Not only do the media have this perverse fascination with war and violence; they also neglect the peace forces at work. Of course, some of this is the result of governmentalism, the fascination with power in addition to violence. How about some fascination with peace? And with people? How about giving them more voice?

As the media work, they amplify the sound of guns rather than muting them. Is this because we have the media we deserve? Hardly. It is more because the people who run them are badly trained, looking only upward in society, registering the sudden and the negative, not the patient, long-term work of thousands, millions of citizens.

(Galtung 1993: xi)

The term 'peace journalism' can be traced back to the 1970s and the work of Johan Galtung, Professor of Peace Studies and Director of the *TRANSCEND Peace and Development Network* (see also Bruck 1993; Roach 1993; Conflict and Peace Forums 1999; McGoldrick and Lynch 2000, 2001; Howard 2002). Galtung memorably likened war journalism to sports journalism, which typically sees its object in terms of a zero-sum game where winning is all. A better model, he argued, would be health journalism. Here the plight of a patient with cancer, for example, would be described but so too would the possible contributing causes – life style, environment, genetic make-up – as well as the range of possible remedies and future preventative measures. This model, he said, would prove more productive in the context of conflict reporting than focusing on violence, negative events and siding with a particular protagonist. Peace journalism is not, say its supporters, based on hopelessly idealist hopes for a conflict-free future. It recognizes the endemic and structural nature of many conflicts in the world but nonetheless seeks to identify and promote constructive responses: 'conflict + creativity', not 'conflict + violence'. The news media, says Galtung, have too long focused on the latter not the former. Embedded within this humanitarian project for peace journalism, then, is a normative critique of mainstream journalism. This is usefully summarized in Table 6.1.

Read in the light of the critical research findings elaborated in the previous chapter, Galtung's critique of war/violence journalism clearly rehearses many of them, including: the media's tendency to dehumanize the enemy, privilege elite views and the focus on the events of war rather than political context, preceding history, aftermath or

Table 6.1 Peace/conflict and war/violence journalism

Peace/Conflict Journalism	War/Violence Journalism
I. Peace/Conflict Orientated	**I. War/Violence Orientated**
• Explore conflict formation, x parties, y goals, z issues general 'win, win' orientation	• Focus on conflict arena, 2 parties, 1 goal (win), war general zero-sum orientation
• Open space, open time; causes and outcomes anywhere, also in history/culture	• Closed space, closed time; causes and exits in arena, who threw the first stone
• Making conflicts transparent	• Making wars opaque/secret
• Giving voice to all parties; empathy, understanding	• 'Us–Them' journalism, propaganda, voice, for 'Us'
• See conflict/war as problem, focus on conflict creativity	• See 'Them' as the problem, focus on who prevails in war
• Humanization of all sides; more so the worse the weapons	• Dehumanization of 'them'; more so the worse the weapon
• Proactive: prevention before any violence/war occurs	• Reactive: waiting for violence before reporting
• Focus on invisible effects of violence (trauma and glory, damage to structure/culture)	• Focus only on visible effect of violence (killed, wounded and material damage)
II. Truth Orientated	**II. Propaganda Orientated**
• Expose untruths on all sides/uncover all cover-ups	• Expose 'Their' untruths/help 'Our' cover-ups/lies
III. People Orientated	**III. Elite Orientated**
• Focus on suffering all over; on women, the aged, children, giving voice to voiceless	• Focus on 'Our' suffering; on able-bodied elite males, being their mouthpiece
• Give name to all evil doers	• Give name to their evil doers
• Focus on people peace makers	• Focus on elite peace makers
IV. Solution Orientated	**IV. Victory Orientated**
• Peace = non-violence + creativity	• Peace = victory + ceasefire
• Highlight peace initiatives, also to prevent more war	• Conceal peace initiative, before victory is at hand
• Focus on structure, culture, the peaceful society	• Focus on treaty, institution, the controlled society
• Aftermath: resolution, reconstruction, reconciliation	• Leaving for another war, return if the old flares up again

Source: Original table by Johan Galtung, in McGoldrick and Lynch 2000.

devastating human consequences. All these observations are well made. But what about the proposed alternative? Here we need to pursue the presuppositions and prescriptions of 'peace journalism' a little further.

Clearly, peace journalism has a Herculean struggle ahead if it is to successfully reconfigure the established media 'war genre' and repopulate it with different voices, views and values. As we know, in times of war the media come under the severest pressure from governments and military to act as a conduit for propaganda war. Much also depends, however, on the degree of political and state consensus and the strength of opposition to particular wars at any point in time as well as the depth of a more general antiwar/peace culture. The media cannot be wishfully sealed from this wider force field of politics and culture much less disembedded from the economic structures and logics that drive its performance. When analysing both war journalism and the prospects for a deeper more humanly meaningful and constructive journalism, therefore, we have to do so informed by understanding of the wider social, political, economic and cultural and technological contexts in which the media operate. Peace journalism's normative critique and prescriptions are seemingly based on an overly media-centric and insufficiently grounded view. Normative critique has to be augmented, if it is to have any political purchase at all, by studies and analysis of actual media performance and their complex interactions and dynamics and how these often impact processes of peace building, conflict resolution and reconciliation.

Blatant war propaganda and lies designed to deceive can and should be exposed as 'false' but the epistemological assumption embedded in peace journalism (see Table 6.1) appears to presume that 'truths' and 'untruths' are self-evident and can be accepted by even those locked in opposition and enmity. This contradicts everything that we know about the way that different histories and identities fuel each other, and how claims to the facts, much less the 'truth', are frequently destined to remain in dispute, notwithstanding (or maybe because of) appeals to 'history', 'evidence', 'reason' and 'expert testimony'. While the media can help in opening up such complexities to wider view, peace journalists, like the rest of us, do not occupy a position of omniscience in respect of the 'truth' or how we can best arrive at it. Much will depend on the interests, vantage points and perspectives of all the parties involved.

While many will agree with peace journalism's laudable aims to give voice to the voiceless, hear the cries of the suffering and witness the human carnage wrought by war and other violent conflicts, images of human suffering as we heard in the previous chapter cannot be presumed to transcend the interests and ideologies of viewers and readers. To focus on structure, culture, the peaceful society and highlight problem resolution are all 'good things' but this cannot simply be taken as an antidote for the negativity and violence of war reporting. Arguably what is needed is a broadening and deepening of war and conflict reporting, not its universal replacement by an idealized view of the world as it should be, nor one that is representationally engineered to conform to a particular view of the 'peaceful society'. Conflicts are endemic, often entrenched and sometimes unavoidably violent. They can also exact terrible human costs. But the chilling winds of history should remind us that 'peaceful solutions' are not always available and nor are they necessarily always the least bloody means of dealing with oppressive states and regimes. If this is so, the news media cannot universally be charged with the responsibility of representationally portraying all conflicts as if they are amenable to peaceful solutions.

Of course advocates of peace journalism may retort there is small chance anyway given the media's predilection for war/violence reporting. This may generally be so, but here we should not underestimate how journalism may in fact already offer more opportunities for increasing the range of responses to war and peace than generalizing claims based on normative critique alone tend to suggest. Peter Bruck, for example, observed in his study of media reporting of the protests surrounding the placement of cruise missiles how the media provide 'discursive spaces that peace activists can exploit' (1993: 94). Too often the progressive possibilities and enactments of the contemporary news media are lost from view in sweeping, normatively informed, statements. The differentiated forms and genres of journalism in fact, as we shall explore later, often contain opportunities for the discursive engagement of opposing views, the representation of different histories and *her*-stories and the recognition of different identities and experiences (see Chapter 9). Suffice to say here, that journalism comprises many different forms and mediums and at least some of these are demonstrably capable of disseminating ideas and images, discourses and debates that can ground deeper appreciation, as well as possible action, in respect of different conflicts, their causes and consequences (see Chapters 4, 8 and 9, and Cottle and Rai 2006). The communicative complexities of actually existing journalism, however, are rarely acknowledged much less empirically pursued and analysed in generalizing critiques. This is an oversight because they may well contain important seeds of hope for the advocates of peace journalism and others interested in expanding the range of views and voices, values and visions found in the news media and which are required for peaceful co-existence.

If different media forms and issues of representational complexity demand closer analysis, then so too do peace processes and peace negotiations and how these are publicly mediatized over time. To date very few researchers have examined the media's performance in such processes and those that have invariably reveal complexities and contingencies that can better ground the criticisms and prescriptions in respect of the media's role(s) in peace processes (Miller and McLaughlin 1996; Howard 2002; Spencer 2004; Wolfsfeld 2004). Gadi Wolfsfeld (2004), in ways not too dissimilar to Galtung, observes how reporting of peace processes is shaped by *news values*, specifically, 'immediacy', 'drama', 'simplicity' and 'ethnocentrism'. These, he suggests, are intrinsically inimitable to the need for calm, incremental progress and the recognition of the multisided composition and cultural complexities that should ideally inform peace negotiations (2004: 15–23). This general observation, however, is only the beginning of the story. The challenge for researchers, argues Wolfsfeld, is to explain how mediatized peace processes can in fact vary over time and circumstances. And here we need to attend to the dynamics and contingencies of peace processes themselves as well as the differing roles that the media can perform within them. This opens up a much more complex view of the possible role(s) of the news media in peace processes and negotiations:

> The key to understanding such variations is to look at the nature of the political and media environments in which the media are operating. Some environments are more likely to produce positive news about peace because they fundamentally alter journalists' working assumptions. The nature of the political environment is important because journalists reflect and reinforce the existing climate of opinion. The nature of the media environment is significant because it helps define the norms and routines for producing news about peace. . . .
>
> The most important political factors are the degree of elite consensus in support of the policies and the number and intensity of crises associated with the process. The greater the degree of elite consensus and the lesser degree of crisis, the more likely it is that the news media will play a constructive role in a peace process. The two variables having to do with the media environment are the level of sensationalism and the extent to which antagonists share a common media. Sensationalism leads to the media playing a more destructive role and having a large number of shared media has the opposite effect.
>
> (2004: 44)

This approach, then, seeks to ground the analysis and potential of media peace reporting in the contexts and contingencies of different political and media environments. As we have already encountered in the work of researchers such as Daniel Hallin and Piers Robinson (see Chapter 5), the degree of elite consensus or dissensus can significantly alter the media's propensity to support or challenge government initiatives, including peace proposals and negotiations. The unfolding nature of 'crises' including destructive events on the ground – bombings, atrocities, military actions and retaliations – can also affect the outcome of such processes. Media competition can lead to media sensationalism and specifically tendencies towards personalization and demonization as well as the pursuit of constant dramatic breakthroughs creating an unhelpful political climate, as can a media environment characterized by communal-based media that reinforce opposed identities and ideologies (see also Fawcett 2002). In such ways Wolfsfeld takes into account a complex set of conditions and contingencies at work in the media's relation to and representation of peace processes.

A detailed study of television's performance in the peace processes leading to the Good Friday Agreement in Northern Ireland in 1998 by Graham Spencer (2004) also points to further levels of complexity in the media's representations of peace processes. Television plays a participatory and not simply a reflective role, argues Spencer, and his study based on in-depth interviews with journalists, identifies four principal ways in which this is so. First, television news performs an 'expansive role in peace politics by broadcasting to all audiences at once' (2004: 604), and this, as we have heard, may be especially important in a media context characterized by a communally divided and partisan press. Second, television news 'has the potential to facilitate diplomacy and force movement in ways that are unattainable behind closed doors away from public scrutiny' and does so by challenging 'intransigence' and raising public expectations for change (2004: 604). Third, 'the emotional and dramatic emphasis of television has a tendency to simplify and exaggerate problems' and this can impact the flow of communications. And fourth, 'the ability of television reporting to function instantaneously creates expectations for action which can pressure politicians to respond quickly, therefore speeding up the process of interaction and dialogue' (2004: 604).

Television also has a capacity to intervene and register within different stages of peace processes. In early formative stages when not all parties may be equally committed to participating in peace talks, television can become the means for 'signalling'. Here, in the absence of direct face-to-face contacts, or because of a reluctance to communicate formally, the news media provide an alternative for dealing with contentious issues and this can increase the pressure of expectation on all the participants to engage constructively:

> Let's not forget that the first real sign of republicans and unionists communicating in any significant way was on television when Ken Maginnis of the UUP (Ulster Unionist Party) spoke with Gerry Adams in the US and Martin McGuiness on *Newsnight*. To see a republican and unionist talking in the same studio was a considerable step. It wasn't so much what they said, the fact that it was disagreeable was understandable, but it was the symbolism of the two sides meeting. That really was a sign of movement.
>
> (BBC Ireland correspondent quoted in Spencer 2004: 612)

Once serious negotiations are under way, however, it is understandable perhaps that either participants or peace brokers will try to avoid the scrutiny of the media and now the media may deliberately be kept at bay:

> (Senator George) Mitchell told me with the review process that he was taking the players away to the ambassador's residence in London and after explained how for the first two days each morning meeting would start with people waving newspapers at each other saying 'Look what you've just said in the *Newsletter*' and 'What's this you've put in the *Irish Times*?' and that it took two or three days to get over that . . . it was seen as vital to minimize media involvement.
>
> (BBC Ireland correspondent quoted in Spencer 2004: 614)

The media's involvement in peace processes, then, can be both constructive and destructive at different stages. In a vein similar to Wolfsfeld, Spencer also maintains that 'the political power of the media is influenced more by levels of political organization and commitment to engage rather than any inherent ability within news to direct what politicians do (or appear to do)' (2004: 621). Even so, he concludes, 'it remains undeniable that television news has played a crucial role in channelling communications between the participants as well as broader constituencies, and that this role has had both positive and negative consequences which are reflective of occurrences and relations within the political environment' (2004: 621). By careful empirical studies such as these, a few researchers have been able to provide a more grounded and productive approach for the analysis of peace-building processes. They have managed to go beyond the good intentions but limited analysis and free-floating prescriptions of peace journalism and provide stronger grounds for political analysis and critique.

Development journalism: deepening participation?

> But what exactly is development news? An inclusive definition is not easy to provide. It is not identical with 'positive' news. In its treatment, development news is not different from regular news or investigative reporting. It can deal with development issues at macro and micro levels and can take different forms at national and international levels. In covering the development news beat, a journalist should critically examine, evaluate, and report the relevance of a development project to national and local needs, the differences between a planned scheme and its actual implementation, and the difference between its impact on people as claimed by government officials and as it actually is. . . . It could almost lead to the humanisation of international news.
>
> (Aggarwala 1979: 180–1)

Development journalism, like peace journalism, is also informed by normatively informed critique. Its origins go back to the debates about the New World Information and Communication Order (NWICO) convened under the auspices of the United Nations in the 1970s, debates which challenged the imbalances of information flows around the world (Macbride 1980; Thussu 1996). 'Development journalism' was, and is likely to remain, an essentially contested term given its intervention within the shifting politics and theorization of 'development' and 'underdeveloped' societies (Servaes et al. 1996; Mohammadi 1997; Thussu 2000). The term registers quite differently, for example, within the competing paradigms of 'modernization theory' and 'dependency theory' as well as more recent attempts to theorize and enhance participatory communications within underdeveloped societies. Today development journalism may have lost something of its former critical edge through its appropriation by dominant state discourses promoting national economic 'development' and/or prestigious 'development projects', but it continues to signal for many continuing communication inequalities and the need for grassroots participation in decentralized and non-hierarchical media. Here development journalism continues to bear the imprint of its former radical alignments with the struggles of the poor, marginalized and dispossessed within underdeveloped societies in Asia, Latin America and Africa.

The differing inflections of development journalism, therefore, are best teased out and appraised in relation to wider debates and theoretical positions on development. Following World War II, modernization theory served as the informing backdrop of much communications theory. Here 'development' was construed in terms that replicated western trajectories of economic and industrial growth: historically evolutionary, unilinear and generally bounded within the context of the nation state. Evident failures by so called 'backward' countries and regions to mirror this western path of economic growth were invariably explained in terms of endogenous obstacles and deficits – whether at the level of culture, education or technology. Communications and journalism inevitably became seen as playing an important role in overcoming such deficits by building a national identity, a sense of collective purpose and transmitting information and ideas expedient to centrally defined goals of economic growth (Schramm 1964). Information transfer premised on views of powerful media effects and, later, the diffusion of innovations via cascading social relations positioned communications and journalism at the forefront of national programmes of development (Rogers 1962). A powerful transmission model of communications thus underpinned the modernization paradigm as well as its neglect of (a) structural issues of media control and access; (b) cultural sensitivity towards the politics of participation; and (c) cultural complexities of media reception.

Based on devastating critique of the modernization paradigm and its obvious political alignment to western political views, values and interests, the dependency paradigm located the problems of underdevelopment very differently. Here unequal exchange relations, the vulnerability of primary producers in world markets and the dependency of former colonized societies on former colonizers, were all seen as the principal structural determinants causing dependency and underdevelopment and these would continue, it was argued, so long as the underdeveloped countries of the 'periphery' remained dependent on the western powers at the 'centre' (Frank 1969; Amin 1976). Through the political economy lens of the dependency paradigm, modernization theory was seen, ideologically, as very much part of the problem, not its solution.

Ideas of media and cultural imperialism also powerfully informed the dependency critique at the level of communications theory (Schiller 1976; Boyd-Barrett 1977). Here western media influence was seen, essentially, as culturally softening up societies, encouraging consumerism and opening up new markets to western imports and ways of life; the latter corroding authentic traditions and indigenous cultures. In the realm of journalism the importation of the ideals, organizational forms and professional practices of western journalism combined with the dominance of western news agencies and the unequal flows of western media products to under gird western, predominantly US, cultural imperialism. Though now under challenge (Tomlinson 1999; Sreberny 2000) this powerful critique continues to have purchase on contemporary international communication flows and the reproduction of inegalitarian global social relations (Golding and Harris 1997; Mohammadi 1997; Thussu 2000).

The strength of the dependency paradigm is located principally in its critique of the exogenous forces bearing down on underdeveloped societies, not in its theoretical prescriptions for change or its analysis of intranational conflicts within, as well as between, the countries of the South. Calls for economic dissociation or the separating of the 'periphery' from the 'centre' have become increasingly unrealistic in today's increasingly interdependent world. Politically the dependency paradigm has also arguably paid insufficient attention to endogenous forces including grassroots movements and alliances needed for processes of development as well as the potentiality of indigenous communications for harnessing and deepening forms of democratic participation.

In today's globalizing world the complexities of changing relations between countries are not always best captured through static concepts of 'centre' and 'periphery', or 'North' and 'South' (Tomlinson 1990, 1999; Urry 2003). It is in this context that Jan Servaes (1995, 1996) has proposed a new paradigm – the 'multiplicity/another development' paradigm – that better attends to the cultural dynamics and multidimensional nature of communications and which resonates with current thinking about development journalism. Building on current theorizing he argues that 'development' should be informed by: (a) ideas of material and non-material needs; (b) endogenous ideas that emanate from each society and community; (c) ideas of self-reliance; (d) current thinking about ecology and sustainable development; (e) ideas of participatory democracy; and (f) structural changes in social relations, economic activities and their spatial distribution (Servaes 1995: 547–8). In the field of communications specifically, he stresses the importance of participatory communication and democratization. Implicitly, these views challenge earlier ideas of development journalism, as defined by Aggarawala (1979) for example, as insufficiently participatory and for remaining wedded to top-down ideas of national development. Development communications today, he suggests, require active grassroots involvement and the recognition of different cultural identities within self-managed media. Here dialogical exchange should take place, both horizontally and vertically, and in relation to local, national, regional, international and global concerns and contexts.

The ideas of 'development journalism' conceived as a promotional vehicle for national development programmes and agendas (*modernization paradigm*), or as a bearer of radical critique of unequal exchange relations (*dependency paradigm*), now gives way to calls for a more complex understanding of media processes and engagement (*'multiplicity/new development' paradigm*). Here the complexity and contradictions of geopolitical dependency, diverse cultural identities and social and political issues all enter the mix of 'development journalism' which, in its political enactment, strives to build and sustain the very forces that can ensure that 'development' takes root in local communities. The principal concern here, perhaps, is that this laudable, humanizing view of communications which sees development journalism as intimately entwined in processes of economic, social, political and cultural change and as responsive to so many different issues and identities may exacerbate the fragmentation and thereby dissipate the very forces required to combat the structural and political forces that cause underdevelopment. How can development journalism sustain the necessary alliances and interconnections between collectives and organizations, different cultures and identities, when the concept and practice of development journalism itself become fragmented in their efforts to enfranchise so many different interests and identities and at so many different levels?

This also raises questions about the relation between mainstream news media and other media organized for development. Aggarwala's definition above, notwithstanding its limitations, presciently suggested that development journalism need not be seen as the exclusive preserve of alternative or indigenous media, but can in fact feature in mainstream media and other journalism forms that can contribute to the 'humanization of international news'. While silences and imbalances remain, mainstream journalism can and occasionally does produce in-depth reports and 'humanizing' features on development issues and affected communities around the globe (Volkmer 1999; Hannerz 2004; Cottle forthcoming). As we have already heard, satellites and contemporary international television, as well as the Internet, are helping to constitute contra-flows and a nascent 'global public sphere' in which global issues and injustices can find increased exposure (Urry 2003).

The latest arguments of development journalism deliberately accent participatory modes of communication based less on a vertical and top-down 'transmission' views of communication and more on horizontal and bottom-up 'ritual' views of communications. These ideas also chime with contemporary positions of democratic theory (see Chapter 9) and notions of media as public sphere (see Chapter 2). Whether the ideas and ideals of development journalism will be able to sustain themselves against the global tides of economic inequality, competing notions of development, fragmenting interests and identities and the changing field of oppositional politics now increasingly organized under a broader rubric and democratic platform of 'social justice' is perhaps the key point. *Pambazuka News*, for example, subtitled a '*Weekly Forum for Social Justice in Africa*' typifies how ideas of development, formerly positioned at the centre of radical politics and critique, now become one among many issues and concerns addressed under the umbrella term of social justice. This on-line, alternative, platform for radical ideas and democratic politics in Africa clearly describes how 'development' becomes subsumed within a more encompassing politics of change when describing itself as follows:

> Pambazuka News is the authoritative electronic weekly newsletter and platform for social justice in Africa providing cutting edge commentary and in-depth analysis on politics and current affairs, development, human rights, refugees, gender issues and culture in Africa.
>
> (http://www.pamazuka.org)

New media organs such as *Pambazuka News,* therefore, signal both the democratic promise and possibly the demise of development journalism radically conceived and positioned at the heart of democratic projects for change. The radical agenda has proliferated and fragmented and requires new forms of democratizing communications. Concerns with processes of democratic deepening and active citizen involvement in communication processes are not confined, however, to underdeveloped or less developed societies. In a very different guise they also animate the ideas and practices of 'public journalism' in the US.

Public journalism: engaging citizens and democracy?

> Public journalism . . . [is] . . . to imagine a different kind of press, one that would: (1) address people as citizens, potential participants in public affairs, rather than victims or spectators; (2) help the political community to act upon, rather than just learn about, its problems; (3) improve the climate of public discussion, rather than simply watch it deteriorate; (4) help make public life go well, so that it earns its claim on our attention and (5) speak honestly about civic values, its preferred view of politics, its role as a public actor.
>
> (Rosen 1999: 44)

Public journalism represents a set of ideas and practices, supported by various journalists and academics, based on a belief in the communicative power of the press to engage citizens and publics in processes of political debate and deliberation and thereby invigorate American democracy. By such means, it is hoped, citizens and democratic politics can be reconnected to government and the perceived tide of growing political cynicism and apathy turned back. Public journalism hopes that citizens can be actively encouraged to re-engage with the political, not as disaggregated voters pursuing individual preferences or self-interests, but as a collective body, as a 'public', affirmed in its sense of community and democratic membership. The intellectual antecedents of public journalism can be traced back a long way in democratic and republican theory but they resonate most forcefully perhaps in the debates sparked by Walter Lippmann's *Public Opinion* and John Dewey's *The Public and Its Problems*, both published in the United States in the 1920s.

Whereas Lippman advanced a sceptical view towards the press and its capacity to enrich public culture, based on the latter's circulation of stereotypes and failure to convey 'correct representations' to an easily distracted readership, Dewey entertained a more positive view, based on the democratic value of public conversation and the role that the press could play in sustaining this. While Lippmann's ideas led him to conclude that, 'The common interest very largely eludes public opinion entirely and can be managed only by a specialized class', Dewey maintained, 'The printed word is a precondition of the creation of a true public, but it is not sufficient. People must engage each other in conversation about issues in the news' (cited in Rosen 1999: 38–9). The academic James Carey, in the spirit of Dewey, nails his colours to the public journalism mast and, arguing against Lippmann's information based or 'transmission view', affirms the ideal of the press as contributing to a reinvigorated ethic of citizenship bridging the gulf between daily life and public culture:

> What we lack is the vital means through which this conversation can be carried on: institutions of public life through which a public can be formed and can form an opinion. The press, by seeing its role as that of informing the public, abandons its role as an agency for carrying on the conversation of our culture. We lack not only an effective press but certain vital habits: the ability to follow an argument, grasp the point of view of another, expand the boundaries of understanding, debate the alternative purposes that might be pursued.
>
> (cited in Rosen 1999: 38)

Public journalism, according to Carey, seeks to make 'public life possible' and cultivates 'an ethic of citizenship rather than cults of information and markets' (Carey 1999: 51). Ideas of civic republicanism resonate in public journalism where citizenship is seen as much more than individual rights and interests; citizenship, rather, is fundamentally about a sense of belonging, moral community and identity. Only through public discourse, engaged debate and deliberation can citizens be reconnected to political processes and reaffirmed as part of a wider community or collective.

Once again we meet a laudable and normatively inspired corrective to established forms of journalism, this time dressed in the clothes of US public journalism. But how valid is it? Some of the major problems posed by the idea of public journalism include the following. Public journalism proclaims itself to be about invigorating democracy but simultaneously positions itself as non-partisan. By default this positions journalism as seemingly above the political fray and concerned with the *procedural conduct* rather than the *substantive issues* at stake in democratizing society. This, at best, represents a very 'thin' advocacy and one that moves complacently within the historically established parameters of liberal democracy and separates journalism off from radical projects for change. The structural imbalances and weighted interests that shape and bend public discourse arguably require a more robust and critically engaged press, one that is prepared to question how existing democratic procedures are often stacked in favour of powerful interests. As a reform movement public journalism is conservative because, as Michael Schudson (1999: 122) has argued, it doesn't propose new accountability systems to ensure democratic procedures within the media or subsidy systems that can sustain alternative voices and views marginalized by lack of media ownership and control. In this sense, public journalism focuses too much on the role of the press but not enough on interrogating and theorizing the structures of civil society and how these shape and set parameters on public engagement. As Schudson comments dryly, public journalism may know about journalism but knows little about its presumed public and the changing structures of civil society.

Daniel Hallin also challenges the implicit apolitical, expert, role that the press has ascribed to itself and which thereby limits its capacity to engage in meaningful processes of political change and dialogue with its presumed 'public' audience:

> Journalists need to move from conceiving their role in terms of mediating between political authorities and the mass public, to thinking of it also as a task of opening up political discussion in civil society . . . it might be time for journalists themselves to rejoin civil society, and to start talking to their readers and viewers as one citizen to another, rather than as experts claiming to be above politics.
>
> (cited in Schudson 1999: 122–3)

Public journalism, in so far as it advances the desire to make democracy work, appears to be based on a presumed golden age of small-town, meeting-hall democracy in which participation and public debate and discussion could meaningfully take place and involve local communities and their agendas. Today the scale, dispersal and general complexity of governance, the fragmentation and fluidity of 'communities', and the pluralized constituencies of interest and identities of difference within and across nation states all pose considerable challenges to the laudable ideas of community involvement in politics.

This last point also implicitly calls for some sort of conceptualization of the 'public sphere' but one that is not presumed to be homogeneous and simply coextensive with the boundaries of local readerships or the nation state. Today's mediatized 'public sphere', as we have already heard, is likely to be composed of different levels, overlapping interests and facilitated through a complex multimedia ecology (see Figure 3.2 on p. 51). It is in and through this complex communicative space that ideas and ideals, including those concerning the 'common good', are communicated and channelled between different publics and government. This needs to be carefully conceptualized and theorized.

Public journalism also appears to be founded on an overly rationalist and language-based view of public deliberation. However, we know that communication, including news, is constituted by rhetoric as well as reason, affect as well as argument, display as well as debate, dissemination as well as discussion, empathy as well as eloquence, visuals as well as views, sentiments as well as scenes. Though public journalism seeks to move beyond the transmission views of 'information-led' journalism (Carey 1989) to more participatory ideals of journalism as enacted public conversation (Carey 1999), it fails to appreciate the multidimensional appeals of journalism and how, for example, all the features noted earlier can provide valuable resources for democratic inclusion. As we have previously seen in discussions of public screens (Chapter 3) as well as the representation of moral sentiments and symbolism embedded in various forms of mediatized rituals (Chapter 4), the symbolic, affective and culturally resonant are also intimately entwined in processes of deliberation, of collective identification and projects for change.

Public journalism, then, helps to sharpen our understanding of the ideals and obstacles of mediatized democracy but it cannot be presumed to be a panacea, either in theory or in practice, for the democratic deficits that are currently found within contemporary liberal democracies (Peters 1999). But the value of its normative critique and political experimentation in practice should not be dismissed. The ideas and practice of public journalism, like those of peace journalism and development journalism, may well hold invaluable lessons for the media's role in future democratizing projects.

Alternative journalism on-line: public connectivity?

> The Internet offers extraordinary potential for the expression of citizen rights, and for the communication of human values. Certainly, it cannot substitute for social change or political reform. However, by relatively levelling the ground of symbolic manipulation, and by broadening the sources of communication, it does contribute to democratization. The Internet brings people into contact in a public agora, to voice their concerns and shape their hopes. This is why people's control of this public agora is perhaps the most fundamental political issue raised by the development of the Internet.
>
> (Castells 2001 164–5)

Net utopians and net dystopians have long waxed lyrical, or hysterical, about the revolutionizing impacts of the Internet on daily life, culture, politics, economy, social interaction, identity and our sense of 'reality' (for a recent, engaged, discussion see Hassan 2004). Fortunately these often inflated, not to say occasionally apocalyptic, theoretical claims are now being subject to more measured and empirically informed examination. This last part of the discussion picks up on themes already broached in respect of media, democracy and journalism and does so by considering the democratizing possibilities of journalism on-line and how the communicative forms of the Internet may possess distinctive, possibly unique, characteristics for the democratization of mediatized conflicts – characteristics that have variously been recognized and enacted by diverse alternative on-line journalisms.

Studies of on-line journalism invariably address the different communicative features of the Internet as a medium, and how these enact or facilitate more participatory modes of audience engagement (Hacker and van Dijk 2000; Wall 2003; Boczkowski 2004; Stovall 2004). Some studies have also examined how the Internet has been incorporated by practising journalists into their work practices and processes (Cottle 1999; Hall 2001; Kawamoto 2003). And we have already heard how the Net has been used by global activists and theorized in terms of its perceived affinity with the often spatially dispersed, politically decentralized, socially fragmented and culturally fluid nature of alternative projects and new social movements (see Chapter 3). This possible elective affinity between the Internet, news social movements and so called cyber protests demands sustained inquiry (Castells 2001; Bennett 2003; Wall 2003; van de Donk et al. 2004) as does the 'prefigurative politics' that inheres in some of the new forms of alternative media organizations sustain (Atton 2002). Some of these aspects will be touched on later. Here we focus principally on the distinctive characteristics of on-line journalism and how these may possibly be transforming the nature and culture of journalism itself. The recent work of Mark Deuze proves particularly instructive in this regard:

> The online journalist has to make decisions as to which media format or formats best convey a certain story (multimediality), consider options for the public to respond, interact or even customize certain stories (interactivity), and to think about ways to connect the story to other stories, archives, resources and so forth through hyperlinks (hypertextuality).
>
> (2003: 206)

Deuze discerns at least four major types of on-line journalism which he categorizes as: 'mainstream news sites', 'index and category sites', 'meta and comment sites' and 'share and discussion sites'. These, he suggests, can be grouped according to a typology structured across two fundamental continuums, the first ranging from 'editorial content' to 'public connectivity', and the second from 'moderated participatory communication' to 'unmoderated participatory communication' (see Figure 6.1).

Mainstream news sites, whether provided by leading newspapers or existing TV networks such as CNN, BBC and MSNBC, offer a selection of daily news and, at most, provide a highly filtered and moderated form of participatory communication (see also Jankowski and van Selm 2000). Typically such sites do not differ much from established mainstream forms of journalism in terms of storytelling, news values or their imagined audiences/readers.

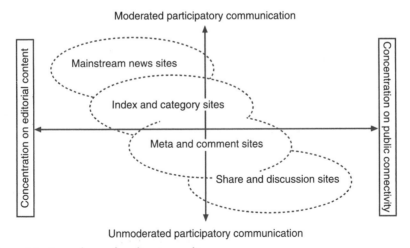

Figure 6.1 A typology of on-line journalism
Reproduced with permission from Deuze, M. (2003) 'The Web and Its Journalism', *New Media and Society* 5(2): 205 © Sage Publications.

Index and category sites are more likely to be associated with on-line search engines such as *Yahoo* than mainstream news providers, and here on-line journalists provide deep links to existing news sites sometimes by categorizing and annotating these into accessible lists and hyperlinked formats. While frequently originating little if any new content these can provide spaces for on-line responses, comment and discussion through, for example, the bulletin board system (BBS). Weblogs or 'blogs' can also be included under this category of new on-line journalism in so far as these often provide personal testimonies, eyewitness accounts and critical commentaries on major news stories and events and can provide readers with further links (see Allan 2004b, 2005). Weblogs, for the most part, however, facilitate minimum participation.

Meta and comment sites provide sites that reflexively monitor and comment on news media sites and media more generally – the Internet's version of journalism as public watchdog(s). Here critical comment and alternative media voices can often come to the fore. Alternative news sites, such as the *Guerrilla News Network* and the *Independent Media Centers* (Indymedia) around the world, offer their own news and will also comment critically on the news provided elsewhere (see Figure 3.2 on p. 51). They generally seek to highlight issues and perspectives on issues marginalized or silenced in the mainstream and can provide opportunities for individuals to upload their own commentary and stories and thereby significantly enhance the means for audience feedback and participation.

Share and discussion sites, finally, as the name suggests, are based principally on the Internet's capacity for the exchange of ideas, accounts and stories and so on and are often centred on a particular theme such as worldwide antiglobalization activism, but all making use of the principle of connectivity – people connecting with other people worldwide.

As we can see in Figure 6.1 Deuze's typology brings some conceptual order to the seeming chaos of on-line journalism, and we can better grasp how these distinctive forms are now supplementing and often challenging traditional and mainstream journalism. They do so, argues Deuze, by communicatively: (a) integrating enhanced public connectivity and participation; (b) changing associated forms of media production and combining roles of producers and consumers (so called '*prosumers*'); and (c) by expanding and shifting prevailing cultural ideas about what 'journalism' is or could and should be. He concludes:

> Different and overlapping types of online journalism may very well change what one perceives as 'real' journalism, as their distinctive features have implications for the way in which media production processes are focused, how news organizations are managed, and how a journalistic culture operates (in relationship with audiences and technologies).
>
> (2003: 216)

Alternative journalism, as we have heard, assumes diverse forms on the Net, is often in flux and variously deploys the distinctive communicative capabilities of the medium

– *multimediality, hypertextuality, interactivity*. As well as replicating the more traditional and 'closed' journalistic culture of mainstream journalism practices, the Net has also spawned a more vibrant, albeit cacophonous, outpouring and posting of views and voices that speak within a more open journalistic culture. These new on-line forms of journalism can be productively typologized, as we have seen, bringing some much needed conceptual order to the seeming communicative chaos of the World Wide Web and the Internet. But there is no substitute for a more grounded engagement with exactly how these communicative forms interact with and mediatize the conflicts of civil society and society more widely (see for example, Dahlberg 2001; Bennett 2003; Wall 2003; Allan 2004b, 2005).

The colonization of the Net by a plethora of alternative and mainstream journalisms as well as the Net's increasing colonization of the everyday life worlds of ever-growing numbers of people around the globe (notwithstanding continuing digital divides), suggests that journalistic culture will inevitably become expanded and through time possibly reconfigured. Unlike the corrective journalisms already discussed which are driven more by normatively informed values and critique, today's on-line journalisms appear to be driven by wider determinants of change located within the changing nature of politics, society and culture and have thereby secured a firmer purchase within the prevailing journalism ecology. If civil society continues, as it surely will, to become increasingly enacted in and through the Net this can only become more pronounced in the future.

Chapter summary

This chapter has examined four influential 'corrective' journalisms, all of which position themselves in opposition to established, mainstream forms and practices of journalism. They all share, as we have heard, a concern to move beyond traditional news values, routinized journalist practices, elite source dependencies and institutionalized ideas of professionalism, and they all seek to augment the range of views and voices, perspectives and problems, discourses and debates finding news representation. All social theories and perspectives tend to be informed by, if only implicitly, normative ideas, values and ideals and this should not be seen as a deficiency. We should all have views about how society is or should be, and these need to be incorporated into the questions that we ask and the questions prioritized and pursued by researchers. However, when media theories and perspectives are based exclusively or even principally on normative values and critique, this increases the tendency towards superficial, often media-centric, arguments which fail to grapple with the complexities, interactions and wider determinants involved.

Wish-fulfilment is no substitute for analysis, and good intentions cannot compete with grounded prescriptions. Deeply held values and preferred viewpoints, even when rhetorically aligned to 'democratizing' media projects, cannot therefore be allowed to go unquestioned or escape critical scrutiny – too much is at stake. Peace journalism, development journalism and public journalism, each in their different ways, can be criticized in such terms. Nonetheless, each has also served to deepen our understanding of the nature of contemporary journalism as well as some of its shortcomings. And each has thereby served to sharpen our sense of what a democratized media could and should look like. All, for example, talk about meaningfully extending access and deepening forms of participation: the ideas of peace journalism encourage us to revisit established news forms and formats and investigate further their communicative possibilities for enhancing understanding and facilitating reconciliation between former opponents and enemies; current ideas of development journalism require us to think seriously about grassroots community involvement in media and self-defined processes of development; and ideas of public journalism demand that we reconceptualize journalism not as the expert transmission of information but as an advocate for public conversation and societal deliberation. All these ideas are surely fundamental for any serious attempt to both understand and deepen the media's contribution to democratizing processes within and across civil societies – now and in the future.

On-line forms of journalism, given their diversity and dispersal by the World Wide Web, are collectively based less on normative critique and more, it seems, on the affinity between the distinctive communicative features of the Internet – multimediality, hypertextuality, interactivity – and the general pursuit of 'connectivity' that informs issue and identity politics around the globe. Of course some of these alternative on-line journalisms are also informed by normative critiques of mainstream media and journalism, but their existence and scope for future development appears to be underpinned as much by the culture and technological capacities of the Internet as by the prescriptive nature of their politics and clearly defined or shared normative goals. The Internet, like civil society, hosts a cacophony of views and values, voices and visions, and it is this as well as its promise of worldwide connectivity that animates a more open culture of alternative on-line journalisms.

This returns us to the necessity to situate, theorize and analyse these developments in relation to the wider contexts and changes now characterizing civil and wider societies – contexts and changes that are all too often ignored in normative-based critiques and shopping lists for media changes. Contemporary debates about the media conceptualized in terms of 'public sphere(s)', 'public screens', 'counter public spheres' or even 'public sphericules' and, following recent enthusiasm for on-line weblogs and warblogs, so called 'blogospheres', all aim to map and encapsulate the complex of communicative forms and interactions between media and publics (see Figure 3.2). These are variously theorized as communicative spaces giving expression to and bringing into being 'publics' in the mediatized dissemination and deliberation of issues, identities and ideas. Alternative journalisms, then, prompt further reflection on the complex ecology of contemporary mediatized societies and how these can enact or disable processes of democratization and democratic deepening (see Figure 2.1 on p. 30).

Finally, though corrective journalisms generally position themselves in opposition to mainstream news media, many also now seek to avoid isolation, marginalization and political irrelevance. Notwithstanding the rise of the Net, mainstream news media remain the biggest game in town. Different journalisms increasingly comment on, feed into or work alongside each other in a complex overlapping news media ecology. Today the rather comforting notion of a singular, nationally deliberating and rationally conceived 'public sphere' is increasingly at odds with the empirical complexities, fragmentations and dispersals now found within our communications environment. Even so, there is no getting away from the fact that democracy and democratization require that people talk and commune with each other as 'publics', and they therefore cannot subsist entirely or exclusively within their own separate, interest-based, 'public sphericules' (Figure 3.2 on p. 51). There has to be a broader interaction and exchange, a broadening and borrowing of issues and agendas, which finds more generalized public expression and refraction in and through overlapping spheres of media engagement. For the most part, the alternative journalisms discussed in this chapter have failed to provide an encompassing conceptualization of the complex communicative spaces of contemporary societies or how they could and should interact within these. Each nonetheless has helped to contribute insights and ideas, both directly and indirectly, for just such a conceptualization and the ways in which journalism can become an integral part of processes of democratization.

Recommended reading

Deuze, M. (2003) 'The web and its journalisms: considering the consequences of different types of newsmedia online', *New Media and Society* 5(2): 203–26.
Glasser, T. L. (ed.) (1999) *The Idea of Public Journalism*. New York: The Guilford Press.
Hall, J. (2001) *Online Journalism*. London: Pluto.
Servaes, J., Jacobson, T. L. and White, S. A. (eds) (1996) *Participatory Communication for Social Change*. London: Sage.
Spencer, G. (2004) 'The impact of television news on the Northern Ireland peace negotiations', *Media, Culture and Society* 26(5): 603–23.
Wolfsfeld, G. (2004) *Media and the Path to Peace*. Cambridge: Cambridge University Press.

7 | MEDIA, 'RISK SOCIETY' AND THE ENVIRONMENT: A DIFFERENT STORY?

Across the last decades of the 20th century and continuing into the 21st, growing public concerns about the environment as well as the conflicts and contentions surrounding the risks manufactured by advanced industrialized societies have found increased prominence in the media. Some commentators have suggested that mainstream media have played a crucial role in building and channelling the manifest upsurge in environmental consciousness and politics across the same period. In the context of this book and its focus on mediatized conflict this is surely interesting, and perhaps surprising. Many studies, such as those encountered earlier when discussing media reporting of demonstrations and protests, moral panics and media events, or war, for example, often point to the media's subservience to the voices, views and values of powerful institutions and authorities. And yet here the media are thought to have performed a more independent and even championing role. This chapter explores exactly how and why the media's environmental coverage may have assumed a more critical stance in comparison to other news issues across recent years. As we do so, further complexities of media performance and the enactment of mediatized conflicts are opened up to view.

At the outset of this book the social theory of Ulrich Beck (1992) was referenced as a powerful source of contemporary ideas helping to make sense of the unprecedented risks and threats that confront people and their environments in late modernity. This chapter begins by first explicating Beck's key ideas of so called 'risk society' as a means of getting a better theoretical fix on contemporary 'ecological hazards' and 'manufactured uncertainties' and why it is that the media occupy such a central position in their public definition and contestation. Beck's overarching theoretical ideas speak to the conditions of our times and they do so in a way that no other social theorist has been able to match. Notwithstanding the inevitable disagreements and theoretical challenges prompted by his thesis of 'world risk society', his work provides a necessary springboard for developing our understanding of environment and risk communications. Recent studies undertaken by researchers in the field of environment and risk communication research also contribute to this growing knowledge and help to redress the underdeveloped nature of some of Beck's social theoretical themes. Three areas of research activity in particular can be singled out as important for further discussion.

Beck coins the concept of 'relations of definitions' to refer to the institutional matrix of institutional and organizational interests, scientific and social rationalities and contending knowledge claims that structure public communications about 'risks' and 'risk society'. Though productive, these ideas now need to be refined and empirically grounded in research that has examined how environmental agendas are built and mobilized over time and how and why they can also disappear from the media's public eye, notwithstanding the continuing or even worsening nature of the environmental threats that they signal. Key debates here centre on theoretical ideas of 'primary definition' and the 'public arenas model' – debates that have relevance far beyond the field of risk and environment communication. With a more refined approach to the study of media–source interactions and the strategic mobilization of news agendas, the discussion then moves to consider the deep-seated and historically forged 'cultural resonances' often embedded in mediatized images of the environment and how these can exert agency in and through today's media sphere. Finally, with the help of some of the most sophisticated studies of audience reception conducted to date, we attend to important questions of how media representations of the environment and ecological risks enter into people's everyday lives, their thoughts and feelings, ideas of citizenship and collective actions.

'Risk society', ecological hazards, media

> The risk society can be grasped theoretically, empirically and politically only if one starts from the premise that it is always also a knowledge, media and information society at the same time – or, often enough as well, a society of non-knowledge and disinformation.
>
> (Beck 2000: xiv)

Ulrich Beck's thesis of 'risk society' focuses on the 'manufactured uncertainties' produced by today's 'Second Modernity', that is, the advanced industrial and technological risks that escape efforts to calculate, calibrate, predict, control and insure against them. The fall out from today's global 'risks', unlike their predecessors in the 'First Modernity' of industrial/manufacturing society, threaten to wreak havoc or even catastrophe on the world. Their peculiar nature, as outlined by Beck, positions the media as a key site in their social definition, construction and possible challenge:

> By risks I mean above all radioactivity, which completely evades human perceptive abilities, but also toxins and pollutants in the air, the water and foodstuffs,

together with the accompanying short- and long-term effects on plants, animals and people. They induce systematic and often *irreversible* harm, generally remain *invisible*, are based on *causal interpretations*, and thus initially only exist in terms of the (scientific or anti-scientific) *knowledge* about them. They can thus be changed, magnified, dramatized or minimized within knowledge, and to that extent they are particularly *open to social definition and construction*. Hence the mass media and the scientific and legal professions in charge of defining risks become key social and political positions.

(1992: 22–3)

The risks from nuclear fallout and industrial toxins, environmental despoliation, genetically modified crops and global warming, among many others, are historically unprecedented in terms of space, time and their potential magnitude of harm. Blown by the weather systems the fall-out from Chernobyl, for example, soon circumnavigated much of the globe; and Agent Orange in Vietnam as well as the deadly toxins spewed out at Bhopal in India will continue to maim and kill generations yet unborn. Such ecological hazards, such manufactured uncertainties, are not aberrations of either nature or society argues Beck. They are the circulating and systemic '*bads*' (in contrast to commercial '*goods*') produced by the advanced application of scientific knowledge and technologies and their consequences remain, at best, poorly understood. Today the 'calculus of risk' becomes uncertain; risks are essentially unknown and therefore unpredictable and evade former safeguards and systems of control; they undermine principles of insurance and they are potentially catastrophic.

Though the risks of manufactured uncertainty can have low probability, when actualized they can be globally devastating: 'society is living on top of the volcano', says Beck, and this is produced and stoked by mankind's own activities. It is in this context that Beck argues: 'The public eye of the media takes on a key significance in the risk society' (2000: xiii). Specifically, the media shine a spotlight on the 'organized irresponsibility' and the 'social explosiveness of hazard' and help to visualize and dramatize the consequences of manufactured risks. Given the often invisible nature and competing claims about risks, whether voiced by scientists, politicians or lay people – Beck's so called 'voices of the side effects' – they can also give vent to the complex arguments and rationality claims, both scientific and social, in contention. Not that the media spotlight is allowed to roam and illuminate unopposed in the risk society. The growing army of public relations officials and experts, or the 'argumentation craftsmen' of modern industry and the 'provident state' (1992: 32), argues Beck, all engage in information-management strategies and damage limitation in their unending battle to ward off the destructive effects of contestable scientific knowledge and unmanageable compensation claims. This produces the 'dance of the veiling of hazards':

The system of institutionally heightened expectations forms the social background in front of which – under the close scrutiny of the mass media and the murmurs of the tensely attentive public – the institutions of industrial society present the dance of the veiling of hazards. The hazards, which are not merely projected onto the world stage, but really threaten, are illuminated under the media spotlight.

(Beck 1995: 101)

Beck's (2001) more recent formulation of 'world risk society' continues to position the media as a powerful lens that can publicly illuminate 'the unseen side-effects of industrial production' and help turn these into 'global ecological flashpoints'; and, in so far as these are not amenable to calculation and control, so the media spotlight contributes to the erosion of the very basis and legitimacy of the system itself (2001: 33).

The social theory of world risk society, then, provides a profound critique of late-modern society and the systemic nature of environmental risks, ecological hazards and potential catastrophe. Understandably it has attracted widespread interest and generated considerable academic debate. Clearly, it chimes powerfully with contemporary ecological concerns and the rise of a new environmental consciousness and, as we have heard, it also theoretically positions the media centre stage in the field of risk communications and ecological politics. Beck's thesis is more encompassing than risk communication in the media, however, and, like the work of Anthony Giddens and other major contemporary social theorists to which his ideas are often compared, its broad theoretical sweep ranges across historical and social trajectories of change that include processes of globalization, individualization, detraditionalization and 'reflexive modernization' (Beck et al. 1994). Given its speculative and relatively abstract formulations it has not gone without criticism. Issues raised include its historical periodization of so called 'first' and 'second modernities'; conflation of different risks and ecological hazards to essentially catastrophic ones; tendency to displace concerns of class and traditional fault lines of inequality under the guiding rubric/slogan of 'risk society' ('poverty is hierarchic, smog is democratic'); and seeming slippage between ontological statements about the reality of 'risks' and epistemological claims about how we come to know about them (Goldblatt 1996; Cottle 1998b; Elliott 2003; Mythen 2004).

These and other criticisms contribute to a deeper appreciation of the strengths and weaknesses of Beck's social theory but take us beyond the scope of this chapter. We can productively engage further, however, with his stated theoretical ideas on the media. Beck's social theoretical ideas are formative for mass communication researchers but they remain empirically underdeveloped. Here, then, we turn to the work of communication researchers to build a deeper understanding of the complexities and dynamics of the mediatized risk society.

Relations of definitions: agenda building beyond primary definers

Beck's concept of 'relations of definitions' refers to the matrix of interests and ideas and the different rationality claims (both scientific and social) that publicly define, contend and challenge within the risk field including the media. The concept deliberately plays on the earlier Marxist notion of 'relations of production' and emphasizes the institutionalized and ideational premises of public knowledge and contending discourses about risk. His writings are relatively silent, however, on the exact configuration and dynamics of the institutional and other interests comprising these 'relations of definitions' as well as how these compete and contend for access, public recognition and legitimacy within the public sphere and with what differential resources and capacities. We have heard, for example, how scientists and experts become key players contesting the intellectual high ground of risks and their consequences, but who exactly these 'claims makers' are, how they relate to each other institutionally, professionally, politically, and by what information strategies and rhetorical moves is surely also an important part of the explanatory picture (Hansen 1991, 1993; Hannigan 1995; Anderson 1997, 2000; DeLuca 1999; Wykes 2000). Here we need to revisit positions and debates on media access to arrive at a more grounded and complex understanding of how 'relations of definitions' actually enter into the media sphere of risk communications.

In the 1970s and 1980s a number of researchers argued forcefully, and not without supporting evidence (see Chapter 2), that media access tends to be routinely and systematically dominated by elites who are thereby granted a privileged opportunity to publicly define and interpret major events in ways consonant to the reproduction of the existing capitalist social order: 'Access is structured and hierarchical to the extent that powerful groups and individuals have privileged and routine entry into the news itself and to the manner and means of its production' (GUMG 1980: 114). A particularly influential theorization of this 'systematic authority skew', and one that has proved influential to this day, conceptualizes this in terms of 'primary definers' and 'primary definition'. Here political, social and cultural elites through their privileged access to the media set the boundaries and definitions of social discourse and are thereby enabled to prescribe in relation to society's problematic events and processes. While other opinions and views are not necessarily excluded from the media they nonetheless have to engage within the parameters of discourse set down and elaborated by these 'primary definers'; in such ways they are both structurally and discursively disadvantaged (Hall et al. 1978).

Stuart Hall and his co-authors also elaborated a two-pronged explanation for such an ideological state of affairs:

> These two aspects of news production – the practical pressures of constantly working against the clock and the professional demands of impartiality and objectivity – combine to produce a systematically structured over-accessing to the media of those in powerful and privileged institutional positions.
>
> (1978: 58)

We have already encountered numerous research studies which lend some empirical support to this thesis – whether the arguments of *Manufacturing Consent* advanced by

Herman and Chomsky (1988), the classic studies of protest and demonstration by Halloran et al. (1970) in the UK and Gitlin (1980/2003) in the US, or numerous studies which have observed the routine access granted to political leaders and military spokespersons, not the voices of opposition, dissent or casualties, in times of war. While the primary definer thesis continues to command some support, especially in respect of elite-dominated conflicts, it can nonetheless be challenged on a number of theoretical, conceptual and empirical grounds. Essentially it proves too blunt and insensitive to the complexities and contingencies involved in media source interactions and the communicative strategies deployed therein.

Philip Schlesinger has argued convincingly that different fields of media–source interaction, though often structurally weighted to the advantage of dominant groups and interests, are nonetheless often contested and therefore less closed in terms of representational outcomes than the primary definer thesis suggests:

> it is necessary that sources be conceived as occupying fields in which competition for access to the media takes place, but in which material and symbolic advantages are unequally distributed. But the most advantaged do not secure a primary definition in virtue of their position alone. Rather, if they do so, it is because of successful strategic action in an imperfectly competitive field.
>
> (1990: 77)

Schlesinger elaborates exactly why the conceptualization of primary definers is theoretically insecure and why we need to adopt a less media-centric and more sociologically refined and politically contingent understanding of media–source interactions. Specifically, the primary definer thesis is criticized for not taking sufficient account of: (a) the contention between official sources; (b) the behind-the-scenes manoeuvrings of sources rendered methodologically invisible by cultural readings of media representations; (c) the competitive and shifting nature of key sources *within* privileged elites; (d) the longer-term shifts in the structure of access; and (e) for assuming a unidirectional flow of definitions from power centres to media (1990: 66–7). To these we may also want to add the increasingly complex media ecology of news and journalism with its emergent contra-flows and cross-over genres (see Figure 3.2 and Chapter 8), alternative on-line journalisms (see Chapter 6) and the distinctive cultural forms of tabloid journalism (see below) as well as the spectacular nature of mediated public crises (see Chapter 4). All these seemingly permit or even encourage different and sometimes distinctly less than deferential, 'hierarchies of access'. And we have also heard earlier how yesteryear's 'folk devils' (Cohen 1972) have become increasingly media savvy and learned how to manipulate and 'fight back' in the media (McRobbie 1994). In all these ways, therefore, the primary definer thesis is theoretically less robust than once presumed.

These more complex views on source power and strategic activity have found empirical support in a range of studies examining different competitive fields, whether HIV/ Aids (Miller and Williams 1993), criminal justice (Ericson et al. 1989; Schlesinger and Tumber 1994), the voluntary sector and non-governmental organizations (Deacon

1996, 2003), government policy opposition (Deacon and Golding 1994), trade union-ism (Davis 2000, 2003; Manning 2001) and the historically changing political field of the Troubles in Northern Ireland (Miller 1993, 1994). In their different ways these and other studies have helped to shift attention away from media-centred views to examine the complex of vying interests and temporal dynamics shaping both processes of news entry and the media representations that result. Studies of source strategies and media interactions, therefore, discover complexities and contingencies where once social dom-inance alone was presumed to be a sufficient guarantee of successful news entry and the control over news agendas. This is clearly documented in the field of environmental news coverage (Hansen 1991, 1993, 2000; Anderson 1993, 1997, 2000; Peters 1995; Kitzinger and Reilly 1997; DeLuca 1999; Wykes 2000).

Adopting a social constructionist approach to the study of social problems Anders Hansen (2000: 55), for example, notes how environmental issues depend on processes of successful claims making and how the media constitute a prime public arena in which an array of voices, definitions and claims of claims makers compete for access and public legitimacy. As Spector and Kituse famously argued, social problems are not static conditions but 'the activities of groups making assertions of grievances and claims to organizations, agencies and institutions about some putative conditions' (1973: 146). Environmental problems can also productively be approached and exam-ined as the outcome of a dynamic social process of definition, negotiation and legitim-ation which involves claims, claims makers, and claims-making processes in both pri-vate and public settings. For environmental issues to become successfully mobilized they have to first (a) command attention; (b) claim legitimacy; and (c) invoke action (Solesbury 1976).

Questions of media framing, of how the media selects and accesses claims makers and presents/evaluates environmental issues and arguments, that is, it 'frames' them, are often critical in such processes:

> Framing essentially involves selection and salience. To frame is to select some aspect of a perceived reality and make them more salient in a communicating text, in such a way as to promote a particular problem definition, causal interpretation, moral evaluation and/or treatment recommendation for the item described.
>
> (Entman, cited in Hansen 2000: 55–6; see also Gamson and Modigliani 1989; Hannigan 1995)

The Greenpeace protest surrounding the proposed dumping of the redundant oil rig, the Brent Spar, by the multinational Shell/Royal Dutch in the Atlantic in 1995, for example, illuminated how commanding attention for an issue does not necessarily translate into securing legitimacy in the media. A study by Hansen notes how Greenpeace com-manded news attention with their publicized occupation of the derelict installation and how this produced sympathetic headlines such as: 'Murder at Sea: Scandal of Dumped Rigs That May Wipe out Marine Life: Greenpeace Seize Oil Rig to Highlight Danger of Leaving Deserted Rigs to Rot at Sea' (*Daily Mirror* 1 May 1995).

However, more was required than a publicity stunt if the issue was to move beyond commanding attention to secure legitimacy and invoke action. Here, argues Hansen, Greenpeace's influence as a claims maker was also dependent on its strategic ability to gather and disseminate information (2000: 60). The Brent Spar action was deliberately timed, for example, to coincide with intergovernmental discussions at the North Sea Conference in June 1995 and this gave Greenpeace an opportunity to present information and to influence and frame the agenda in this and other key political arenas including the British Parliament and the G7 Summit held that year. Not that Greenpeace's tactics met with universal media approval. The British *Daily Telegraph*, for example, framed the protest action as follows: 'Civil disobedience: Protestors take law into their own hands – campaigns have targeted poll tax, animal exports and new motorways/more and more demonstrators are willing to act illegally to further their various causes' (*Daily Telegraph* 5 June 1995). As Hansen points out, this 'threat to democracy frame' is the newspaper's own and is not based on a quoted primary source or guest writer. Similarly, other newspapers also aligned themselves to their imagined readerships and political outlooks. The *Daily Mirror*, in stark contrast to the *Telegraph*, for example, sought to take credit for Shell's reversal on its earlier decision to dump the Brent Spar in the North Sea and effectively proclaimed itself as the champion of this, and other, environmental causes: 'Glad Oil Over – *Daily Mirror* Victory as Petrol Giant Halts Rig Sinking' (*Daily Mirror* 21 June 1995).

Clearly, from the headlines above as well as the reports and editorials that followed, sections of the media chose to adopt a combative or championing stance in respect of Greenpeace's action and they appear to have done so independently of 'primary' sources. Ideas of primary definition are rendered considerably more problematic when we examine particular instances of media framing and, as in this case, we can also find that the media are capable of taking an independent and, on occasion, even championing line on environmental issues and causes.

Importantly, in addition to drawing attention to processes of claims making and media framing, Hansen's study also invites us to consider the interrelationship between different public arenas. In this instance, how different media and political arenas interacted to condition the public elaboration of a particular environmental issue in the media. As the analytical focus moves to a consideration of environmental agenda building in multiple arenas, the research frame considerably broadens. Examining how agenda building takes place through time and in a context of competing institutions and interacting arenas takes us considerably beyond media-centric and relatively atemporal views of media 'agenda setting'. It begins to open up a more sociologically encompassing and grounded conceptualization of the field of risk and environmental communications.

Here the 'Public Arenas Model' (Hilgartner and Bosk 1988) serves to specify some of the complexities at play and provides a useful framework for the analysis of the 'rise and fall of social problems', including environmental issues and concerns. It identifies six interrelated features of public arenas that affect the communications environment in which social problems and their claims makers compete for media, public and policy attention:

The public arenas model
1. Dynamic process of competition among social problem claims;
2. Institutional arenas where social problems compete for attention and grow;
3. Carrying capacities of these arenas;
4. Principles of selection (such as drama, novelty, cultural and political factors, organizational factors);
5. Patterns of interaction among different arenas;
6. Networks of operatives.

(Hilgartner and Bosk 1988)

When applied to the media we can readily see how these identified factors may be at work and determining the rise and fall of environmental issues in the media. In the context of news, claims and claims making about different social problems jostle for recognition and access and do so in mediums with different carrying capacities (time/ space) and content dispositions. Their chances of inclusion or exclusion will depend in part on such principles of selection as the operation of news values (drama, conflict, negativity, visuals, celebrity etc.), whether the social problem is already politically recognized or culturally resonate, and whether established links exist between the media and claims-making organizations. The 'networks of operatives', say environmental correspondents, may also entertain broadly sympathetic views about the environment and this too will influence processes of story selection and inflection (Lowe and Morrison 1984; Anderson 1997), as will the provision of 'information subsidies' (Gandy 1982) or 'video subsidies' to resource-strapped competitive news media by source organizations such as Greenpeace.

When combined with empirical studies of environmental source fields and the communicative strategies deployed within different public arenas, social constructionist approaches to claims makers and claims making opens up a more complex vista on environmental agenda building. This considerably improves upon Beck's underdeveloped views on 'relations of definitions' as well as earlier neo-Marxist notions of 'primary definition'. Before we leave this part of the discussion, however, a further dimension of relevance needs to be addressed. This concerns the differing epistemologies or ways of knowing often embodied in different risk positions occupied in risk society. Beck usefully draws attention to the differences between scientific and social rationality and how these different ways of knowing inform public discourses about risk. His description of the so called 'voices of the side-effects' powerfully opens up these epistemological distinctions to public view:

What scientist call 'latent side effects' and 'unproven connections' are for them their 'coughing children' who turn blue in the foggy weather and gasp for air, with a rattle in their throat. On their side of the fence, 'side effects' have *voices, faces, ears* and *tears* . . . Therefore people themselves become small, private alternative experts in risks of modernization. . . . The parents begin to collect data and arguments. The 'blank spots' of modernization risks, which remain 'unseen' and 'unproven' for the experts, very quickly take form under their cognitive approach.

(Beck 1992: 61)

Here Beck's victims of environmental risks begin to articulate forms of social rationality based on their immediate experiences and feelings, social relations and subjectivities, on their 'lay knowledge' (see also Coleman 1995; Wynne 1996). Their 'cognitive approach' or way of apprehending and making sense of their plight, challenges the scientific rationality of experts and scientists which is generally based on an epistemology of impersonal and analytical logic, statistical and probabilistic claims and scientific tests of 'proof' (the latter often an unrealistic goal in the complex field of risk interactions given the uncertain state of 'knowledge' about risks). As Beck's examples of 'social rationality' indicates, however, lay people of necessity have to gather their own evidence and formulate their own arguments and proofs if they are to effectively take on the logics, obfuscations and denials of the 'argumentation craftsmen' of risk society. Social rationality has to inveigle itself into the jurisdictions and discussions of science and technocracy and become publicly elaborated. Here we may want to ask whether popular culture and the media constitute a serviceable terrain for this necessary elaboration.

Countless popular cultural forms by definition and audience appeal position themselves in relation to the lifeworlds of ordinary people and are thereby generically disposed to give expression to something of their experiences and feelings, collective concerns and moral values. Tabloid journalism is well known, for example, to be oriented towards consumerism and entertainment rather than the arguments of government and political debate; it is disposed to play up the sensational and the sexual rather than deliberate institutional issues and agendas; it endorses and promotes celebrity and stardom rather than deference to political elites and monarchy; its discourse is couched in terms of a moral economy of deviance and populist opprobrium rather than the intricacies and indexes of the financial markets; it valorizes the 'private' and proximate lifeworlds of home and intimate relationships, sports and the human interest story rather than the 'public' and remote systems world of government, economy and international affairs; and it does so through expressive means of communication based more on visual display and affect, everyday idioms, commonsense opinions and emotions rather than written discourse, expert views, detailed analysis and cool argument (Dahlgren and Sparks 1992; Sparks and Tulloch 2000). Is it possible that popular cultural forms, such as television news, provide openings for Beck's 'voices of the side effects' and give vent to the claims and arguments, value positions and experiences that help to constitute forms of social rationality?

Research that has pursued such questions found, with few exceptions, that this was not generally the case (Cottle 2000b). Based on a sample of television news environment items the author mapped the analytic and experiential, collective and personal modes of speech delivered by different environmental news actors. Though ordinary or lay people were found to be relatively numerous in many forms of television news and frequently symbolize the 'human face' and consequences of ecological hazards, rarely are they granted an opportunity to advance rational claims – whether 'social' or 'scientific'. Television news, rather, positioned ordinary people to symbolize or (literally) 'stand for' ordinary feelings and responses to the consequences of environmental risks, not to articulate a form of 'social rationality', much less discursively challenge 'scientific rationality'. With few exceptions only, the contention of different rationality claims surrounding and informing the field of risks was found to be preserved for politicians, officials and experts and corporate spokespeople (Cottle 2000b: 33–8).

In world risk society where a cognitive and communicative division of labour increasingly characterizes contemporary science, ordinary people become 'ensnared in relations of epistemic dependence', says James Bohman, and this produces political situations in which 'asymmetric information is increasingly salient' (2000: 47–8). This division of labour has to be made 'more democratic and open to public deliberation without thereby falling into a form of technocracy', or 'the rule and domination by those with epistemic and communicative advantages' (2000: 48). Nowhere is this democratizing task more urgent than in the field of ecological hazards and manufactured uncertainty. The struggle for media access and the opportunity to advance forms of social rationality and challenge the claims of experts and scientists, politicians and 'argumentation craftsmen' becomes a struggle intimately entwined in processes of reflexive modernization and world risk society. Though research findings suggest that the opportunities to do so are underdeveloped in the mainstream media, the 'voices of the side-effects' nonetheless have a powerful cultural ally on their side in the struggle for democratizing risk communication – the subject of the next section.

Cultural resonance and the rhetoric of environmental images

> The cultural blindness of daily life in the civilization of threat can ultimately not be removed; but culture 'sees' in symbols. The images in the news of skeletal trees or of dying seals have opened people's eyes. Making the threats publicly visible and arousing attention in detail, in one's own living space – these are the cultural eyes through which the 'blind citoyens' can perhaps win back the autonomy of their own judgement.
>
> (Beck 1992: 119–20)

The roots of contemporary environmental sensibilities are both historically long and culturally deep (Cottle 1993b, 2000b; Macnaghten and Urry 1998) and these sustain cultural resonances and symbols daily circulated within the media – resources that can also fuel environmental protests and projects of change. Ulrich Beck's observation above is surely right: culture does 'see' in symbols. Pick up any newspaper, watch any television news programme and we are likely to encounter a succession of images that either visually endorse and celebrate 'nature' or symbolize it as under threat. Powerful cultural dualisms structure contemporary outlooks and 'structures of feelings' in respect of nature and environment (Williams 1985). These can be traced a long way back, even to the advent of modernization and the new division of labour that separated the urban from the rural, the town from the countryside, impersonal association from community, and society from nature. Today such dualisms are often informed by romantic ideas of a more humanly meaningful, organic and harmonious life thought to have preceded the alienated, atomized and individualized existence ushered in by the industrial revolution. The destructive side of progress and civilization, from dark satanic mills (Blake) and alienation (Marx), to anomie (Durkheim) and association (Tönnies) finds its beneficent Other in culturally resonate ideas of the environment and these continue to inform social imaginaries of how we should live closer to nature (Eder 1996; Lash et al. 1996; Anderson 1997; Macnaghten and Urry 1998; DeLuca 1999; Allan 2002b; Cottle 2000b, 2004c).

There are different ways, however, of apprehending and appropriating nature(s). Phil Macnaghten and John Urry (1998) observe how nature has variously been seen and approached as landscape, as object of scientific study, as threatened and in need of protection, as providing resources for life, and as source of spiritual renewal and communion. Urry's (2002) seminal work on the 'romantic tourist gaze' specifically identifies how nature has become an object of spectacle, contemplation and aesthetic consumption. This tourist gaze has in part become democratized by the advent and popularization of photography (Sontag 1979) as well as through other visual media including television. Raymond Williams's ideas of 'mobile privatization' are pertinent here (1974: 26). As both a technology and cultural form television is supremely situated to construct a globalizing tourist gaze through 'armchair travel' facilitated by holiday shows, natural history programmes, routine and spectacular environmental news stories or the scenes of global disaster communicated via such global news providers as CNNI and BBC World. The point here, then, is that visual media routinely circulate and globalize images of nature as spectacle and/or as under threat and these help to infuse contemporary sensibilities about nature as well as environmental anxieties with moral and affective force.

Contemporary western outlooks on nature(s) and the environment, then, draw upon the deep reservoirs of cultural meanings and these find frequent and routine expression in the media, whether advertisements and women's magazines, films and natural history programmes or current affairs programmes and news representations. In the field of journalism a conventionalized 'rhetoric of the image' (Barthes 1977) is also often semiotically at play. Here images of the environment 'relay' meaning at the level of the visual and frequently do so without the 'anchorage' of words, even though the two may unfold in parallel. An established 'rhetoric of environmental images' principally visualizes nature and the environment by two, often interrelated, means: (a) the *spectacularization* of nature as scenically pristine, pure and untainted by human actions – as 'sacred'; and (b) through symbolic and 'profane' scenes of the environment as *under threat*. Table 7.1 illustrates how the rhetoric of environmental images is often at play within news representations and how this serves to discharge and invoke deep-seated cultural sensibilities (based on Cottle 2000b):

Table 7.1 Environmental images and news representations

BBC1 News	*Visuals*
(*News presenter to camera*) Environmental groups are increasingly concerned about the impact of poisonous flood water near Europe's biggest national park in southern Spain. Toxic waste escaped on Saturday from an industrial reservoir near the Corton Donana national park in southern Spain threatening to destroy plants and wildlife.	(*News presenter in studio*) Still: dead fish, belly up Still: map of Spain/location of national park.
The surrounding farmland has been devastated. Local farmers say that it could cost them up to £8 million.	Still: dead fish, belly up.
(*Correspondent voice-over*) This is the aftermath of the toxic spill, it has choked everything in its path.	Video: close-up of boot turning over dead animal lying in mud.
For José Antonio Deluna and his wife Carmen, these are days of despair.	Video: pull-back from dead animal to couple walking in front of mud-devastated fields.
Much of their 30-hectare farm is now under a sea of mud. José Antonio should have started harvesting his peach crop this week, now he's afraid that he may never be able to work his land again.	Video: three panning distance shots of mud stretching into tree lined distance.
(*Voice of José Antonio with translator's voice-over*)	
'For us this is total ruin, this is our business and our home. We don't even know whether we will be able to stay living here because we won't be able to farm'.	Video: couple interviewed in front of muddied fields.

BBC1 News	Visuals
(*Correspondent voice-over*) These pictures from the environmental group Greenpeace show how far the toxic tide material has spread. They say it is a disaster for land and for health. The full effects won't be known for five or six years.	Video: aerial panning scenes of industrial reservoir and burst banks, following 'sea' of mud across devastated landscapes.
(*Eva Hernandez: Greenpeace representative*) Heavy metals are now in this place, in the water, in the ground and only in a few years will we be able to know what is happening to the bird population, the fish population.	Video: Interview of Greenpeace representative in front of lush green vegetation.
(*Correspondent voice-over*) The cost of this toxic spill is high and rising.	Video: mid-shot to close-up shot of dead fish, belly up.
Voladin Aspera, the Swedish mining company involved, are bringing in senior executives as a government inquiry begins.	Video: distance to mid-shots of birds circling to land on mud-covered fields.
(*Correspondent direct to camera*) The problems here are just beginning. The toxic waste is continuing to seep into the soil.	Video: correspondent standing in front of mud-devastated fields.
Hour after hour it is causing greater contamination. Local people say it's not only livelihoods that have been destroyed here, but lives too.	
Orla Guerin, BBC News, Seville.	

Source: BBC1 News 27 April 1998, lead story.

Attending to the choreographed use of visual images in this typical television news presentation we can see how a succession of symbolic images are displayed to underwrite the accompanying words while simultaneously invoking cultural feelings about nature and its industrial defilement. The repeated still image of the dead fish, belly up, visually frames the item at the outset and is returned to later on in the video film report from which it originates. (Incidentally, we can also note how once again ordinary voices appear to have been deliberately positioned to symbolize the human effects of this disaster but are granted no opportunity beyond describing their immediate circumstances to advance claims and arguments.) The succession of scenes, visibly, makes use of the established rhetoric of environmental images which connect with an

Table 7.2 Visualization of nature and verbal narrative

HTV News	Visuals
(Newscaster voice-over) An investigation's been launched after fire broke out at a controversial chemical plant in Wiltshire today.	Video: pan from fire engines in a tree-lined street to factory perimeter fence and visible tall chemical containers inside.
Workers were evacuated from Premier Environmental Waste in Westbury as a precaution but no one was hurt.	Video: scenes of assembled workers outside. Video: two yellow-suited, hooded firefighters walking towards camera down street with hoses.
Fire crews wearing chemical suits were called in to make the area safe.	Video: steam rising up into sky from opening in blackened metal tanks.
It's thought flames took hold when chemicals were accidentally mixed.	Video shot: rusty metal factory gates and stacked drums inside.
Today's blaze is the latest in a string of fires and chemical leaks at the factory.	Video shot: chemical drums, different colours and conditions stacked in yard.
The Environment Agency is looking into the cause of today's incident.	Video: middle-distance shot of fire engines in tree-lined street. Video: scene of firefighters near fire engines.

Source: HTV News 25 June 1997.

environmental sensibility emotionally stirred by images of nature as industrially defiled and under threat. Given its deep-seated cultural resonance, this visualization of nature can also assume a more independent existence from the verbal narrative. Consider Table 7.2.

The 20-second news report illustrated in Table 7.2 includes eight different visual scenes. Though each purports iconically to establish the factual accuracy of the news narrative, when examined in sequence and juxtaposition these same images clearly also serve to 'relay' a further set of overlaid meanings. Situated within an otherwise normal tree-lined street, and set against the summer green foliage, the opening scene and panning shot help to connote something of the environmental threat posed by the adjacent chemical factory – a scene that resonates, in other words, with the tensions of a cultural opposition between 'nature' and the risks posed by industrial/chemical technologies. The sense of the abnormal is also visually reinforced, as is the sense of invisible manufactured threat, with the dramatic image of the two firefighters decked out from head to foot in bright yellow protective suits with blackened visors (see Image 7.1). When appearing with the voice-over declaring, 'as a precaution, but no one was hurt', the drama of this visual image relays a different, perhaps less comforting, meaning. When followed by the scene of smoke (or could it be something more sinister?) wafting up into the blue sky from blackened metal tanks, the sense of threat from chemical emissions finds further symbolic purchase (see Image 7.2). Following this, scenes of industrial infrastructure and their intrusion into an otherwise 'clean' and 'safe' environment also work to reinforce the unstated meanings – images of chained and rusting metal gates, dented and paint-peeling drums, chemical containers stacked in precarious heaps.

In such ways, then, even a 20-second news report can pack in a succession of culturally resonate images relaying an environmental sensibility towards nature as

Image 7.1
Source: ITV West News, 25 June 1997 (Courtesy of ITV West).

Image 7.2
Source: ITV West News, 25 June 1997 (Courtesy of ITV West).

under threat. Such images do not only feature in isolated news reports but now flow across news programmes, TV programmes more generally and other media as a matter of routine.

An aesthetic/contemplative sensibility is also regularly invited through the camera's gaze that looks out on and *spectacularizes* scenes of nature as pristine, timeless and 'sacred', scenes that are also indulged in news features about environmental projects, ecotourism, wildlife and wilderness and much else besides (Cottle 1993b, 2004c). The rhetoric of environmental images, therefore, is based in considerable measure on deep cultural reservoirs of meaning within the surrounding culture and these impart to news media images much of their affective and moral force. While this is generally so, a few qualifying observations are also needed.

Notwithstanding claims about their 'universal' meanings and audience appeals we cannot of course presume that environmental news agendas will be the same in different countries and cultures (Hansen 1991; Chapman et al. 1997), or that images of the environment and risks will always be read in the same way by everyone. Semiotic signs can discharge different codes and meanings in different contexts and at different times.

Scenes of (1) mechanized forest clearing; (2) the construction of roads through former wilderness; (3) massive urban development projects; or even (4) the bloody slaughter of whales and baby seals can all take on different meanings when read, say, through social optics of (1a) employment and jobs; (2a) the need for regional transport systems; (3a) Third World aspirations for economic progress and development; or (4a) traditional indigenous practices. We should also acknowledge, and research, the strategic manipulation and mobilization of symbols (see Chapter 8), and how these have been constructed and possibly later challenged within the media, and sometimes politically neutralized through their wider circulation and/or commoditization (Lester 2005). New symbols are constantly being forged by environmental protestors and these feed into the changing repertoires of protest addressed earlier (see Chapter 3). It is also the case that industrial and corporate interests are increasingly using their public relations capacities to circulate countering (but interestingly also often environmentally inflected) symbols in the media sphere. The recent work of Libby Lester is exemplary in this regard, historically recovering the strategic deployment of constructed symbols of 'wilderness' in the protests fought out in Tasmania from the 1970s to the present and how these have continued to play a significant role in the changing dialectic between movement and media over time (Lester 2005 forthcoming).

The main finding here, however, and notwithstanding these qualifying observations, is that the news media trade for the most part, both commercially and symbolically, in an environmental sensibility that resonates with deep-seated cultural 'views' of nature and environmental hazards. To what extent this constitutes an immanent critique of industrialism, capitalism, progress and essentializing views of nature (DeLuca 1999), rather than a more inchoate, often romanticized, cultural disposition towards 'nature' which often remains politically underdeveloped is a moot point. There is no doubting, however, the incorporation of deep-seated sentiments and views in media visualizations of the environment and these constitute a potent resource for environmentalist critique and possible action.

Audiences, the everyday and citizenship

Adding some weight to the textual claims above concerning the salience and affect of environmental images are a number of recent studies of audience reception focused either in whole or in part on environment and risk communication (Corner et al. 1990; Burgess and Harrison 1993; Corner and Richardson 1993; Buckingham 2000; Kitzinger 2004). In their study of how television viewers made sense of the nuclear power debate in the UK, Corner and Richardson usefully set out their view of the recent paradigm shift in the field of media and audience research, which now guides most audience reception studies:

By placing a more thoroughly theorized notion of meaning as social action at the centre of the analysis of public communication, research has been routed away from both functionalist linearity of 'message flow' and structuralist fascination with a semiotically imperial 'text'. A concern with the *pragmatics* of mediation has thus begun to appear, alert to the disjunctions and variables of the public communication process but still wishing to pursue substantive, empirical research and to work with hypotheses which accord the media effectiveness and power.

(1993: 222–3)

Sensitized to the contingencies of meanings, of how different viewers actively make sense of and evaluate television programmes, Corner and Richardson engage with different audience groups and elicit three key themes and responses from their programme viewers. It is noteworthy that these also mirror and lend further evidential support to the themes highlighted in the discussion so far. The first of these concerns how 'expert' and 'ordinary' discourse features across the selected programmes and in the responses of their programme viewers. While science and expert testimony can still call forth deference in some, for many audience members it is likely to produce lay scepticism:

> Mediated personal testimony can have a powerful effect upon viewers, against the grain of scientific discourse. The role of the ordinary person, particularly in programmes dealing with the consequences of particular events (Bhopal, Three-Mile Island, Chernobyl) is extremely important. Lay accounts can offer a density that scientific abstraction cannot match, as viewers hear about, and also see, the crops that failed, the animals that starved, the children who fell sick and lost their hair.

(1993: 222–3)

A second theme concerns 'symbolic resonance' and the way in which certain images convey meaning at an implicit/connotative level and how these prompted and influenced viewers' perceptions and feelings. Here the writers point to the 'imagery of threat' (endorsing the argument in the last section) and how this was enacted through particular types of visualization, and sometimes with supporting music. A televised scene of a lake adjacent to a nuclear power station, for example, was filmed steaming because of the increased temperature caused by the coolant from the plant. This visual image clearly registered in the minds of their respondents as suggesting 'radiation' and points to the power of visual symbols and how these can undercut accompanying verbal statements claiming, as in this case, that nuclear power is safe (1993: 227).

And the third principal theme that arises from this audience study is the way in which viewers' responses to the programmes are informed by overlapping interpretative frames. Four frames of reception in particular are identified: (a) the personal frame (relating to personal experience or temperamental predispositions); (b) the political frame (filtered through a political grid including environmental concerns); (c) the evidential frame (assessing arguments, evidence, narrative); and (d) the civic frame (judging according to balance and fairness). Evidently processes of audience reception and sense making involve multiple dimensions and interpretative dispositions and these defy simplistic notions of message transmission or sociologically blunt predictions based on social categories of class, occupation or indeed political orientation – the *pragmatics* of reception confound such easy generalizations.

A more recent study by David Buckingham (2000) also uncovers multiple layers of complexity in his study of young people and their reception of television news, including news about environmental issues. 'Talk', says Buckingham, 'needs to be interpreted, not as a straightforward reflection of what individuals really think or believe, but as a form of social action' (2000: 98). He notes, for example, how the expressed views of young people in a general discussion about news may suggest apathy and alienation both in their lives and in respect of news programmes, but once focused in respect of particular news items about particular concerns, such as the environment, a less cynical (but also less autonomous) relationship to television news begins to emerge. Again audience perceptions of programme fairness and balance, the 'civic frame', come to the fore as do considerations of the symbolic nature of news visuals and how these can both emphasize and displace certain meanings. One of Buckingham's young respondents commenting on an environmental news item, for example, said how the producers showed 'what they perceived as the impact of the factory, smokestacks and fires burning and all this' but then critically observed that the producers did not show 'the impact of joblessness – people on the street starving'. Others were equally sensitized to the rhetoric of environmental images as in this discussion about a news story on a pulp mill and its environmental impacts:

> *Dartagnan*: Did you see the outline of the bridge and the lake and everything, with the sun setting? And then you see the tops of waste plants, something dumping into the lake . . .
> *Patrick*: Yeah, but they showed some other plant, where it was a huge plant and nothing around it, it was just like mud and dirt and nothing and just dumping and the smoke coming out. And it wasn't a very good picture . . . They used really good camera angles, I thought, in there, especially with sun and everything. I mean, everybody pictures that – you look up, these big, tall trees and then the sunshine through, and it's beautiful.
>
> (2000: 145–6)

These selected extracts cannot, of course, do justice to either the complexity of Buckingham's research or the complex views and responses advanced by his young subjects, but they indicate nonetheless that reception studies have much to contribute to our understanding of the complex ways in which media representations of the environment enter into people's sense making and become resources for both talk, critical responses and possible future environmental action. In fact, it is probably true to say that environment and risk coverage is positioned at the cutting edge of audience reception research because it is these very concerns that reach into the everyday lifeworlds, identities and practices of ordinary people and they can therefore open a valuable window on how people incorporate and make sense of media images and ideas in their everyday lives and actions.

A focus group study by Phil Macnaghten and John Urry (1998) provides further insights into the dimensions that mediate the complex relationship between environmental concern and action. They demonstrate, for example, how environmental issues and risks are generally apprehended and made sense of in relation to local, particularized settings and through embedded identities. Contrary to survey findings that suggest that the environment may have become less salient as an issue in people's thinking over recent years, their qualitative focus group discussions reveal in fact a widespread and possibly growing anxiety or 'ontological insecurity' (Giddens 1990) about the world's ecology and the impact of this on their lives, and the lives of their children in the future. Importantly, their research reveals how (a) people make sense of environmental issues within particularized local and embedded identities, whether as mothers, rural dwellers, or global or British citizens; (b) that environmental issues are distinguished not only by a local and global continuum but also by rational/instrumental and moral/symbolic dimensions; and (c) ambivalent attitudes towards personal action relate to a pervasive sense of lack of personal agency and a marked lack of trust in institutions responsible for managing environmental change (Macnaghten and Urry 1998: 245–6).

Arguably the principal challenge for media researchers and all those concerned about the environment and the risks of late modernity is to better understand how mediatized environmental risks connect – cognitively, affectively, socially, culturally, politically – with the everyday lifeworlds, identities and wider environmental concerns of ordinary people, and how these mediations can empower responses and action in the future.

Chapter summary

This chapter took its opening cue from Ulrich Beck's social theory of risk society before proceeding to develop ideas and arguments based on empirical research which help to illuminate the complex mediations involved. Beck's thesis provides a particularly rich source of arguments and ideas addressing contemporary concerns of ecology, politics and media, but his arguments can be developed and refined further in respect of the environmental and risk communications field. This is necessary if we are to not only map but also understand and explain the rise and fall of environmental agendas in the media and how these resonate with audiences, many of whom are already environmentally aware and concerned.

Beck's conceptualization of 'relations of definitions' is productive and pertinent to the field of risk communications with its contending claims, media frames and scientific and social rationalities. This now needs to be better grounded by studies of the strategic interventions of different media sources and their position within institutional fields as well as examination of the competition for access and legitimacy that takes place within and across different public arenas. Only then can we begin to account for the rise and fall of environment and risk agendas in the media and the impact of claims-making processes and agenda building over time. The evident successes of new social movements and pressure groups in mobilizing environmental and risk issues in the media documents how the media need not be regarded as an unassailable citadel monopolized by political elites and powerful corporations. That said nor can we underestimate the continuing structural imbalances and commercial and technocratic logics that remain antithetical to the democratization of the risk communications field.

In global risk society, the uncertainty, prevalence and universalizing consequences of risk potentially position everyone as 'representative' spokespersons for entry into the media arena, whether as the 'voices of the side effects' advancing experiential testimonies and critiques based on heartfelt and humane forms of 'social rationality' or the experts, scientists, politicians and 'argumentation craftsmen' espousing statistical and probabilistic claims based on the procedures and logics of 'scientific rationality'. Cognitive and epistemic disadvantages based on social position in relation to the science and technocracy of risks should not be allowed to shape and delimit the contours of public debate or go unchallenged within the media. Notwithstanding the cultural affinities evident between popular media forms and everyday lifeworlds Beck's 'voices of the side effects' in fact according to recent research find few opportunities to put their views and arguments across in the public domain though they are accessed to symbolize the harmful consequences of environmental degradation and risks.

The media also routinely deploy a conventionalized 'rhetoric of environmental images' in their visualizations of nature and the environment. Whether depicted in terms of the *spectacularization* of nature as pristine, timeless and pure, or through symbolic images of the environment as *under threat*, these culturally resonant images provide an affective and potentially critical charge to the discourses and politics of risk now circulating within the media and throughout wider society. They are underpinned by historically forged and culturally deep reservoirs of meaning, 'structures of feeling' organized around dualisms of the rural–urban, tradition–modernity, community–association and nature–society. Such cultural resonances are plainly at work within contemporary representations of the environment and they play a part in sustaining widespread environmental awareness and anxieties. These image rhetorics are available to be harnessed by protests and the politics of the environment and they often are within the media. Even so, their semiotic charge and political impact can shift when interpreted in different contexts and through differing interpretative frameworks.

Concerns of risk and environment, we have also heard, figure prominently in people's everyday lifeworlds and the latter mediate the play of expert and ordinary discourse and environmental symbols. Media audiences make sense of media forms and representations through complex layers of meanings and multiple overlapping interpretative frames, whether personal, political, evidential or civic. Whether environmental risks are global or local in scope for many they are experienced 'close to home' and they register most forcefully in local and particularized settings and via embedded cultural identities. It is here that the feelings of 'ontological insecurity' (Giddens 1990) produced by risk society and the lack of trust in authorities and officialdom to manage Beck's 'civilization of threats' become most keenly felt and sometimes articulated. The media have a responsibility to not only illuminate the '*bads*' of global risk society but also to democratize risks by enfranchising all those who are affected by them to enable them to have their say in how the risks spawned by late modernity should be managed or curtailed in the future. Media researchers can continue to play an important part in opening up to view some of the complexities and contingencies involved.

Recommended reading

Allan, S. (2002b) *Media, Risk and Science*. Buckingham: Open University Press.
Allan, S., Carter, C. and Adams, B. (eds) (2000) *Environmental Risks and the Media*. London: Routledge.
Anderson, A. (1997) *Media, Culture and the Environment*. London: UCL Press.
Beck, U. (1992) *Risk Society*. London: Sage.
Buckingham, D. (2000) *The Making of Citizens: Young People, News, Politics*. London: Routledge.
Corner, J., Richardson, K. and Fenton, N. (1990) *Nuclear Reactions: Form and Response in Public Issue Television*. Luton: John Libbey.

FROM 'TERRORISM' TO THE 'GLOBAL WAR ON TERROR': THE MEDIA POLITICS OF OUTRAGE

The relation between terror, insurgency and the media has long exercised politicians, commentators and academics, many of whom have either argued for or against claims that the media serve to encourage acts of violence targeting innocent civilians. We shall revisit this heated debate presently. Following the terrible events of 11 September 2001, now immortalized simply as '9/11', questions of the media's relation to terror assumed a new global urgency; especially for those who became exposed to threats of terrorism for the first time or who found themselves caught up in a vortex of state and military responses, many of them violent and conducted in their name. Nine days after the 9/11 atrocities in the US, President George W. Bush announced in his state of the union address his intentions to engage in a global 'war on terror'. 'Our war on terror begins with al Qaeda', he said, 'but it does not end there. It will not end until every terrorist group of global reach has been found, stopped and defeated' (cited in Tuman 2003: 96).

Post 9/11 this ill-defined and infinitely elastic definition of a 'global war on terror' decisively moved the world into a new and dangerous phase. Military invasions in Afghanistan (2001) and Iraq (2003) followed with the deaths of many thousands of combatants and innocent civilians, and new draconian security measures such as the Patriot Act were introduced in the US in a growing climate of fear. Meanwhile, terrorist atrocities have continued around the world with indiscriminate bombings in Bali (2002 and 2005), Turkey (2004), Madrid (2004), Jakarta (2005) and London (2005) – among many others. The 'successful' invasion of Iraq by the 'coalition of the willing' also prompted chilling acts of mediatized barbarity when insurgents videotaped hostages pleading for their lives before beheading them on camera. Coalition forces engaged in deadly military operations in Iraq, such as the siege of Fallujah in November 2004, long after the staged declarations of the US President of 'mission accomplished'. They did so amidst circulating images of military personnel torturing detainees in Abu Ghraib prison and the continuing incarceration of over 600 'terrorist suspects', without trial in defiance of international law, in Guantanamo Bay. We also now know that the improbable links alleged between Saddam Hussein and al Qaeda, like the existence of Iraqi weapons of mass destruction (WMD), both prominent justifications for the 2003 Iraq invasion promulgated through the mass media (Allan and Zelizer 2004; Miller 2004), were entirely without foundation (see Chapter 5).

The US war on terror, as well as its asymmetric enemies, therefore, has positioned 'terror' at the centre of the new world (dis)order and high on global news agendas. Given the high stakes involved for so many people, so many countries and even for the idea of democracy itself, the role of the media in this unfolding maelstrom of terror demands careful scrutiny. The 'battle for hearts and minds', say researchers, is no less apparent in the media's portrayal of insurgency and acts of terror than in wartime. But the media can also perform a more progressive role in relation to violence and terror. They can do so by engaging publics in discussion of the causes, contending claims and human consequences of terror and violence as well as the risks of ill-conceived political over-reactions or tendencies for the military to 'overkill'. In such ways, arguably, the media can help to 'democratize violence'. These themes are addressed in the first part of the chapter.

The second part of the discussion addresses the symbolic, often spectacular and staged nature of mediatized terror – one of the circulating dark signs of globalization – as well as the 'media politics of outrage' that this has spawned. How images of human suffering, death and destruction are circulated by contemporary media and are subject to forms of control, censorship and countering images can be examined in respect of the US global 'war on terror'. For reasons that will be elaborated, the war of images and, specifically, the contention over circulated images of terror and violence is only likely to increase in the future.

From the 'oxygen of publicity' to the 'democratization of violence'

A view widely promulgated by counterinsurgency experts and some politicians has become orthodoxy, a seeming default position in debates about 'terrorism' and the media. Acts of 'terrorism' are here seen as instances of a generalized, if indistinct, phenomenon of 'international terrorism', a phenomenon moreover which at heart is thought to be accounted for with reference to the mass media. In the context of the Troubles in Northern Ireland in 1985, the then British Prime Minister, Margaret Thatcher, famously articulated this view when she declared, 'democracies must find a way to starve the terrorists and hijackers of the oxygen of publicity on which they depend'. The 1988 Broadcasting Ban followed that muzzled proscribed political organizations and the media (Henderson et al. 1990; Miller 1995). Four questionable assumptions inform this widely held media/terrorism orthodoxy.

First, it works with an implicit 'retail', as opposed to 'wholesale', understanding of 'terrorism' (Herman and Chomsky 1988; Herman and O'Sullivan 1991; Schlesinger 1991). All too often 'terrorism' is defined as, and delimited to, the violence and terror perpetrated by individuals and groups, not states (Taylor 1986). This view has prevailed over the years notwithstanding the disproportionate numbers of state killings compared to those by non-state actors and insurgents. Such selective accounts of 'terrorism' has led some commentators to conclude that 'terrorism' can be seen as an ideological ascription invariably used in a context supportive of state, and often western, interests (Herman and O'Sullivan 1991). Clearly, if terrorism is semantically and ideologically confined to those groups challenging state authority, all too easily the state, no matter its historical or contemporary involvement in brutal acts of violence and terror, can portray itself as reacting with legitimate force to illegitimate violence, when in fact the opposite may be the case.

A second feature of the orthodoxy is the assumption that 'terrorists' secure attention, recognition and legitimacy through media exposure. This flies in the face of considerable evidence, both international and comparative, to the contrary (Paletz et al. 1982; Paletz and Schmid 1992; Miller 1994). Research findings in fact suggest that though the generality of media coverage grants terrorist *acts* and *consequences* attention, and may thereby be implicated in insurgency efforts to disseminate fear, media coverage typically fails to provide *explanation, reason* or *political motive.*

A third, related, belief is the idea that the mass media effectively serve as a propaganda platform for terrorists and their causes. Again, evidence is in short supply, though this has not inhibited calls for censorship based on such claims. Evidence suggests that the media are anything but disposed to grant 'terrorists' an opportunity to advance their political aims or claims for political legitimacy. In her seminal study of the British reporting of the Troubles in Northern Ireland, Liz Curtis elicited the BBC's informal policy towards the IRA in the 1980s and quotes the BBC's Director of News and Current Affairs as follows:

> Nobody involved in the journalistic coverage of terrorism is other than sympathetic to the victims or repelled by the perpetrators of terrorist crimes. We do not deal impartially with those who choose to step outside the bounds of the law and decent social behaviour. Not only do they get very much less coverage than those who pursue their aims legitimately, but the very manner and tone that our reporters adopt makes our position quite plain . . . such exposure provides them not with a platform but with a scaffold.
>
> (1984: 148)

This, of course, is simply one policy response by a particular media institution at a particular historical moment. When set alongside other empirical studies of British media organizations and professionals (Schlesinger 1978; Bolton 1986; Miller 1994; Butler 1995) and their output (Elliott 1977, 1980; Rolston 1991; Taylor 1991; Miller 1994; Elliott et al. 1996; Rolston and Miller 1996), as well as findings from studies of international broadcasting organizations (Paletz and Tawney 1992), and their editors and reporters (Blaisse 1992; Schmid 1992), a considerable body of evidence documents that Curtis's finding is not atypical. Far from providing a propaganda platform for 'terrorists', then, it appears that most media organizations and media professionals actively set out to be less than impartial, given their acknowledged bias towards constitutional politics (Bolton 1986: 108).

The fourth questionable feature of the orthodox view is the claim that the media encourage, albeit unintentionally, further acts of terrorism. That they serve, in other words, to promote the contagion of terrorism (Brosius and Weimann 1991). A considered assessment of the 'contagion hypothesis' based on a review of two decades of research and argument, however, concludes:

> During the past two decades the literature associating media with terrorism and implicating media as a contagion of such violence has grown rapidly. When carefully dissecting that literature, however, one finds it contains no credible evidence that media are an important factor in inducing and diffusing terrorist acts . . . As one reviews the literature it becomes shockingly clear that not a single study based on accepted social science research methods has established a cause–effect relationship between media coverage and the spread of terrorism.
>
> (Picard 1991: 50)

The failure to produce findings supportive of such a direct causal link should not surprise anyone who has followed the media 'violence–effects' debate over the years. Underpinned by dubious theories and concepts, an insufficiently reflexive methodology and crippling blindspots in respect of terrorist motivations and political aims as well as the contingencies of political process, action and response, the media 'contagion hypothesis' is destined to remain just that. A counter position, 'coverage as preventative of terrorism', provides a more plausible claim in so far as the media give public expression to and debate, or ignore and denigrate, aggrieved social groups and their aspirations for political recognition, accommodation and change (Picard 1991; see Chapter 9). This, though, is very different from asserting that the media 'cause' acts of terrorism.

From these criticisms of the media/terrorism orthodoxy a more productive approach for the study of media, insurgency and terror begins to emerge and one that has relevance to the post-9/11 world and the global war on terror. Media researchers have usefully drawn attention to the representational and symbolic processes involved in publicly labelling groups as 'terrorists'. Few will choose to describe themselves as terrorists. At the level of political meaning 'terrorism' becomes a matter of judgement and interpretation, a key to which is often the claim to political legitimacy. This is not to suggest that any or all acts of political violence have equal claim for acceptance or that some are not morally repugnant (perhaps most are) but that such evaluations can only be based on judgements about 'context', 'aims', 'cause' and '(in)justice'.

The terms 'terrorist' and 'terrorism', in current media and public discourse, are generally used to delegitimize the political aims and actions of insurgents. Semantically the terms 'terrorist' and 'terrorism' function as lexical foot soldiers in the 'propaganda war' and are often deployed by states, via the media, to pave the way for the suppression of dissent; helping to legitimize militaristic violence or even prepare the way for military 'overkill' (Schlesinger 1991; Gerbner 1992; Keane 2004). The liberal press and sections of the broadcasting media have also warned against the threat posed by state excesses when targeting insurgents located within civilian populations and periodically turn 'miscarriages of justice' and, for example, the British government's undeclared 'shoot to kill' policy in Northern Ireland into *causes célèbres* and potential political scandals (Miller 1990; Murphy 1991).

When democracies are challenged by new forms of transnational and so called 'apocalyptic terror', as well as by more traditional acts of insurgency, it is imperative that state responses which can lead to the exacerbation of terror and undermine democracy itself are publicly scrutinized. Public communication, deliberation and debate at such times are vital if democracies are not to forfeit their democratic legitimacy by disproportionate or misjudged violence. John Keane argues persuasively, for example, that the 'democratization of violence' requires first and foremost that we 'always try to understand the motives and context of the violent' (2004: 167). Few studies, however, have sought to examine how different media, genres and formats can contribute to the public debate and deliberation necessary when civil society becomes subject to a vortex of violence and terror. Fewer still have sought to seriously consider how some of these media forms can provide opportunities for enhancing public understanding of the issues, interests and identities at stake.

Exceptionally, a study by Philip Elliott (1980) analysed the heavily symbolic and ritualized forms of press performance in the Troubles in Northern Ireland (see also Wagner-Pacifici 1986 and Chapter 4). Elliott with co-authors also examined how television's 'discourses of terrorism' are mediated through the more 'open' spaces of current affairs, documentary programmes and dramas (Elliott et al. 1996). These programme forms can provide opportunities for views and voices rarely heard in news reports and they also provide less predetermined or 'tight' formats for the exploration of the different perspectives and political outlooks in play. Factuality programmes and re-enactments, drama-documentaries and also some fictionalized media forms can all perform an invaluable role in publicly representing the contexts and causes of political violence as well as dramatizing the undercover manoeuvres of the state in its secret war against terror and clandestine meetings and insurgency decision making. These programme representations often have as much to do with the nature of conventional media forms, the pragmatics and temporal gestation of media production and the degree of authorial or programme independence from the commissioning media outlet than the crude operation of censorship and ideological influences (see Table 8.1).

David Butler (1995) acknowledges these differing opportunities of programme form but also argues that such a typology can appear too formalist and too atemporal or

Table 8.1 The major forms of actuality television

Programme form	News bulletin	News magazine	Current affairs	Documentary
Examples	*News at Ten* (ITV) *BBC News*	*Nationwide* (BBC1) *Newsnight* (BBC2)	*Panorama* (BBC1) *TV Eye* (ITV)	*Heroes* (John Pilger)
Frequency	Daily	Daily	Weekly	Irregular
Item length	Short (news item)	Short (pro-gramme item)	Long (pro-gramme theme)	Long (pro-gramme subject)
Presentation techniques	Visual clips, brief interviews	Short film report/studio interview	Film report/ studio discussion	Film report
Presenter's role	Reader	Reporter/ interviewer	Reporter/ chairperson/ interviewer	Storyteller
Programme identified with	The broad-casting organization	The produc-tion team	The produc-tion team	An individual presenter/ producer

RELATIVELY CLOSED ← — — — — — — — — — — → RELATIVELY OPEN

Source: Reproduced with permission from Elliot, P., Murdock, G. and Schlesinger, P. (1996) 'The State and "Terrorism" on British Television', in B. Rolston and D. Miller (eds) *War and Words: The Northern Ireland Media Reader*, p. 345. Belfast: Beyond the Pale Publications.

static, and thereby underestimates how the state's 'aperture of consensus' imposed on the media can wax and wane through time and in response to changing political conditions (see also Hallin 1986, 1994; Bennett 1990; Robinson 2001). In the context of the Troubles in Northern Ireland, how programme forms represent contending official, alternative and oppositional political discourses may in fact, suggests Butler, be more fluid and historically contingent than Elliott et al.'s schema suggests (Butler 1995: 10). Even so, this heightened sensitivity to the mediating forms and discursive opening or closure of different programme forms, or the 'politics of representation' more textually conceived in contrast to the 'representation of politics' more propagandistically conceived, remains a productive optic through which to interrogate the media's representations of political violence.

Television news also demonstrates representational complexity in this regard. David Altheide (1987) has reported, for example, how 'event type' reports associated with regular evening news broadcasts tend to focus on the visuals of the aftermath and tactics of terrorism, while 'topic type' formats associated with interviews and documentary presentation are more likely to include materials about purposes, goals and rationale, again pointing to the complexities and impacts of media formats. The communicative complexity of television news was opened up even further in a recent study of six countries and how their television news services simultaneously mediatized the global War on Terror in and through a standardized and (seemingly universal) communicative architecture of television journalism forms, with consequential results for how the mediatized War on Terror becomes publicly known (Cottle 2005b).

Similarly, a study of British current affairs programmes in the aftermath of 9/11 demonstrates how public speech and wider deliberation were enacted by a strict minority of British programmes which constituted rare but meaningful 'agorae' or public spaces for the airing and engagement of opposing views and did so at a time when a culture of fear and emerging fortress mentality was narrowing public discourse (Cottle 2002). One memorable programme, for example, used live satellite link-ups to facilitate intercultural exchanges across geopolitical, cultural and religious divides, and brought together studio-based audiences in New York and Islamabad shortly after 9/11 and just before the US invasion of Afghanistan. The discussion and exchanges that ensued proved electrifying and arguably 'democratizing' in the provision of images and ideas, rhetoric and reasons, arguments and affect, emotions and experiences, discourses and debate silenced elsewhere.

Lest we should assume, however, all current affairs and documentary programmes depart from dominant political agendas, which as Butler reminds us many do not, we can also acknowledge the ideologically powered use of filmic codes and visual dramatization and how these techniques can add emotional intensity to factuality programmes and their meanings. Consider, for example, the following from Fox News Channel following the US military occupation in Iraq in 2004:

War stories: under fire in Iraq
Host: I'm Oliver North this is *War Stories* coming to you from a marine base in Iraq. We're here with the second battalion, fourth marines the unit that has inflicted more damage on the enemies of democracy and taken more casualties than any other in Operation Iraqi Freedom. Tonight we'll take you along on the dangerous missions the one thousand marines of 2–4 run every day. We're there when they're ambushed by the enemy and you'll see first hand how our troops respond to these deadly attacks. From IEDs (Improvised explosive devices) that detonate without warning, to hours-long gunfights in enemy-held buildings at a hundred and twenty degrees. It's the anatomy of battle in the war on terror . . .
(Dressed in Fatigues, helmet in hand leaning against a tank, footage of battles . . .)

Oliver North: . . . Though badly wounded with shrapnel in his face, arms and leg, Carton refused to leave his men. 'He didn't want to go and I wasn't going to ask him to go that's something that you just don't do, you don't ask the commander to leave his command. And the Captain stayed in the fight until the end. . .'.

(Feature footage of ongoing battle, captain limping with bloodied cheek staying in charge.)

Oliver North: Mark, when you think about that moment when you almost got killed does that make you rethink what you're doing out here?

Captain: Not at all. If for nothing else I'm out there because those boys are out there. So there's no other place for me.

(Featured interview with wounded Captain, scarred and bloodied cheek and neck, bandaged arm.)

(Fox News Channel, *War Stories: Under Fire in Iraq*, 20 September 2004)

While Oliver North's brand of close-up and personal patriotism may, for some, be considered to be a peculiarly myopic public eye on the War on Terror, and one seemingly blinded to the wider politics that drive such military adventures, it nonetheless exhibits a different and possibly revealing insight into the nature of military thinking played out on the ground in Iraq as well as in the Fox News Channel's programme presentations.

Other programme forms provide a less closed perspective. The UK's *Question Time*, broadcast by the BBC to a large national audience, for example, is modelled on a parliamentary agora that remains under the control of the programme host (Speaker) Sir David Dimbleby. Programme producers invariably exhibit a form of professional TV 'agoraphobia' or the fear of wide-open programme spaces and feel compelled to steer and control programme flows and agendas (Cottle 2002). *Question Time* is no exception, but even so this particular format can produce meaningful exchanges that are disseminated into the public domain. Here, the precariousness of live unscripted speech, opportunities for challenging dominant political and programme presuppositions, agenda-shifting and the public airing of dissenting views and opinions all manage to break through the production controls and professional containments built into the programme logic and design. Consider the following extracts from a broadcast discussion prompted by a question about hostages taken by insurgents in Iraq:

Question Time
Presenter: Good evening, welcome to this the first edition of a new series of *Question Time* . . . the rules are the same as ever: the audience will ask straight questions and the panel will give answers. And, um, the panel don't know, needless to say, what questions are going to be put to them. So let's have the first question tonight.

Kay Amona: Is it too much to ask for the release of two female scientists in exchange for an innocent British life?

Simon Hughes, President Liberal Democrats: . . . no government, no prime minister of any party could say we're going to give in to demands from people who are clearly warped individuals who are claiming divine authority for something that cannot be right in the eyes of God, cannot be right in the eyes of God. And I think we have to be very clear about that. Just one other thing. Behind the scenes I am sure there is all the work that anybody can manage being done to try to identify where this person is being held, where Ken is being held, and to try to release him, as you expect to be done by intelligence services and the secret services. But the answer is, although of course any saved life might be a price worth paying – even if we have to let other people go free who've done terrible things – it isn't something you can judge tonight on its own, and if you do it once then the people who took this man and are holding him and have beheaded two people horribly, are likely to think that they can get away with it again. (Audience applause)

Richard Dreyfuss, Hollywood actor: . . . This is all from the consequence of this war which has made ourselves all the more secure and relaxed in that region. We're all much more secure because of this war and we haven't ignited anything provocative or anything terrible because we've done this war, this good war thing . . . (Audience mirth)

Further panel discussion . . .

Presenter: Let's not get away from the question. There's a number of you wanting to speak. I would like to bring in several but if you could keep your remarks fairly succinct I think it would be good because we have a lot of questions tonight. I'll go to the man in the front row first.

Man in front row: The people of Iraq were attacked by what the UN General Secretary called an illegal war. They say you cannot negotiate with terrorists, what about the terrorists who tortured the people in Abu Ghraib? What about the terrorists who held thousands upon thousands of Iraqi men, women and children without trial, without any due process, in their jails? They're murdering them, they're devastating them left, right and centre. The people of Iraq are turning around and saying we cannot, we cannot negotiate with the terrorist George Bush, so therefore we are going to use our way of getting back at him.

Peter Hain interrupts: But are you saying that that is the equivalent of people beheading somebody on live television, are you saying that the abuses, are you saying that the abuses at Abu Ghraib, which were unacceptable . . .

Man in front row: Where is the difference between beheading someone and shooting them in the head, shooting them in the back, hitting a crowd, hitting a crowd of people who are standing on the pavement with helicopter gun ships or using depleted uranium shells on them, or blanket bombing Baghdad. What is the terrorism, tell me what is the terrorism, what is the terrorism?

Peter Hain: What is your conclusion? Sorry, what is your conclusion from this about this particular case?

Man in front row: My solution is that they should not have been there in the first place. Tony Blair and George Bush illegally went to war and it is a consequence of their illegal acts that this poor man is now facing death. (Applause)

Presenter: All right I don't want this discussion to become about democracy in Iraq or the future of Iraq, because it is specifically about the events surrounding Kenneth Bigley, that's what the question is about and that's what I'd like to stick with. . . . The woman next to you, on your left there, in the red shirt.

Woman in red shirt: We keep on about Ken Bigley and if we do nothing it will happen again, it's going to happen again anyway because the Americans are still bombing civilians and they are dying and we don't care about them. (Applause) . . .

(UK: BBC1 *Question Time*, 23 September 2004)

As we can see this contrived forum for public speech and debate, though clearly steered and controlled by the programme host and producers, nonetheless generates productive encounters between opposing views and values, and begins to provide opportunities for the public advancement of some of the contending political perspectives and arguments surrounding the War on Terror. Though such communicative spaces are relatively infrequent and often marginalized in programme slots outside 'prime time', the communicative architecture of such programme forms and formats can contribute to processes of public dissemination and deliberation. As such, these need to be acknowledged by researchers and, where possible, defended and deepened in the future (see Chapter 9). Such programme forms and openings can play a productive role in the democratization of violence post 9/11 and they are vitally needed in a context where the politics and presuppositions of the global War on Terror demand to be subject to rigorous public debate and sustained discussion.

Media, terror spectacle and the politics of moral outrage

The war on terrorism is a war of images. Just as the September 11 attacks were calculated not simply to wreak terrible destruction but to create a global media spectacle by targeting symbols of American prestige and power, so too the response of the US and UK governments has been highly image-conscious.

(Hammond 2003: 23)

Not since the surprise air attacks on Pearl Harbor at the outset of World War II had US dominance visibly come under such an assault on its home territory. On 9/11, potent symbols of US hegemony – economic, political and military – came under attack with devastating, shocking results. The awful scenes captured by television encapsulated for many '9/11' and were 'moving' in both senses (see Images 8.1 and 8.2).

In their mediatized repetition two repeated televisual arcs particularly came to symbolize 9/11: the surreal images of jet airliners flying incongruously into the Twin Towers above the New York streets; and, later, the accelerating rush of the Twin Towers dropping floor by floor towards the ground amidst a huge billowing cloud of debris and dust. After seeing their replay time and again, such scenes could only be viewed by

Image 8.1 America Remembers
Source: CNN *International*, 7 September 2002 (© CNN).

most western audiences with a knowing and tragic sense of inevitability. The world's news media quickly disseminated them around the globe and they thereby entered into collective, cultural memory, periodically renewed by the media's ability to store, arch-ive and recycle these same images time and again. Their shocking nature prompted diverse responses and even some soul searching as to what justifications or belief systems could possibly propel people to commit such a crime against humanity (Zelizer and Allan 2002).

Such scenes were produced as a calculated act of political communication enacted on the global stage. Mediatized and globalized, as any assault on the US mainland and its symbols of prestige and power would be, they signalled to US and western audiences that American power whether at home or abroad was not beyond reach and nor were US citizens immune from transnational terrorism or the production of a culture of fear. But more importantly perhaps, by their globalized circulation these same images also communicated a powerful political message to the followers and would-be recruits of al-Qaeda and other opponents of US and western power. To these different publics they proclaimed that the geopolitical dominance of the US, and the Occident more widely, was neither unopposed nor invincible and that western influence and intervention in the Arab world would increasingly be paid for in blood.

Image 8.2 America Remembers
Source: CNN *International*, 7 September 2002 (© CNN).

Spectacular and symbolic images of the War on Terror have continued to play a prominent part in the ensuing War on Terror, with images deliberately manufactured and globally circulated as part of the wider propaganda war. The late French sociologist, Pierre Bourdieu, defined symbolic violence as the ways by which institutions and language encode and enact a 'gentle, invisible form of violence' which informs relations of communication which are also relations of power and domination (cited in Thompson 1984: 43). When applied to images specifically, various features and artifices such as selection and omission, juxtaposition and framing, focus and perspective, cropping and digital manipulation, can all enact forms of 'symbolic violence'. They may do so, for example, by symbolically occluding or symbolically annihilating the presence, interests and identities of the Other (most conflicts tend to produce and *mis*recognize 'Others'), or by valorizing, affirming and mobilizing group identities and allegiances premised on ideas of dominance, right or legitimacy again premised on a silent Other. We shall consider a number of images of symbolic violence later.

The global War on Terror and recent evolutions of transnational asymmetric warfare have also led to 'less gentle' images with the calculated production of deadly media enactments. Here the deliberate manufacture and global circulation of images of death and destruction, terror and torture provides a more blatant and cynical use of communicated violence. Violent symbols are here produced and disseminated in support of strategic aims and interests. The following now addresses some of the ways in which media images of 'symbolic violence' and 'violent symbolism' have come to perform a prominent, often terrifying, role in globalized media war and why such images are likely to become increasingly produced and globally circulated in the future.

Image wars: symbolic violence and violent symbolism

The invasion of Iraq, it will be recalled, began with a night-time bombing campaign of Baghdad labelled by the US military 'Shock and Awe'. This was captured by the world's press (see Image 8.3) and TV cameras and then repeatedly replayed often to accompanying music by transnational and national news broadcasters such as BBC

'A free Iraq will have policies the US dislikes. This is called independence'
Neal Ascherson, page 13

'Saddam has been helped materially by the ineptitude of his opponents'
Said Aburish, page 14

The **GuardianWeekly**

A$3.95 inc gst / NZ$4.95 **Thursday March 27 to Wednesday April 2 2003** Vol 168/No 14/Printed in Sydney

Shock and awe . . . smoke covers Saddam Hussein's palace compound in Baghdad as the Iraqi capital comes under attack from Stealth bombers and cruise missiles last week Photo: Ramzi Haidar/EPA

Image 8.3 *The Guardian Weekly*, 27 March–2 April 2003 (© Guardian Newspapers Limited 2003. Photo: AFP/AAP).

World and CNNI. Some used these scenes to head up their 24/7 news and special 'Iraq War' programmes. Spectacular scenes of pyrotechnic explosions bursting across the night sky demonstrated for the benefit of coalition audiences the awesome power of the military bombardment, but did so in an aesthetized display that denied (and symbolically annihilated) the human carnage piling up beneath the lit up night sky.

When the Arab TV network Al-Jazeera broadcast images of Iraqi civilians, women and children killed, maimed and hospitalized (symbolically recognized) from this and other bombardments the channel came under a barrage of US criticism and flak. Symbolic violence is politically encoded and part of the propaganda war; images of violence whether symbolic or iconic are likely to be contested given their capacity to record, bear witness and recognize the human devastation and miseries occluded in the officially sanctioned views.

The highly symbolic and, as it turned out, highly staged scenes of Saddam Hussein's statue being pulled down by 'rapturous' Iraqi civilians when US troops entered Baghdad (9 April 2003) figured prominently in the war of images (see Image 8.4). This scene was followed by a further staged media event in which President George Bush, dressed in military fatigues, announced for the benefit of attending media and cameras 'mission accomplished' on the deck of USS *Abraham Lincoln* (1 May 2003). In his speech the US President deliberately invoked these earlier 'historic' images and declared: 'In the images of falling statues, we have witnessed the arrival of a new era', and, 'In the images of celebrating Iraqis, we have also seen the ageless appeal of human freedom' (cited in Hammond 2003: 25). The scenes referred to were later found in fact to have been populated by a relatively small group of supporters of the proposed US interim government and a wider angle lens on these same events depicted how the seemingly 'rapturous crowd' was in fact a rather more dispersed and less animated group than at first appeared – findings that reinforce earlier studies that have observed how the media can visually exaggerate, dramatize and frame events through close-ups, occluding the wider context which can invite a very different interpretation of the events depicted (Lang and Lang 1953; Halloran et al. 1970; Cottle 1993a: 101–7). President Bush's 'mission accomplished' speech soon began to ring hollow as more US soldiers began to die in the occupation of Iraq than in the initial invasion. (At the time of writing in 2005, over 2000 coalition troops are known to have died; civilian and insurgent deaths are thought to exceed 20,000.) These staged images, high in symbolism, were clearly designed to support coalition propaganda purposes. As we have already heard earlier in respect of the Hollywood style filming and construction of 'Saving Private Jessica Lynch' (see Chapter 5) no expense or effort was seemingly spared in their media propagation.

Propaganda images, high in symbolism, did not only emanate from the United States and the coalition. Though lacking sophisticated public relations capabilities and media technologies, insurgents in Iraq produced their own low budget, DIY, 'shock and awe' images. As a form of political communication these proved to be devastatingly effective

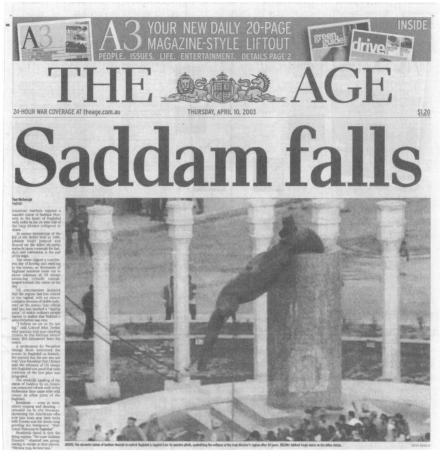

Image 8.4 *The Age*, 10 April 2003
(© The Age 2003/Paul McGeough. Photo: Reuters TV/Picture Media).

and affective (see Image 8.5). The use of violent symbolism took a new and terrifying turn when insurgents began to take foreign workers hostage, forcing them to plead for their lives before beheading many of them in cold blood all in front of the camera, then posting their productions on the Internet for all the world to see, download, rebroadcast and republish (see Image 8.5).

These local productions were staged and choreographed to undermine US claims to victory, embolden opposition groups and sap the morale for continuing coalition occupation in Iraq. The fact that the staged violence was real, doubled up on the capacity of film and photography to record and witness events as well as communicate symbolically. In these crude DIY productions, the iconic and symbolic merged in a terrifying spectacle which could only augment their chilling effects. They shocked and

4 Insight

THE AGE • SATURDAY, SEPTEMBER 25, 2004

TERROR AND SECURITY

Savagery hits home in a divided nation

The beheadings of US hostages have horrified their countrymen – and galvanised them, too. **Caroline Overington** reports.

Life on the Upper West Side of Manhattan is the antithesis of life in Baghdad. The neighbourhood is leafy and calm. Its citizens are mostly Christian, white and liberal. They voted five-to-one against President George Bush in 2000.

In the run-up to this year's election, many New Yorkers in this neighbourhood are wearing "Beat Bush" badges. They consider themselves educated people, conscious of events in the wider world.

In recent days, they have recoiled in horror at the barbaric images of sobbing US hostages being beheaded in Baghdad. Like many Americans, they opposed the war in Iraq from the outset. But if the terrorists committed these acts in an effort to shift US opinion on the war, it may have had the opposite effect.

Just hours before a second US hostage was murdered this week, Bush told journalists in New York that he would not let "these thugs" control Iraq's future. On the streets, there is support for …

… this has happened, we should evaluate our policy. I'm not even sure that is what the terrorists are trying to achieve. For them, it's about power. It's about killing Americans."

If the US were to withdraw, Schertz felt sure that "terrorists would use that as propaganda and the situation would worsen".

Anne Schiltz, 35, a working mother, was sitting in the park with her young son. She says she was initially "conflicted" over whether the US should invade Iraq. "I'm not a Bush supporter," she says. "I think Kerry has explained very clearly that he would make a huge effort to get international support, maybe get the UN involved. But that still means the US will be staying. I think only the most radicalised Left thinks we can just pack up our bags and leave. We have a responsibility now."

In the state of Georgia, where one of the murdered hostages, Jack Hensley, used to live, there was outrage on the streets, according to local newspapers. The Reverend Randy Mickler, a pastor at the 8000-member …

The terrorists wanted to kill my brother to hurt my family.

TY HENSLEY, brother of murdered hostage Jack Hensley

IRAQ: How do we end the nightmare?

What is the way ahead for Iraq? **Larry Schwartz** this week spoke to eight experts for their insights on the future of the troubled country.

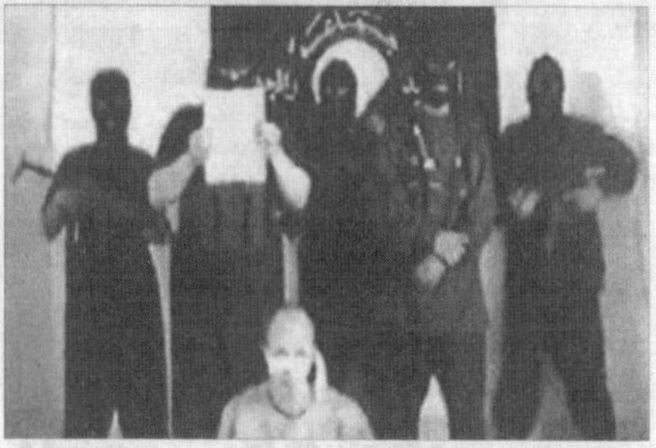

CHRIS REUS-SMIT

ALLAN BEHM

HUGH WHITE

WAYNE COLES-JANESS

AHMAD SHBOUL

AMIN SAIKAL

SUSAN WINDYBANK

DAVID WRIGHT-NEVILLE

Image 8.5 *The Age*, 25 September 2004
(© The Age 2004/Caroline Overington/Larry Schwartz. Photo: AP/AAP).

assaulted moral sensibilities and communicated a dreadful message to all international workers and their countries of origin to leave Iraq or risk fearsome reprisals. Calculated violent symbolism was at the heart of this latest tactic in image politics and asymmetric warfare:

> Terrorists have been quick to understand that the camera has the power to frame a single atrocity and turn it into an image that sends shivers down the spine of an entire planet. This gives them a vital new weapon.
>
> (Ignatieff 2004: 2)

Scenes of death, human destruction and dying, already discussed in Chapter 5 are conventionally shown sparingly, if at all, within 'disembodied' media wars. But the fast-changing ecology of international communications as well as the development of video and digital cameras along with increased ease of access to communication systems via the Internet have all rendered efforts to contain and control the circulation of images across time and space that much more difficult (see Figure 3.2 on p. 51). Political flak inevitably followed the televised scenes of captured US troops, clearly vulnerable and fearful for their lives, as well as shots of dead comrades, taken from Iraqi television and replayed by Al-Jazeera in March 2003 (see Image 8.6).

The US Secretary of Defense, Donald Rumsfeld, publicly pronounced that the Geneva Convention makes it illegal for prisoners of war to be 'shown and pictured and humiliated' and put pressure on the US media to suppress the video. No such pressure or arguments had been voiced previously, however, when the networks ran pictures of dead, surrendering and captured Iraqi soldiers which had often been accompanied by US statements that many Iraqi troops were unwilling to fight for Saddam Hussein.

It is important to note in this context that scenes of dead, dying and decomposing bodies are not always excluded from our television screens, notwithstanding producers' guidelines and professional codes of practices concerning taste and decency (see

Image 8.6 *The Age*, 25 March 2003
(© The Age/The Washington Post 2003. Photo: AFP/AAP/Al-Jazeera).

Chapter 5). At the time of writing (April 2005), an image of a dead body takes pride of place on many newspaper front pages and is no less inconspicuous on mainstream and primetime television screens around the world. The dead body of Pope John Paul II, evidently, is regarded neither by media or governments as in anyway contravening the policies and sensibilities of taste and decency. The media coverage of the devastating Tsunami that brought death and destruction to so many coastline communities in South and South East Asia at the outset of 2005 also did not hold back in showing scenes of mangled bodies and the mass dead. Much, clearly, depends on political context as well as the prevalent belief by governments and military in the 'Vietnam syndrome' (see Chapter 5). The latter continues to cast a heavy censoring shadow over the decimated and terrorized bodies of war.

Even so, powerful media images increasingly leak out into the mainstream media, often by haphazard means. When they do, images that were often recorded for 'private' or 'home' purposes can wreak havoc on the best laid public relations plans and the battle for hearts and minds. The release to the media of graphic video and photographic images recording US military personnel torturing, terrorizing and degrading Iraqi prisoners at Abu Ghraib prison seriously called into question the US administration's stated war aims and its proclaimed codes of conduct (see Images 8.6 and 8.7).

The US had claimed to be fighting a war in part to depose a regime that routinely resorted to torture in prisons such as Abu Ghraib. Here, caught on camera for all the world, including Iraq, to see were scenes of US torture and degrading behaviour. Michael Ignatieff reflects on the role of new digital technologies in the practices of torture:

> Besides the terrorist as impresario, let us remember that we also have the torturer as video artist. The Abu Ghraib pictures were never just for private use. Some were meant as a spur to other torturers. And some were supposed to be shown to other prisoners to warn them what awaited if they did not cooperate. The digital image, moving or still, has become an instrument of coercive interrogation.
>
> (2004: 2)

A historical line can in fact be traced back to earlier photographs of US racist lynching where perpetrators were similarly photographed grinning and smiling, without shame, beneath the strung up and burnt bodies of their victims. In her essay 'Regarding the Torture of Others', widely disseminated in mainstream newspapers and available worldwide on the Internet, Susan Sontag also points to the historically unprecedented nature of these latest circulated images:

> The lynching pictures were in the nature of photographs as trophies – taken by the photographer in order to be collected, stored in albums, displayed. The pictures taken by American soldiers in Abu Ghraib, however, reflect a shift in the use made of pictures – less objects to be saved than messages to be disseminated, circulated. A digital camera is a common possession among soldiers. Where once

Image 8.7 The *Guardian*, 30 April 2004
(© Guardian Newspapers Limited 2004/Julian Borger. Photo: Courtesy of Splash News).

photographing war was the province of photojournalists, now the soldiers themselves are all photographers – recording their war, their fun, their observations
of what they find picturesque, their atrocities – and swapping images among
themselves and e-mailing them around the globe.

(2004: 3)

Following the release and circulation of the Abu Ghraib pictures around the world, the
US government went into damage control, seeking to cauterize the opening wound that
threatened to contaminate the country's stated war aims and its claims to legitimacy.

Though clearly constituting 'torture' under the Geneva Conventions (Sontag 2004), the actions of the soldiers were referred to only as 'abuse', and low-level military personnel were court-martialled. But the symbolic damage had been done and the images have continued to prompt deeper questions about the systemic nature of the military's treatment of prisoners not only at Abu Ghraib but other US-controlled prisons in Iraq, Afghanistan, and at Guantanamo Bay in Cuba, and from how high up in the military chain of command these practices had been authorized.

The increasingly porous way in which damaging images can leak into the public sphere has been theorized by John Thompson (1995) as the historical 'transformation of visibility'. Elite institutions and the powerful have increasingly become exposed to public scrutiny and criticism via today's media and its unrivalled capacity for elite surveillance. Unlike in medieval times where the powerful few simply represented, that is displayed and paraded, their power before the many (Habermas), or more modern times where the powerful could regulate, administer and survey the many through new disciplinary regimes and systems of monitoring and control (Foucault), today's media enact a new visibility where the powerful become subject to the critical gaze of the many and are thereby rendered publicly vulnerable to scrutiny, criticism and disapproval. Media gaffs, embarrassing revelations and damaging exposés, including the disclosure of damaging information and images, are all perpetual risks confronted by the powerful who increasingly find themselves 'caught on' or 'caught out' by cameras. In such mediatized times it is perhaps not surprising that political and other forms of scandal are on the increase (Thompson 2000; see also Chapter 4). The communications ecology of contemporary media is both globalizing and reconfiguring the social relations between the powerful and the powerless (see Figure 3.2 on p. 51). The production and circulation of symbolic, often damaging, images has become an integral part of these developments.

Contra-flows and cross-over genres

The US media benefited from Al-Jazeera's unique capacity to report from inside Afghanistan, Iraq and other countries inhospitable to, or untrusting of, western media and broadcast these materials to a wider western audience; and they were also keen to rebroadcast video releases delivered to Al-Jazeera from Osama bin Laden given the huge public interest in these. Content-sharing deals with Al-Jazeera and other non-western networks, therefore, increasingly complexify the tendency to characterize the media in bipolar terms of 'mainstream' and 'alternative' (see Figure 3.2 and Chapter 6). So called 'contra-flows', or 'reverse flows' of media products from disadvantaged and former colonized countries to diasporic and mainstream audiences in former colonizer countries have long been observed in entertainment media – soaps, pop music, cinema – but these emergent flows have yet to be fully explored in respect of contemporary developments in news media and other forms of factual television (Boyd-Barrett and

Rantanen 1998; Volkmer 2002). Al-Jazeera as well as other 24/7 global news networks such as CNNI broadcast content originating from outside western countries and cultures, and thereby expand, or at least inflect, to some appreciable degree the range and breadth of views on world events. To what extent this truly constitutes a 'global public sphere' (Volkmer 1999, 2002), however, remains more debatable.

Much depends on how or in what ways content originating elsewhere becomes replayed, reappropriated and repositioned by the receiving medium and this demands careful empirical analysis (Azran 2004). Nonetheless, the broadcasting media environment today is reconfiguring and the Internet with its profusion of different journalism sites and so called 'blogospheres' renders the control and containment of ideas and images increasingly difficult (see Figure 3.2 and Chapter 6). And here, as we have already heard, Al-Jazeera as well as other emergent regional and global networks are beginning to make themselves felt in the new media environment and have disseminated images and ideas that western governments and interests may prefer to see controlled and censored (see Chapter 5).

Adel Iskander and Mohammed El-Nawawy argue in their study of Al-Jazeera that this Arab-based network has been no less than a 'hurricane in the media landscape' and they coin the phrase 'contextual objectivity' to make sense of its particular journalistic stance and presentation. The latter, they suggest, seeks to provide 'objective' news reports, dissociated from obvious partisanship and political interests, while nonetheless recognizing and responding to its target Arab audience and its cultural expectations. This dualism of journalistic identity, summed up in the authors' use of the image of the Minotaur, half beast, half human, is not peculiar, they argue, to Al-Jazeera – it has just become more visible when viewed from the taken-for-granted standpoints of the West:

> Contextual objectivity, the perpetual tension between the decontextualized message of the news deliverer and the nuanced and coloured perceptions of the receiver of news messages, can be witnessed on virtually every news bulletin of war on every media outlet in the world today, not the least CNN and Al-Jazeera. It permeates every story, and has become increasingly emblematic of the struggles for the construction of mediated messages.
>
> (Iskander and El-Nawawy 2004: 321)

In a context in which Arab views and evaluations predominate and where scenes of bloodshed and oppression have long emanated from occupied Palestine, it is not surprising that gruesome images from the invasion of Iraq would figure prominently in both Al-Jazeera's presentation as well as their audience's evaluations. Al-Jazeera undoubtedly represents a significant development, both regionally and internationally, in terms of global and diasporic news flows and contra-flows and implicitly, sometimes explicitly, challenges western news claims to 'objectivity'.

A further development also underlines the increasingly porous nature of today's media ecology where government attempts at propagandistic control and containment of controversial war images have not gone unchallenged. A spate of critical and oppositional TV documentaries and independent films has made it into the mainstream media and distribution outlets. Most notably perhaps are the television programmes, books, films, videos, DVDs and website of the US director/producer Michael Moore.

Delivered in the guise of satire, polemical critique and popular entertainment, Moore's productions have proved to be extraordinarily successful in reaching mainstream audiences. Films like *Bowling for Columbine* (2002) and *Fahrenheit 9/11* (2004) have delivered caustic critiques of US culture, politics and economic power and become box-office successes before moving on to generate significant video and DVD sales and replays on major TV networks in different countries. Moore's inimitable style blending genres of journalism and entertainment, evident in *Fahrenheit 9/11*, also contributes to today's 'transformation of visibility' and poses a challenge to the 'symbolic violence', the silences and annihilations, distortions and deceits, encoded within mainstream representations following the events of 9/11 and continuing with the US War on Terror. As the back cover of Moore's *Fahrenheit 9/11* DVD describes:

> Moore uses his characteristically deft humour and uniquely persistent style to launch an unflinching inquiry into the Bush government's foreign policy. Combining rare footage, expert testimony and his one-of-a-kind dogged hunt for answers to tough questions, Moore takes on the burning issues facing America today. His camera turns a skeptical lens on President George W. Bush and his inner circle that ignored the Saudi connection to 9/11 and instead rushed headlong toward war on Iraq.

Cross-over films such as *Control Room* (Director/producer Jehane Noujaim, 2004) have also proved extremely successful in terms of audience reach and in this case provide an inside view of Al-Jazeera's difficult, occasionally dangerous, struggles to broadcast their distinctive news. Popular documentaries such as *Out Foxed* (Director/producer Robert Greenwald, 2004) have also exposed and criticized Rupert Murdoch's US Fox News channel for its overt political agenda setting, shoddy journalistic practices and partisan support for the Bush administration and its global War on Terror. And a number of other hard-hitting documentaries produced in different countries but broadcast internationally and thereby maximizing audiences, have also exposed and criticized the propaganda strategies of the coalition in the lead-up, conduct and post-invasion stages of the Iraq war. Together they point to the existence of meaningful media spaces that can still be found and won within today's increasingly commercialized media sphere.

Current affairs and documentary TV, though under considerable pressures – commercial, political and cultural – arguably remain democratizing assets in the broadcasting repertoire of communicative forms as we have already heard, and emergent contra-flows and commercially successful cross-over films can also occasionally buck dominant marketplace trends (Thussu 2000; McChesney 2003). The struggles over images and ideas conducted in the media today take place in an increasingly complex global media ecology (see Figure 3.2 on p. 51).

Chapter summary

This chapter has reviewed some of the principal research findings and arguments concerning questions of media and terrorism. We have seen how research generally does not support simplistic arguments that propose a strong causality between media and terrorism, which is not to suggest that the media are not a powerful and perhaps indispensable conduit for communicating terror in the modern era. However, conceived politically and as a tactic, 'terrorism' has to be understood contextually and labels such as 'terrorist' invariably obfuscate the reasons and motivations of those involved. The word 'terrorist' generally functions to depoliticize and delegitimize insurgents and deliberately positions them outside the sphere of political discourse, rational explanation and non-violent engagement. In the short term this may prove expedient in the state's efforts to combat terror through military force but is unlikely to prove successful in the longer term given the exacerbation of violence and accumulated grievances that such a strategy inevitably generates. Here the media may be able to perform a more productive role in the social pacification of violence by giving vent to felt grievances and publicly examining the arguments and opposing interests and identities involved. While it would be naïve to presume that media-enacted public speech and deliberation can necessarily produce reason, consensus and negotiation between deep-seated enmities and opposing interests, especially when 'fundamentalist' beliefs remain impervious to the point of view of Others, the media's possible role in the 'democratization of violence' should not be discounted. Acts of terror represent a frontal assault on democratic states and civil societies and demand careful and considered responses if democratic rights and freedoms are not to become sacrificed in knee-jerk reactions propelled, or legitimated, by a surrounding culture of fear. Here the communicative forms of the media can play an important part in the public elaboration of the contexts, causes and consequences of acts of terror, from wherever they emanate, as well as the actions and reactions that may follow.

The US global War on Terror and the rise of transnational terrorism as a new form of asymmetric warfare has pitched the world into precarious and dangerous times, and the media once again are positioned centre stage as mouthpieces or screens for propaganda war. Image war has become a salient feature of this new turn in world history, especially the global circulation of spectacular, staged and symbolic images. The War on Terror, as we have seen, has produced a succession of memorable, mediatized images that variously enact symbolic violence and/or deploy violent symbolism; both frequently based on deliberately staged, choreographed and circulated images designed to capture news interest and mobilize audience sentiments and feelings. The War on Terror has become in large measure a war of media images, from the aestheticized spectacle of the 'shock and awe' bombing of Baghdad to the chilling DIY 'shock and awe' of videotaped beheadings circulated by insurgents on the Internet; from the US administration's no expense-spared staged announcements of 'victory' to the deliberate DIY filming of 'violent symbolism' produced by low-grade US military personnel at

Abu Ghraib. These and many other images collectively point to the prominent role of images and symbols in today's global media ecology where insurgents and soldiers as well as states and military machines have access to media technology and the media sphere. It is in this mediatized space and without shame that staged images characterized by symbolic violence and violent symbolism are produced, circulated and harnessed to strategic war aims.

In a world of globally communicating images, the costs of not winning the image war can be high and the efforts at control are not always successful. The historical transformation of visibility has recently taken a new turn, at once both democratizing and tyrannical. Democratizing in so far as the availability of new digital technologies, ease of visual recording and access to communication systems now enfranchises everyone from foot soldiers to torturers who potentially bear witness to acts of inhumanity (including their own) anywhere in the world; and tyrannical in so far as these same means and developments have produced a new 'amoral economy' where the production and circulation of symbolic violence and violent symbolism increasingly becomes staged in the battle for symbolic ascendancy and political impact. On the basis of these recent developments, the historical transformation of visibility facilitated in part by new communication technologies may be thought to be less than an unmitigated democratic advance.

Finally, we have also heard how the changing global ecology of broadcasting including the 'contra-flows' of new networks, the most celebrated of which is Al-Jazeera, have unsettled western news orthodoxies and, occasionally, informed western news agendas. The commercial successes of independent 'cross-over' films and documentaries produced in one country but increasingly broadcast by major networks across many, have also managed to secure an important foothold in the media sphere and occasionally disseminate oppositional ideas and images that challenge dominant state and corporate interests. Alongside existing programme forms and formats these developments are also very much part of the continuing historical transformation of visibility in today's globalizing media sphere, though for the time being these may often prove of more symbolic, than statistical, significance and cannot be taken to constitute a sea change.

Recommended reading

Cottle, S. (2005b) 'Mediatizing the Global War on Terror: Television's Public Eye', in A. P. Kavoori and T. Fraley (eds) *Media, Terrorism, Theory: A Reader*. Oxford: Rowman and Littlefield.
Silberstein, S. (2002) *War of Words: Language, Politics, and 9/11*. New York: Routledge.
Tuman, J. (2003) *Communicating Terror*. London: Sage.
Zelizer, B. and Allan, S. (eds) (2002) *Journalism After September 11*. London: Routledge.

IDENTITY POLITICS AND CULTURAL DIFFERENCE: ON MEDIATIZED RECOGNITION

The rise of identity politics, new social movements and single-issue campaigns in western countries over recent decades was noted at the outset of this book as one of the defining features of late modern societies – a feature that also positions the media centre stage in the cultural politics of civil societies. Whether it concerns ethnic, racialized and indigenous minorities; varieties of feminisms and struggles centred on gender, gay politics and sexualities; new religions and resurgent nationalisms or countless other identity-based campaigns this new politics of difference invariably seeks access to the media stage. It is here that wider recognition is sought and claims and aims are advanced. Social theorists explain this new politics of difference in relation to underlying processes of sociohistorical transformation, including economic restructuring, globalization, detraditionalization, individualization and increased social reflexivity (Hall and Jacques 1989; Giddens 1990, 1994; Beck et al. 1994; Castells 1996; Beck 1997; Urry 2003; see also Chapter 1).

This cacophony of views and voices has also been conceived more philosophically, and politically, as an emergent 'politics of recognition' in contrast to the established 'politics of redistribution' (Taylor 1994; Benhabib 2002; Frazer and Honneth 2003). Historically struggles aimed at equality and redistributive justice have been mounted on the basis of class struggle and focused on economic inequalities, state politics and welfare systems. Today a new politics of recognition, it is said, is principally conducted on the cultural terrain of civil society and centres on the symbolic realm of public representations, communication and interpretations. In today's mediatized societies it is probably inevitable that the media will be seen as a key, possibly principal, means by which cultural differences and agendas can be publicly recognized and acknowledged. Minorities and marginalized groups can variously become publicly recognized and valorized in the media or, as is often the case, misrecognized and devalued – or worse. This last substantive chapter sets out to explore important theoretical arguments about the politics of recognition and its enactment in and by today's media before examining how the media can contribute to the public representation of marginalized and vulnerable cultural groups – groups too often represented elsewhere as social outsiders, cultural strangers, as 'Others'.

To date numerous studies have documented how journalism marginalizes, denigrates and even demonizes certain social groups, positioning them as social pariahs or stigmatized outcasts and depositing them into dustbin categories labelled 'social problems', 'unworthy', 'despicable' or 'dangerous'. This story has been told many times before under the overarching concerns of media and deviance (Cohen and Young 1981; Ericson et al. 1991). Findings here are well known and documented, whether in respect of early news studies of protest and demonstration (Chapter 3), labelling and moral panic theory (Chapter 4), war journalism (Chapter 5) or mediatized 'terrorism' (Chapter 8). A voluminous literature also documents similar findings in respect of the media's representations of 'race', racism and ethnicity (e.g. van Dijk 1991; Cottle 2000a; Downing and Husband 2005), gay and queer politics (e.g. Watney 1987; Gauntlett 2002), gender and feminism (e.g. Tuchman 1978; van Zoonen 1994; Carter et al. 1998; Myers 1999; Dines and Humez 2002), as well as countless other marginalized groups and alternative projects. Such studies remind us of the need for continuing ethical vigilance and media scrutiny. This is because when media representations enter into fields of conflict structured by deep-seated inequalities and entrenched identities, they can become inextricably fused within them, exacerbating intensities and contributing to destructive impacts. These media depictions do not, however, exhaust the nature of today's media's representations.

Though today's media are positioned in fields structured by dominance, they are neither institutionally monolithic nor ideologically closed. Journalism, as discussed across preceding chapters, is far from historically static and it is certainly not hermetically sealed from the wider power plays, struggles and contentions in society. Indeed, it is these contentions and conflicts that provide journalism with much of its *raison d'être* as well as the raw materials for public elaboration and circulation. Different conflicts and contentions, as we have also heard, can create 'openings' as well as 'closures' and, evidently, some media forms and journalism representations are capable of breaking the mould. They sometimes do so by 'fleshing out', that is, embodying and humanizing the status of former Others, repositioning them inside the imagined social universe of collective care and politics and acknowledging their denied humanity. In such ways, former Others can be symbolically rehabilitated, past stereotypes can be fractured and identities begin to be fleshed out and repositioned as active subjects.

While not denying the inadequacies and distortions of much of the media's output, nor the damaging consequences of these representations for different cultural identities, this last discussion deliberately focuses on how some media forms can perform a more progressive role in the public recognition of marginalized cultural groups. Here the media provide important resources for the recognition of differences and in so doing can contribute to the democratization of civil societies. Too often these 'exceptional' media forms are ignored or overlooked by media academics whose critical sites are focused elsewhere. They now need to be acknowledged, better understood and defended against the erosions and incursions of contemporary media and market logics and, where possible, deepened and extended in the future. When deployed in the public representation of asylum seekers, refugees and indigenous minorities, terrorism suspects, victims of war and famine, for example, journalism's communicative modes of *deliberation* and *display* can prove to be important allies in processes of cultural recognition and political change. But first, a few more words on the theorization of the politics of recognition.

Theorizing the politics of recognition

> The struggle for recognition finds new purchase as a rapidly globalizing capitalism, accelerates transcultural contacts, fracturing interpretative schemata, pluralizing value horizons, and politicizing identities and differences.
>
> (Frazer and Honneth 2003: 1)

The concept of 'recognition' in its current usage harks back to Hegel's phenomenology of consciousness and the ideal reciprocal relationship in which each is interdependent on the other, yet both are separate. It is in and through intersubjective communication and the recognition of the other that the subject becomes validated and known, both to himself/herself as well as to others. This conceptualization informed Charles Taylor's influential essay, 'The Politics of Recognition', which articulated what was thought to be at stake. He argued:

> A number of strands in contemporary politics turn on the need, sometimes the demand, for *recognition*. The need, it can be argued, is one of the driving forces behind nationalist movements in politics. And the demand comes to the fore in a number of ways in today's politics, on behalf of minority or 'subaltern' groups, in some forms of feminism and in what is called the politics of 'multiculturalism'.
>
> The demand for recognition in these latter cases is given urgency by the supposed links between recognition and identity, where this latter term designates something like a person's understanding of who they are, of their fundamental defining characteristics as a human being. The thesis is that our identity is partly shaped by recognition or its absence, often by the *mis*recognition of others, and so a person or group of people can suffer real damage, real distortion, if the people or society around them mirror back to them a confining or demeaning or contemptible picture of themselves. Nonrecognition or misrecognition can inflict harm, can be a form of oppression, imprisoning someone in a false, distorted, and reduced mode of being.
>
> (1994: 25)

Taylor's essay productively brings to the fore the importance of 'recognition' in social relations and how this is thought to have evolved historically from a medieval system of *honour* premised on status hierarchy to modern notions of *dignity* based on equal human rights and equal recognition; the only basis, he says, for democracy. Questions of recognition, in other words, are not trivial matters; they are simultaneously onto-logical and political and go to the core of social being and claims to democracy. Ideas of 'recognition' have long informed major philosophical treatise and theoretical out-looks, whether Jean Paul Sartre's existential ruminations on 'The Look' in *Being and Nothingness* and Simone De Beauvoir's feminist views on the objectification of the male as a positive norm positioning the female as Other in the *Second Sex*; Frantz Fanon's disquisition on 'The Fact of Blackness' in *Black Skin, White Masks* and Edward Said's excoriating critique of the Occident's constructions of 'the Orient' and Islam in *Orientalism* and *Covering Islam*; Ervin Goffman's interactionist sociology elaborated in *The Presentation of Self* and *Stigma* or, more recently, Judith Butler's ideas on the performative nature of gender and identity developed in *Gender Trouble*. In these, and other, major works ideas of 'recognition' – and *mis*recognition – are posited and theorized as inextricably bound up with ideas of self and relations of dominance and oppression. Clearly, when aligned to the new politics of difference, the concept also resonates with the importance of public recognition in the struggles of diverse cultural minorities and lends weight to the ideas and practices of 'multiculturalism' – conceived in the broadest and most encompassing of ways. Ideas of recognition, then, lend considerable support to minorities and others seeking to enhance their representation within the media – whether in terms of improved media access and portrayal (Hall 1988; West 1999), or through increased media control and employment opportunities (Cottle 1997, 2000a). Here, representationally, things become a little more complicated.

Despite the seeming synergy between philosophically informed ideas of 'recognition' and the new politics of difference, the fit may be less snug than at first presumed. A number of problems can be briefly noted, each of which goes to the heart of the politics of recognition and what can be expected or advocated in the context of media practices and performance. Critical benchmarks inevitably shift depending on how we con-ceptualize and theorize ideas of mediatized recognition and the politics of difference. Each of the problems intimated below points to the necessity for a more politically differentiated, sociologically grounded and culturally nuanced understanding of pro-cesses of public 'recognition', as well as the need for a clearer sense of how exactly the politics of recognition becomes *mediatized* in and through established media forms.

First, the evident heterogeneity of identities all presumed to be demanding 'recogni-tion' is collapsed under the catch-all categories of 'identity politics' and the 'new politics of difference'. This is troublesome because not all of these struggles and claims necessarily share the same concern with (much less ontologically based need for) 'rec-ognition'. The politics and strategies of minority advance vary enormously in and across, for example, different social movements, single-issue campaigns and ethnic or gender-based struggles. There is a sociological and political complexity buried, therefore, within the new 'politics of recognition' and this needs to be empirically recovered and better theorized in respect of the mediasphere (fortunately sociological studies produced under the 'media contest' paradigm, are beginning to provide just this level of detail and theorization – see Chapters 2 and 7).

Second, we can also question whether the 'politics of redistribution' and 'politics of recognition' really are so distinct in practice. Particular struggles seemingly centred on 'redistribution' in fact often involve claims for cultural recognition, and the pursuit of cultural recognition often produces rhetorical and performative claims which can only enhance the pursuit of collective goals and interests. Claims for distributive and representational justice, therefore, are often more interwoven than the overarching conceptualization of twin politics suggests. It follows that the tendency to succumb to either economic or cultural reductionisms in their respective theorizations is also unhelpful given the entwined material/economic and discursive/cultural dynamics involved (Frazer and Honneth 2003).

Third, there appears to be an unfortunate homology in Taylor's conception of 'recognition' that regards group demands and needs for 'recognition' in the same terms as individual needs for expression and respect (Benhabib 2002). But not all collective identities and projects depend on public recognition in the same way – some will have learned to resist, oppose and deflect hurtful images and even found solidarity in their opposition, while others may be deeply wounded and incapacitated by them. Cultural identities are also often less clearly defined, bounded and centred than arguments for cultural recognition may suggest. If individualist ideas of authentic self-expression are complicated by the different social positions inhabited and performed by individuals, when these ideas are extrapolated to the cultural and collective level they become even more insecure and problematic.

Fourth, moving away from essentialist ideas of individual and collective identity as relatively fixed and stable, renders notions of media 'recognition' and 'representation' far from straightforward. Once we go beyond essentialist categories and theorizing, which it seems we must when confronting the complexities, contingencies and flux of embattled and enclave cultures, so the new politics of difference fragments the possibility of a singular authentic 'representation'. Some time ago Stuart Hall (1988) articulated such ideas when addressing the demise of 'the essential black subject', the rise of 'new ethnicities' and the cultural politics of black representation in Britain. A common experience of marginalization and racism, he argued, had earlier led to the category of 'black' being deployed by black Britons as a category of resistance and hence the subordination of ethnic and cultural differences to this politics of opposition. This produced critiques of the 'unspoken and largely invisible "other" of predominantly white and aesthetic discourses' and was animated by the 'concern not simply with the absence or marginality of the black experience but with its simplification and stereotypical character' (1988: 27). Similarly in the US, Cornel West has argued that African Americans had earlier sought to 'contest the bombardment of negative, degrading stereotypes put forward by White supremacist ideologies' and had sought to 'highlight Black "positive" images over and against White supremacist stereotypes' (1999: 262–3).

Over time, however, this politics of representation has given way to a more complex aesthetic as well as a more discursively informed notion of representation, one in which categories of 'race' and ethnicity become the site of multiple, overlaid and often contending discourses and projects. With the demise of 'the essential black subject' as a stable or politically fixed ethnic identity, so the category of 'race' as well as unspoken codes of dominant White ethnicity can become exposed for what they are: racializing and ideological constructs (Hall 1988; Julian and Mercer 1988; Mercer 1994). The politics of recognition, in the context of new ethnicities (Hall 1988) and the new cultural politics of difference (West 1999), thereby moves beyond representational interventions designed to substitute positive images for negative stereotypes, and encourages the creative production of new cultural forms, new aesthetics of expression and pluralized representations that depict and deconstruct portrayals of difference – problematizing simple *reflectionist* ideas of representation.

Fifth, this attention to the emergent politics of representation in the media signals the need to move beyond the rationalist and deliberative emphases that often character-ize philosophical ruminations on the same (Benhabib 2002; Frazer and Honneth 2003). Exceptionally, Iris Young (1996) has sought to counter this rationalist bias within much contemporary theorizing with a call for increased sensitivity to the ways in which greetings, rhetoric and story telling, for example, can inform communication and the development of mutual recognition and understanding (Young 1996). Story telling, she argues, can serve mutual understanding by revealing, (a) particular experi-ences; (b) distinct values, culture and meanings; and (c) particularized views of the social totality including those on other social perspectives. This account usefully reminds us that mediatized recognition need not be understood in terms confined to rational, deliberative exchange. Communication is multidimensional and can assume many different forms. Reason and rhetoric, images and ideas, analysis and affect, narrative and story are *all* often infused in the processes and forms of mediatized recognition today.

So it is clear that we need to attend much more carefully to the processes and forms of mediatized 'recognition' than has so far generally been the case. Arguments developed by theorists of deliberative democracy undoubtedly help here, refining our sensitivity to the ways in which words and talk, claims and counterclaims publicly define and defend interests and projects for change and, indeed, in a democratic polity are obligated to do so with reference to ideas of the 'common good' (Benhabib 1996, 2002; Habermas 1996; Dryzek 2000; Gutmann and Thompson 2004). When identities and interests rub up against each other in the mediasphere and are communicatively obliged to elabor-ate, justify and defend their respective claims and aims, then we, the audience, find invaluable resources for deliberation and improved understanding of the differences in play. However, mediatized recognition cannot be confined to rationalist and/or parliamentarian presuppositions concerning the public elaborations of reason and debate and the formation of public opinions and consensus – indispensable as these may be. We also need to attend to the media's more expressive capacities; its aesthetic and emotional appeals and ritual forms of communication (see Chapters 4 and 7). Here visualized histories and *her-stories*, dramatized narratives, experiential accounts and emotive testimonies can also contribute to the cultural valorization of different ways of being and how different people make sense of themselves and others in the world (Smith 1979; Campbell 1987; Bird 1990; Corner 1995; Dahlgren 1995; Cottle and Rai 2006).

When enacted in the mediasphere the politics of recognition is variously performed in established communicative modes of *deliberation* and *display*. Whereas the former is based on the circulation of information, reasoned accounts, rational arguments, investigation, discussion and debate, the latter communicates by the presentation of image and visualization, narratives of self and collective discovery, stories of 'roots' and 'routes', and dramatized re-enactments as well as expressive and aesthetic appeals. Journalism, as we shall see, communicates by both these modes of 'deliberation' and 'display' and thereby can infuse the mediatized politics of recognition with claims and arguments as well as expressive and moral force. These communicative complexities, however, have yet to be properly acknowledged and researched. To help illustrate something of these complexities of *mediatization* and as a way of opening up to view the more progressive possibilities that inhere within some mainstream forms of journalism, the following demonstrates how television journalism has sometimes repositioned former Others – indigenous people, asylum seekers and refugees, terrorism suspects, victims of war and famine – as human subjects demanding wider recognition, respect and political response. For the purposes of this discussion we focus on the medium of television, though press journalism is also capable of performatively championing, as well as publicly denigrating, Others, whether incarcerated asylum seekers or impoverished and politically abused Aboriginal people (see Images 9.1 and 9.2).

Mediatized recognition, symbolic rehabilitation and the Other

Many governments across recent years have developed particularly harsh, some would say punitive, regimes designed to reverse the flows of migrants, refugees and asylum seekers who are looking for sanctuary and new opportunities for themselves and their families. Australia's record is particularly noteworthy given the extraordinary lengths to which the Liberal (conservative) government of John Howard has gone in incarcerating men, women and children in 'detention centres' in the Australian desert or remote islands before returning them, often after many years, to their countries of origin and charging them with the costs of their own incarceration. In its enthusiasm to detain and deport 'illegal immigrants' the Australian government has also wrongly incarcerated and deported mentally ill Australian citizens.

Image 9.1 *The Age*, 16 April 2005
(© The Age 2005/Michael Gordon. Photos: Michael Gordon/The Age Photo Sales).

There is little doubt that the Australian media, like many media in western countries, have tended to perform a less than independent and critical role in the mediatized politics surrounding refugees and asylum seekers or, to use the Australian government's preferred term, 'illegal immigrants'. There are strong grounds to suggest that John Howard's election victory of 2001 was snatched from defeat by playing the 'race card', specifically by media-circulated claims – that we now know to have been untrue – that 'boat people' had deliberately thrown their children overboard in order to be picked up by the Australian Navy to gain entry to Australia (Marr and Wilkinson 2004). Many Boat People had drowned in the perilous journey from South East Asia and elsewhere to Australia, and those that managed to make it to Australian waters became interred in detention centres deliberately cited in remote locations including the islands of Nauru off-shore (see Image 9.1).

Not all the Australian media, however, have reproduced the government's preferred symbolic representation of 'illegal immigrants' as a collective Other or endorsed their discursive reification as an undesirable and indivisible threat confronting Australian culture and way of life. Some television programmes sought to get behind government-led headlines and give image and even identity to the normally invisible Other of the news, visualizing their human plight and documenting the injustices that strict policies

Image 9.2 *The Sunday Age*, 15 May 2005
(© The Age 2005/Russell Skelton. Photo: John Donegan/The Age Photo Sales).

of incarceration and denial of legal process had produced (the following draws in parts on Cottle 2005c).

Image to the invisible, voice to the voiceless

Four Corners, a mainstream and popular current affairs series produced by Australia's main public service broadcaster, the ABC, managed to give human face and voice to some of the detainees normally rendered invisible by the government's refusal to allow them media access on spurious grounds of protecting their privacy!

Four Corners: About Woomera
Protestors on roof of building wave banner 'We refugees have request – from Australian people for help'.

Debbie Whitmont, Reporter: These pictures were filmed by guards at Woomera Detention Centre in February last year. They show scenes children, adults and staff witnessed, sometimes daily, in an Australian detention centre. For Woomera this isn't an unusual day. There are demonstrations in three of the compounds and, here, a 19-year-old Afghan man has climbed into the razor wire . . . Those who starved or harmed themselves in Woomera weren't a small minority. And, ultimately, most were found to be genuine refugees and given temporary visas . . . One man sees the camera as a chance to speak to people he's never met – ordinary Australians, outside Woomera. . . . He tries to explain that the detainees have nothing left to use but their bodies to plead their desperation.

Man: We are crying, we are screaming. And we are all, 'What to do?' We have nothing. This is what you want? This is Australia say to us? Please help us and listen as we are suffering inside. We don't want to make any rampage. We don't want any things to this (sobs). We all came from bad condition. We want help.

ABC, *Four Corners*, About Woomera, 19 May 2003

This programme about refugees and asylum seekers incarcerated in Australia's notorious detention centre, 'Woomera', in the South Australian desert, was a powerful indictment of the Australian government's anti-asylum seeker policy, and helped to place in the public domain images and voices that had not been aired previously. Clearly, the programme manages to get behind the news headlines about 'riots' in detention centres and begins to reveal something of the motivations and injustices animating these desperate attempts for public recognition and action.

Claims, reason and public argumentation

Some forms of television journalism act as a public interlocutor, demanding answers from policy makers and authorities. In so doing, they help to produce rhetoric and explanation that are essential for 'deliberative democracy' (Dryzek 2000; Benhabib 2002; Guttmann and Thompson 2004) and, as in this case, the politics of recognition also when the claims and aims of Others are being publicly contested. Ethnomethodologists and conversation analysts can provide refined tools for the analysis of mediated talk and interaction including the institutionalized parameters of television interviews and how these structures are reproduced and/or challenged through turn taking, agenda setting, agenda shifting, evasions and so on (Clayman and Heritage 2002). Here we can simply observe how a brief exchange between a news presenter and the Australian Minister for Immigration responsible for the Australian Government's detention centres elicits basic arguments and defensive propositions:

Lateline: child detainees

Tony Jones, reporter: Immigration Minister Philip Ruddock has defended the detention of children, saying there is no other realistic way of dealing with asylum seekers. Mr Ruddock claims the separation of children from their parents would cause more psychological harm than keeping them in detention.

Tony Jones: How are you going to rebuff this almost united body of medical opinion? Why are you right and all these doctors and psychiatrists are wrong?

Philip Ruddock: Well, I don't think I've ever asserted that, Tony. What I assert is that in detention of unauthorized arrivals as a matter of public policy there is no other realistic way to be able to deal with people who come, whether with families or otherwise, who come without any authority, than to properly detain them, process them, and have them available for removal if they have no lawful basis to be here. . . .

ABC Lateline, 19 March 2002

Here we see how the news presenter's questioning prompts the interviewee to produce reasons and rhetoric, claims and counter claims, as he tries to present a reasoned and reasonable defence to the criticism put to him. As this exchange unfolds, so we, the audience, are provided with resources – propositional, argumentative, rhetorical and performative – with which to recognize and evaluate both the issue in contention as well as the credibility of the interviewee.

Public performance and credibility

A live televised interview has an integral wholeness and dynamic that can generate tension and prompt verbal virtuosity as the protagonists engage each other, get to the heart of the issue and/or produce apparent evasions – again providing materials for more detailed forms of conversation analysis (Clayman and Heritage 2002). Here we observe how the same news interview above developed and thereby contributed further arguments and claims surrounding the asylum debate while also providing a 'display' of public performance that could enter into evaluations of the credibility of the government minister concerned as well as the government's political position:

Lateline: child detainees

Tony Jones, reporter: Can I come back to the question of their mental health, Minister, because that is the question that is at stake here. Can you name one?

Philip Ruddock: It is not the only question, Tony.

Tony Jones: It is the question we're discussing tonight.

Philip Ruddock: No, that's the question you want me to, no, Tony, that's the question you want me to deal with.

Tony Jones: With respect, Minister, that is the question we asked you to come on and deal with. Can you name one medical body that supports your argument that children and their families should remain in detention at risk to their psychological state.

Philip Ruddock: I haven't seen arguments from organizations that believe that it is preferable to have no effective control of our borders in order not to face some difficulties in the management of that process. I haven't seen that argument. That's not what they're arguing. What I am saying to professional bodies and others – if you are of the view that the risk to the child is so great that the child ought to be removed from that environment and be separated from their parents, and that it is in their best interests, I will take that advice, but that's not the advice I received.

Tony Jones: This is the advice we're getting from the people we're talking to. This is the advice the medical bodies, including all the medical committees, appear to be getting. Let me cite to you what we've just heard Dr Raman say, the senior paediatrician from Sydney's Western Area Health Services: 'Young babies are not developing properly, they're not talking, they're not engaging, there's a lack of curiosity'. Another paediatrician writes to the Royal College of Physicians that 'Children at Woomera are living in a chronically deprived environment that's affecting their psychological development'. Does that worry you?

Phillip Ruddock: Of course it worries me. It ought to worry their parents. It ought to worry people who bring children to Australia without lawful authority.

Tony Jones: Minister, they are here in Australia now and with respect, you are their guardian, their legal guardian. Those children . . .

Philip Ruddock: No Tony, I am only the guardian for those children who come unaccompanied. . . .

ABC *Lateline*, 19 March 2002

As even this short exchange reveals, there is an unpredictable quality and dramatic potential within live televised encounters; they contain risks as well as opportunities for the protagonists involved. Here the news interviewer doggedly pursues a line of questioning – an agenda – as the interviewee, equally determinedly, seeks to agenda-shift to safer, less politically damaging, ground. Throughout these verbal twists and turns the audience is positioned, perhaps compelled, to consider where the responsibility (or culpability) should be placed for the plight of children and their families locked up in detention centres – moral evaluations that become infused in the politics of recognition.

Personal accounts, experiential testimonies

When former Others are enabled to put their individual experiences into the public domain, telling their stories through personal accounts of pain, suffering and injustice, the collective Other and its reductionist stereotypes begin to fragment. Here a reporter helps to put a human face to 'terrorism suspects' who have been publicly silenced and literally 'disappeared' in America's global war on terror:

Panorama: inside Guantanamo

Vivian White reporter: The call to prayer at Guantanamo Bay. Over 600 men are being held here by the USA as part of its war against terror. We've been to investigate Guantanamo justice . . .

White: While Alif Khan was inside Guantanamo, branded as an Al-Qaeda suspect, his business rivals grabbed his assets, including these shops, from him. Since his release he's fought to get his property back . . .

Alif Khan: . . . I am not Taliban, not a terrorist, not Al-Qaeda. People handed me over because someone wanted to gain influence – dollars or because of a personal dispute.

White: But Alif Khan was transported from Afghanistan to Guantanamo. This is his testimony.

Khan: They put cuffs and tape on my hands, taped my eyes and taped my ears. They gagged me. They put chains on my legs and chains around my belly. They injected me. I was unconscious. I don't know how they transported me. When I arrived in Cuba and they took me off the plane they gave another injection and I came back to consciousness. I did not know how long I was flying for. It might have been one or two days. They put me onto a bed on wheels. I could sense what was going on. They tied me up. They took me off the plane into a vehicle. We go to a big prison and there were cages there. They built it like a zoo.

BBC1 Panorama: Inside Guantanamo, 5 October 2003

This BBC *Panorama* programme, broadcast in Australia as well as other countries, was the first serious attempt to give a human face and identity to the hitherto invisible 'terrorism suspects' secretly transported by the US military to Cuba and incarcerated without trial at Guantanamo Bay. The programme provided necessary insights into the suffering of countless 'suspects' caught up in the war on terror: by allowing their voices and testimonies to be heard, the programme arguably revealed something of their sense of injustice and denied humanity.

Reconciling the past, towards the present

Memories of past violence, trauma and injustice often inform the struggles and continuing injustices of the present, creating demands for wider recognition of both historical and ongoing pain. Symbolic meetings and events, when mediatized to wider audiences, can assist in public processes of acknowledging the deep trauma and hurt caused by past deeds and contribute to ongoing processes of reconciliation and cultural accommodation and adjustments. Although John Howard's Australian government has felt unable to say 'sorry' to the Aboriginal communities of Australia for white settler genocide and the stealing of land, television journalism has sought on occasion to play a more progressive part in the process of reconciliation, dramatizing past deeds and bearing witness to the pain and hurt felt by family members whose ancestors were victims and perpetrators of violence:

Australian Story: Bridge over Myall Creek
On 10 June 1838 a gang of stockmen led by a squatter rode into Myall Creek Station and brutally murdered about 28 unarmed women, children and old men.

Sue Blacklock: We haven't forgotten them, but we know that they are still here. They're still in our memories, they're in our hearts. They will always be remembered. And it's just a very emotional time for us. And we just want to remember them so they will be at peace.

Beulah: It's a very satisfying experience. We've committed ourselves to follow this right through and to remember our history – the history of the Aboriginals and our history, because it is our history as well. So it is very humbling and it's a privilege . . .

Rev. Brown: We had planned a beautiful memorial, and it remains a beautiful memorial. But to actually have descendants of those who carried out the murder and descendants of those who were killed come together in an act of personal reconciliation as part of the process of . . . of . . . dedicating this memorial was just marvellous. It was something we couldn't have planned, but it was a great gift to us. And a great gift, I think, to the people of Australia.

Des: I was there to say how sorry I was on behalf of all my family, and of all those who would wish me to say I was sorry, how sorry we were. When we said the words and said the prayers, the feeling I had was that I had done something in my life that was really meaningful to those people. The whole day was one where, you know, I really felt . . . it was probably the best thing I'd done. . . . There are still many people who don't want to know about it, but as this happens in various places around Australia I think it'll just expand from there.

ABC, *Australian Story*: 'Bridge over Myall Creek', 26 July 2001

This programme, as we can see, gives expression to the efforts of local communities to acknowledge past injustices by sharing family knowledge and collective memories of the murderous acts committed by white Australians against Aboriginal people. By representing these events in the public arena, the programme performatively extends their reach to wider Australia and contributes symbolically at least to processes of recognition and reconciliation.

Media reflexivity

Today's media occasionally monitor and comment on their own performance and practices. Sometimes this is institutionalized in programmes designed to do just this, such as *Media Watch* in Australia or *Right to Reply* in Britain, or sometimes it takes place in and through existing programmes. Given that today's politicians and other power brokers make extensive use of the media in their battle for hearts, minds and votes, such media reflexivity is vital for deconstructing 'spin' and understanding symbolic and rhetorical forms of power as well as for analysing the media's seeming complicity with powerful interests. Here a war photographer eloquently reflects on his own practice and, in so doing, articulates a compassionate plea for recognizing the Other and also the possible role of the media as a conduit for a more critically engaged public:

Christian Frei: War Photographer
Why photograph war? Is it possible to put an end to a form of human behaviour which has existed throughout history by means of photography? The proportions of that notion seem ridiculously out of balance. Yet that very idea has motivated me. For me the strength of photography lies in its ability to evoke a sense of humanity. If war is an attempt to negate humanity, then photography can be perceived as the opposite of war; and if it is used well it can be a powerful ingredient in the antidote to war. In a way, if an individual assumes the risk of placing himself (sic) in the middle of a war in order to communicate what is happening, he's trying to negotiate for peace. Perhaps that's why those who are in charge of perpetuating a war do not like to have photographers around. . . . But everyone can't be there; so that's why photographers go there. To create pictures powerful enough to overcome the deluding effects of the mass media and to shake them out of their indifference. To protest and by the strength of that protest to make others protest.

The worst thing as a photographer is the thought that I'm benefiting from someone else's tragedy. This idea haunts me; it is something I have to reckon with everyday because I know if I ever let personal ambition overtake genuine compassion then I will have sold my soul. The only way I can justify my role is to have respect for the other person's predicament. The extent to which I do that is the extent to which I become accepted by the Other. And to that extent I can accept myself.

ABC, *War Photographer: Christen Frei*, 15 February 2004

Reflexive programmes such as these, though relatively rare in television schedules, nonetheless encourage a more critical stance to the routine representations of media reporting and reveal something of the dilemmas and ethical difficulties behind the production of news, current affairs and documentary programmes. They can invite a more reflexive stance in relation to the programmes that fill our TV screens and the artifices that go into their production. Such deconstructions, then, are also part of the politics of mediatized recognition where claims and counter claims swirl and spin, distort and deceive, in the mediasphere, but where claims to truth and the integrity of the human subject can also – occasionally – be made.

Bearing witness in a globalizing world

Opening the theoretical discussion of the new politics of difference cited earlier, Nancy Frazer and Alex Honneth (2003) position the politics of recognition in relation to globalizing forces of cultural pluralization and change. They are right to do so. Our increasingly globalizing and interconnected, yet unequal, world impels us to recognize the human needs and plight of others. Bonds of commitment and solidarity are needed if we are to overcome ethnic, nationalist and other fragmenting forces and confront the moral challenges posed by global change. Television journalism, notwithstanding its capacity to trivialize and render into spectacle images of human suffering (Tester 1994, 2001), also has the potential to stir consciences and deepen public understanding of the dynamics of global poverty and social injustices. It can help dismantle historically anachronistic images of the Other (Ignatieff 1998). BBC reporter Michael Buerk, for example, returned to Ethiopia 20 years after helping to bring to public notice the devastating famine which had then galvanized public sympathies and charitable donations worldwide:

> *BBC Ethiopia: A Journey with Michael Buerk*
> Michael Buerk, reporter: This is a story of a forgotten people in a lost land. The story of how hundreds of thousands died of starvation on a planet choked with food. Of tyranny and neglect. Yet it's also a story of how 3 million Iron Age families were saved by the power of television, by our shame that made us feel their pain in a way that has never happened before and has never happened since. It's a story of betrayal . . .
> BBC2, *Ethiopia: A Journey with Michael Buerk*, 11 January 2004

The programme was broadcast in a number of different countries. It deployed the techniques of personalization and narratives of personal testimony – both Buerk's and former Others' – who recounted how their lives and experiences following the first televised famine had changed. The programme also made use of a follow-up discussion online. While the reporter's analysis of the continuing desperate situation in Ethiopia inevitably remains open to political criticism, the programme nonetheless sought to move beyond simplistic depictions of Third World as 'Other' and, through its humanizing rhetoric and narratives, provided scenes and stories that helped to visualize the continuing plight of many in Ethiopia. It is simply deficient and morally vacuous to assume that such programmes have no part to play in the changing consciousness and politics of understanding that condition our responses and ability to interact with today's globalizing world. The media's capacity to 'recognize', to 'bear witness', and communicate the conflicts and injustices perpetuated within a globalizing world has to be taken seriously and the communicative forms in which and through which this takes place need to be better understood. They are central to the mediatized politics of recognition.

Chapter summary

This chapter has considered contemporary arguments about the politics of recognition, pursuing these into the mediasphere. Notwithstanding continuing disagreements over the theoretical standing of the politics of recognition in contrast to the politics of redistribution, issues of identity and calls for cultural recognition have found increased salience in contemporary societies (and social theory). The media are positioned centre stage in the contentions of civil societies and have become a prised terrain from which to secure enhanced recognition and advance claims and aims. Countless studies of journalism have documented how mainstream news outlets delegate who is permitted to speak, what views are heard and how these are visualized and performed. It is certainly true that sections of the media frequently define and portray various groups and identities as 'deviant', 'outsiders' and 'Other', rendering them 'speechless' and stripping them of their identity and humanity in stereotypical or spectacular news visualizations.

However, the media are neither uniform nor static and television journalism's communicative modes of deliberation and display can sometimes flesh out former Others, embodying them as active subjects deserving of recognition and political response. Evidently there is a complexity, as well as political opportunity, embedded in the communicative forms and appeals of contemporary journalism. Our brief excursion into television journalism's forms and communicative modes has found more complexity than is often acknowledged or anticipated in overarching paradigms of mediatized conflicts (see Chapter 2). Arguably researchers should attend more carefully and empirically to these important *mediatizing* properties of communication in the future. This is not only because these features exist and therefore need to be better understood and examined but also because they are of obvious political importance and possible impact. The communicative forms of the media not only condition and constrain media representations, they can also enable and enact processes of deliberation, constitute the public display of differences and thereby even contribute to processes of 'democratic deepening' (Giddens 1994).

Mediatized recognition, as we have seen, assumes different forms and expressions in the contemporary media and is enacted through communicative modes of display and deliberation. It is by these communicative means that television journalism occasionally gives *'image to the invisible'* and *'voice to the voiceless'* and circulates different *'claims, reasons and arguments'* and generates *'public performances'* that invite deliberative and evaluative audience responses. It is by these same means that *'personal accounts and experiential testimonies'* can be publicly heard and heard in ways that personalize the human meaning of oppression and the disrupted biographies and stunted life chances that it causes. And so too can these powerful communicative forms also 'recognize' collective hurts and play a performative role in processes of *'reconciling the past'* as well as necessary processes of *'media reflexivity'* and *'bearing witness in a globalizing world'*. These brief observations and examples demand further exploration and more systematic analysis than is possible here (Cottle forthcoming), but they point nonetheless to something of the communicative forms and complexities involved in contemporary processes of mediatized recognition. Together they document how the Other can be symbolically rehabilitated and repositioned within the mediasphere, talking back and challenging those who would seek to deny them their humanity by locking them up – whether figuratively or literally – inside reified collective categories and/or remote, hidden places.

The study of mediatized recognition, then, demands that we attend to the complex forms and flows of contemporary media and explore further the possibilities of journalism's powerful communicative modes of deliberation and display. We must also, however, seek to reintegrate the study of these mediating forms and circulating representations into the wider struggles for media access, media control and media agendas (Cottle 1997, 2000a). Here the cultural politics of recognition becomes less a matter of abstract philosophical debate and more a practical concern and political intervention that is forced to steer a difficult path through the structures of media ownership and control, logics of media organizations and markets, strategic power of different media sources and surrounding cultural fields of contention – the more recognizable *terra firma*, perhaps, of the politics of redistribution.

Recommended reading

Benhabib, S. (2002) *The Claims of Culture*. Princeton, NJ: Princeton University Press.

Carey, P. (1998) *The Faber Book of Reportage*. London: Faber and Faber.

Clayman, S. and Heritage, J. (2002) *The News Interview*. Cambridge: Cambridge University Press.

Cottle, S. and Rai, M. (2006) 'Between Display and Deliberation: Analyzing TV News as Communicative Architecture', *Media, Culture and Society* 28(2) 163–89.

Frazer, N. and Honneth, A. (2003) *Redistribution or Recognition?* London: Verso.

Hall, S. (1997) 'The Spectacle of the "Other"', pp. 223–79 in S. Hall (ed.) *Representation: Cultural Representations and Signifying Practices*. London: Sage.

MEDIATIZED CONFLICT: CONCLUSIONS

Though conflicts for the most part originate in the social world beyond the media, it is through the different media of journalism and the circulation of news that many of them become publicly known and, often, pursued. It is here, as we have seen, that conflicts are variously defined, framed and visualized; elaborated, narrativized and evaluated; moralized, deliberated and contested; amplified and promoted or dampened and reconciled; conducted and symbolized; enacted and performed. In a word: mediatized. This concern with *media doing* has granted this book its centre of gravity as we have moved through selected case studies and different positions of theory to build a more multidimensional understanding of mediatized conflict. We have explored different complexities and contingencies, determinants and dynamics, mechanisms and meanings. As we have done so, we have also begun to glimpse how the media can variously open up, or close down, the public elaboration of conflicts and how these thereby contribute to, or curtail, processes of democratization.

In this context, current social theoretical concerns with the 'democratization of democracy' and 'democratic deepening' (Giddens 1994; Beck 1997; Castells 1997) demand that we pay closer attention to exactly how the media enact and discharge conflicts; how they give voice to, and visualize, contending interests and identities. Here traditional liberal democratic notions of 'representation' prove too thin and radical discursive (or postmodern) views of 'representation' are often too textually dependent (or free-floating) to map the complex articulations of economic, political, social and cultural power condensed in mediatized conflict. The individualist and rationalist presumptions as well as delimited field of the 'political' characterizing representative democratic theory fail to recognize, much less engage with, the complexities of communicative action and its multiple sites of elaboration and enactment, including the media. And ideas of media 'representation' approached through a lens of discursive democracy, where media representations seemingly register straightforwardly hierarchical formations of discourse, also fail to ground these in relation to the contexts of media production and how different media and forms of media elaboration impact their final public enactment. Some of these complexities have surfaced across preceding chapters.

How competing discourses are encoded by professional practices within competitive and institutionalized settings and in interaction with different media sources; how these become shaped and enacted in changing media ecologies, different media and established cultural forms; and how these register with socially differentiated and culturally embedded audiences (potential publics) over time, and with what possible consequences and impacts, are *all* integral elements for understanding mediatized conflict today. This complexity, then, demands a more encompassing, multidimensional and dynamic conceptualization than hitherto. Such an approach also needs to better understand the powered and performative nature of media involvement *within* conflicts while also resisting the temptation to succumb to a media-centric view that simplistically collapses either the mainsprings or trajectories of conflict into a self-referential world of media representation, discourse and intertextuality. Conflicts, it is argued here, are ontologically based in the social world while nonetheless maintaining that in *mediated societies* they are often known, represented and even discharged through the media. This is a delicate and sometimes difficult line to tread and too often theorists fall by the wayside: either into the traditional fields of political and social analysis where conflicts are rarely given their mediatized due or, alternatively, over the virtual (post-journalism) cliff of accelerating media signs and semiotic flux where conflicts seemingly only exist in their media representation and discourses. While it is absolutely essential to hold on to the ontological reality of conflicts rooted in the *terra firma* of the wider social world, in today's mediated societies we necessarily also have to attend to how, why and with what possible impacts they become played out in the media.

The media's performative representation and enactment of conflicts, as we have heard across earlier chapters, assume diverse expressions and different forms. They include, for example, the salience granted to certain news events and issues (and not others) as well as the lexical choices, syntactic structures and frames used to describe them. They become institutionalized in the media's reliance on authority sources and their 'definitions of the situation' as well as the range of voices and views finally accessed onto the media stage. They register in the professional deployment of journalism forms and formats and the live encounters and argumentative exchanges that these produce. They are visually encoded in the selections, cropping, editing and juxtaposition of images as well as the narrativization of news events as 'stories' and how these are crafted to resonate with cultural myths. They feature in how some groups are stereotyped and stigmatized, positioned as deviant or Other and how others are granted legitimacy, respect and publicly valorized. So too is media performativity found in the moral sentiments and cultural symbols professionally 'written into' news stories and the part that these play in summoning emotions, publics and collective projects for continuity or change. It also steers and orchestrates exceptional media phenomena – moral panics, conflicted media events, media scandals and mediatized public crises – and amplifies public anxieties, reveals deep social schisms and, potentially, unleashes transformative energies. So too is media performance instantiated in the partisan nature of the daily press (both broadsheets and tabloids), the 'middle-ground' dispositions of TV journalism and the radical challenges and critiques advanced by independent cross-over genres and international contra-flows as well as the identities conducted and sustained by the Internet. Sensationalized and exaggerated media representations stoke the fires of conflicts while others deliberately dampen down tensions and promote processes of peace and reconciliation. And media performance also features in the ways in which conflicts are portrayed to resonate with the private, everyday life worlds of ordinary people while others are clearly oriented in ways that rationalize and legitimize the public actions of the state – whether in times of peace or war. In all these, as well as countless other, ways the media are involved in the constitution and conduct of mediatized conflict; they are *doing something* over and above 'reporting' narrowly and naïvely conceived.

To understand mediatized conflict we also need to situate and theorize media and conflicts within wider contexts and trajectories of change and examine them in their complex multidimensionality. Here paradigms and positions of media theory, as we have seen, can help by providing guiding frames of reference, sensitizing concepts and focused research agendas. On the basis of the discussion and findings above how can we not, for example, acknowledge the general explanatory purchase of the manufacturing consent paradigm as well as our selected exemplar of the 'propaganda model' (Herman and Chomsky 1988) when considering the media's role in the lead-up to the invasion of Iraq in 2003, or indeed war reporting more generally? Not to recognize the blatant, often cynical, deployment of political power, military controls and media censorship in times of war as well as their evident synergy with the commercialized logics and cultural semiotics of an increasingly entertainment-led media is willfully myopic. Similarly, how could we not recognize the insights of the media culture paradigm and, say, the textual acuities of Kellner (1995, 2003) when he recovers the play of discourses as well as appeals to identity encoded within high-profile media events and media spectacles? And how could we also not admire the analytical insights of the media contest paradigm and Wolfsfeld's (1997, 2003) 'political contest model' when researching how different challenger groups can sometimes win some control of the communications environment and do so by deploying culturally resonant symbols that dent the organized public relations capabilities of authorities and dominant sources?

Paradigms and theoretical approaches need not always be seen as mutually exclusive even though we cannot simply collapse them into one another because of differing social ontologies, epistemologies, methodologies and political commitments (see Figure 2.1 on p. 30). We can acknowledge how each helps to sharpen sights on particular objects of enquiry and sometimes on different dimensions of the same object given their overlapping interests. And we can also acknowledge how paradigms and theories sometimes analytically engage with different *levels* of the same media phenomena whether, for example, economy/marketplace, culture/discourses or source-power/communicative strategy, and thereby can provide complementary insights. Clearly theoretical differences are important, productive even, and in the context of research and serious enquiry they will colour how we look and what we will see. But the very fact that depth findings are produced by researchers working within different paradigms should tell us that each has something to contribute and that no one paradigm or theoretical approach is likely to have a monopoly on insight and understanding.

Too often theoretical debate succumbs to sterile posturing rather than productive engagement where theorists can refine rather than simply rehearse extant positions of theory. Paradigms and theories are indispensable for research – they help us see and understand – but each has its blindspots and weaknesses too and positions of theory constantly need to be updated and, where possible, refined or replaced on the basis of research engagement. We can illustrate some of these concluding thoughts by reviewing the principal findings, both empirical and theoretical, which have emerged from the preceding discussions of mediatized conflict and underline how each builds on established paradigms as well as pointing to new research developments.

Principal findings, new developments

Classic studies of the news media's reporting of major demonstrations and protests (Chapter 3) lend considerable support to the manufacturing consent paradigm and its general expectation that (a) establishment views and voices define and frame such events in the media and (b) that they do so in ways supportive of the existing political order while often (c) denigrating or delegitimizing the claims and aims of demonstrators (Halloran et al. 1970; Gitlin 1980/2003; Murdock 1981). Explanations of the mechanisms at work for this ideological reproduction of consensus are grounded in the market imperatives of news organizations, professional journalist practices and dependency on powerful sources, the operation of news values and the event orientation of news. These empirical findings and theoretical explanations undoubtedly have continuing purchase on more recent mediatized demonstrations and protests.

Further complexities and contingencies, however, now need to be recognized and incorporated into our theorization of similar events today. Geopolitical interests and political alignments of different news organizations, for example, clearly inform how different demonstrations and protests are framed, defined and visualized in the media (Fang 1994). And the successful deployment of dramaturgy (McAdam 2000) and changing repertoires of protest (Scalmer 2002) also opens up to view a more politically contingent and contested state of affairs in the struggles between protestors and demonstrators, news organizations and wider cultural fields. Current debates centred on 'public spheres' or 'public screens' (Craig 2002; DeLuca and Peeples 2002) also productively figure in this research context, emphasizing not only the discursive complexities that contend within news representations of 'antiglobalization' protests but also the ways in which visuals, spectacle and immediacy may hold more radical charge than previously theorized – challenging once again the expectations of the manufacturing consent paradigm. The rise of the Internet as a medium and tool particularly well suited to contemporary global activists who are spatially dispersed, non-hierarchical, loosely politically affiliated and culturally diffuse also exceeds the theoretical parameters and expectations of the same paradigm and complicates the theorization of contemporary communication flows (Bennett 2003; see also Figure 3.2).

Classic moral panic theory (Chapter 4), in both its interactionist and neo-Marxist formulations (Cohen 1972; Hall et al. 1978), continues to speak to periodic, exceptional, mediatized phenomena and usefully directs researchers to consider important features of mediatized conflicts more generally. These include attending to their dynamics as they unfold through time and how interests and identities can become caught up in exaggerated fears, behavioural responses and institutional reactions, and the ways in which moral sentiments and affective appeals are often incorporated into media representations and how these are capable of summoning publics and policing boundaries of 'normalcy' and 'deviance'. Moral panic theory, however, does not exhaust the differentiated nature, forms and political impacts of exceptional mediatized phenomena, either empirically or theoretically. Studies of conflictual and consensual media events (Dayan and Katz 1992; Fiske 1994a; Hunt 1999), media scandals (Lull and Hinerman 1997; Thompson 2000) and mediatized public crises (Alexander and Jacobs 1998; Cottle 2004a) usefully draw on positions of theory based in both the 'media culture' and 'media contest' paradigms and deploy these to productively explore how some exceptional mediatized crises and their ritualized and spectacular forms give vent to deep-seated conflicts. These exceptional phenomena can sometimes open up to public view questions of injustice, inequality and identity and can even release transformative energies into processes of change – findings that have particular bearing, as we saw in the mediatized Stephen Lawrence crisis, in changing fields of 'race' and racism.

War journalism (Chapter 5), as we might expect, continues to provide considerable empirical support for the manufacturing consent paradigm whether inflected instrumentally in terms of elite and military controls imposed on the media (Knightley 2003), or enacted via the structural determinations of the marketplace and commercial imperatives (Herman and Chomsky 1988). However, even here, we discerned further levels of complexity including countervailing tendencies and contra-flows. Hallin's theoretical challenge to the 'Vietnam syndrome' and the 'oppositional media thesis', based on his detailed study of the Vietnam war and how growing US elite dissensus emboldened media reporting through time (Hallin 1986, 1994), provides support for a more politically contingent understanding of media–state interactions, as have later theoretical positions such as the 'indexing model' (Bennett 1990) and 'policy interaction model' (Robinson 2001). Sociological and anthropological studies of the phenomenology of war and professional mythology of war correspondents also take us deeper into the social construction of war and the inscription of professional identities within the cultural milieu of war correspondents (Morrison and Tumber 1988; Pedelty 1995).

24/7 real-time reporting, contra-flows and cross-over genres and the changing nature of globalized information war itself, also present new challenges in the mediatized battle for hearts and minds. Today these are prompting new efforts by states and military to control the media whether through 'embedding' or the Pentagon's production of Hollywood-type productions and video releases targeting the news media (Thussu and Freedman 2003; Allan and Zelizer 2004). Contention inevitably surrounds media wars, and the flows of images of body horror are only likely to increase this contestation in the future given the growing capabilities of DIY and global media (Figure 3.2). Audience research tells us however, that the likely impacts of images of body horror (Taylor 1998) cannot simply be read off the images themselves but need to be contextualized in relation to preceding audience outlooks and ideologies (Morrison 1992) as well as the depth and adequacy of earlier media coverage (Philo and Berry 2004).

Examining alternative journalisms – peace journalism, development journalism, public journalism and online journalism – has provided us with a different vista on mediatized conflict. Here we have considered how 'corrective' prescriptions based principally on normative critique stand up to scrutiny (Chapter 6). The advocates and outlooks of peace journalism (Galtung 1993) and development journalism (Aggarwala 1979) often concur with critical findings about the deficiencies and distortions of mainstream journalism including its dependency on dominant sources, operation of western news values and event orientation towards the violent, disruptive and negative. Normative critique alone, however, was found to be a poor basis from which to advocate, much less implement, change. Empirical research examining the media's actual performance and roles in peace processes (Spencer 2004; Wolfsfeld 2004) finds more complex dynamics at work. These variously facilitate and enhance, or sensationalize and undermine, peace negotiations at different stages and within different media environments.

Public journalism's advocacy of democratic forms of journalistic engagement (Rosen 1999), of journalism as 'public conversation' (Carey 1999), though in many ways laudable in its democratic ambitions, is also ultimately found wanting on the basis of its delimited, overly rationalist and complacent parliamentary understanding of democracy and democratic communications as well as its impoverished theorization of the impact of inegalitarian structures and fragmented nature of contemporary civil societies. On-line alternative journalisms, in contrast, are underpinned by the Internet's distinctive capacities as a medium (Deuze 2003) as well as its elective affinity with contemporary cultural formations that reposition 'the political' within civil societies and cultures. In these respects, alternative journalisms on-line appear to have the most chance of gaining ground within the current ecology of news journalism and influencing, or at least broadening, the parameters of what journalism can and should be.

Attending to normative critiques and corrective journalisms, then, helps to sharpen our theorization of democratization in and by the media and also helps to identify some of the considerable hurdles and difficulties that will be encountered along the way. Doing so also invites us to imagine different media futures and how exactly the media can or should enact processes and forms of democratization. This, in turn, begs a more elaborate engagement with political ideas and theoretical debates about the exact constitution, and nomenclature, of public sphere(s); of what forms these would/should take and how best they could be organized and sustained in practice (see Figure 2.1, p. 30 and Figure 3.2, p. 51). The ideas of corrective journalisms, then, are based more on normative critique and future imagining than developed positions of theory and supporting research and in these respects exceed established paradigmatic approaches while also failing to match their grounded analysis of the complexities involved.

Recent research into the communication of risk society (Beck 1992) and the environment brings to the fore further complexities and dynamics of mediatized conflict reporting (Chapter 7). Here we saw how social constructionist views on the rise and fall of social problems have attuned researchers to the discursive nature and competing frames characterizing media representations (Anderson 1997; Hansen 2000), and also how these can be theorized as the outcome of processes of agenda building pursued in different public arenas (Hilgartner and Bosk 1988). Media representations of risk and environment are here theorized in relation to fields of interaction, contest and struggle as well as in respect of their encoding within the textual and visual forms of the media. These findings invite us to move beyond relatively static theoretical ideas about 'primary definers' and dominant news agendas and empirically pursue how different forms of knowledge, different social and scientific rationalities, find expression in and through the media. Arguably the media contest paradigm, with its dynamic models of political communication, theorization of media–source interactions and conceptualization of media as multipurpose arenas, has contributed enormously to this more complex and multidimensional view. But so too has the media culture paradigm with its sensitivity to the textual, cultural and the symbolic and how deep cultural resonances of nature and the environment are embedded in media visualization and the 'rhetoric of environmental images' (Cottle 2000b). Qualitative approaches to audience reception have here also made their mark, revealing how different identities and frames of reference rooted in the everyday mediate the media's environmental portrayal and inform the pragmatics of reception and sense making (Corner et al. 1990; Buckingham 2000).

Journalism post 9/11 and the reporting the US global War on Terror (Chapter 8), like war journalism and reporting of terrorism generally, clearly reproduce agendas and representations that support state interests and policies – lending credence, once again, to theoretical motifs and predictions of the manufacturing consent paradigm.

While there is certainly ample evidence to support this view, researchers have also begun to identify and theorize further levels of complexity and new developments. Attending more closely to the 'politics of representation', or the textual forms and discursive possibilities contained within the different forms of journalism as well as fictional forms such as drama, TV series and films, reveals more discursive complexities and openings than often predicted (Elliott et al. 1996). In the context of the US War on Terror these media forms and resources, though rarely deployed, are arguably much needed for the 'democratization of violence' (Keane 2004). The escalation in staged forms of symbolic violence and violent symbolism following the US invasion of Iraq in 2003 also points to a terrifying and deadly manifestation of John Thompson's thesis of the 'transformation of visibility' (Thompson 1995). This has come about with the availability of new media technologies and the production of deadly DIY media productions by 'auteur terrorists' (Ignatieff 2004) and circulated around the globe via the Internet and satellite broadcasters. When combined with emergent contra-flows from regional broadcasters such as Al-Arabiya and Al-Jazeera, the stunning commercial successes of political oppositional cross-over genres as well as the international circulation of critical documentaries and current affairs programmes, it seems the media communications environment is not entirely closed or impervious to the communications cross-traffic emanating from different political and cultural outlooks and geopolitical vantage points (see Figure 3.2 on p. 51).

Finally, the discussion of mediatized recognition and identity politics (Chapter 9) has challenged generalizing views of the news media as necessarily the purveyor of stereotypes and demeaning representations of minority groups, cultures and outsiders. Symbolic annihilation and denigration certainly continue to characterize many media representations and where this is so undermine group claims for public recognition and social acceptance or, worse, create a climate in which fear and hatred can flourish. But this story, like the contestation for recognition more widely, is not destined to remain fixed for all time. Mainstream media are capable of producing public representations that give identity to image, voice to the voiceless and these can play an important part in the symbolic rehabilitation of former outsiders or Others – whether, for example, asylum seekers, terrorism suspects, aboriginal people or victims of war and famine. Forms of compassionate journalism, too often overlooked by critical researchers, are playing a performative part in the politics of recognition and do so through journalism's powerful communicative modes of display and deliberation. These communicative complexities demand closer attention and theorization and, where possible, they should be actively deepened and extended in the future if journalism is to contribute to processes of democratization within civil society and in an increasingly reflexive, post-traditional and globalizing world.

Taken together, therefore, these research findings and new research directions position mediatized conflict as profoundly implicated in the conduct and multiple contentions of contemporary societies. Mediatized conflicts exhibit, however, considerable differences and they are characterized by multiple dimensions, dynamics that play out over time and political contingencies. Researchers today, necessarily, are obliged to consider the changing formations, flows and frames of multi-medium journalisms. They have to attend to the contingencies and dynamics of mediatized conflicts as they unfold through space and time. They must examine how contending interests and identities deploy communicative power both strategically and symbolically and they need to become attuned to how ritualized forms of expression and the differing communicative modes of journalism colour and shape mediatized conflict. And they also have to be aware of and attend to how different social contexts, the culturally situated-*ness* of audiences and the 'pragmatics of reception' all impact sense making and shape the public circulation of ideas and images, discourses and debate.

This book began by simply noting some of the multifarious, often devastating, conflicts that characterize the contemporary world. In truth we have only managed to touch on some of them. Selections and compromises, inevitably, had to be made, though I would also want to defend the final choice of case studies discussed as 'representative' of some of the best research 'out there' and illustrating important positions of theory and empirical findings. We have, in fact, managed to cover considerable ground – both theoretical and empirical – and together the studies reviewed have brought to the fore many of the principal complexities that need to be addressed when studying mediatized conflict. Based on this foundation we are arguably better equipped to engage with the very latest mediatized conflicts, their determinants, dynamics and democratizing possibilities.

We live in a rapidly globalizing world and themes of globalization have surfaced in many of the studies and conflicts addressed across this book. The unprecedented perils as well as democratizing potential that inhere within processes of globalization demand serious and sustained attention by media scholars, and this will only become more so in the years to come. The world's interlocking media systems are themselves, of course, some of the principal drivers of the changing cultural formations and communicative flows that both characterize and help constitute processes of globalization. How these new media configurations communicate 'global conflicts' – global ecology, human rights, humanitarian disasters, trade flows, poverty, US hegemony and the continuing global War on Terror – conflicts whose origins and ramifications traverse national and even international borders, is, and will remain, a matter of the utmost concern.

Researchers studying global crisis reporting in the future will no doubt find many of the theoretical frameworks and empirical findings deployed and delivered by earlier researchers – and elaborated in this book – of continuing relevance. The unprecedented scale and potential human consequences of many of today's global crises, however, as well as the complexities of their mediatization in today's global media also encourage the development of new frameworks, concepts and methodologies. Media researchers must respond to these latest global developments and rise to the research challenges that they inevitably pose. How and why different global crises are mediatized in the world's media and with what possible impacts and consequences is perhaps THE central question for future media research. *Global Crisis Reporting* (Cottle forthcoming) will pick up on and develop further the complexities discussed in *Mediatized Conflict*, and will do so in today's context of a rapidly changing and globalizing world.

REFERENCES

Abercrombie, N., Hill, S. and Turner, B. (1980) *The Dominant Ideology Thesis*. London: Allen and Unwin.

Adorno, T. and Horkheimer, M. (1944/1972) *The Dialectic of Enlightenment*. London: Verso.

Aggarwala, N.K. (1979) 'What is Development News?', *Journal of Communication* 29: 180–91.

Alexander, J.C. (1988) 'Culture and Political Crisis: "Watergate" and Durkheimian Sociology', pp. 187–224 in J.C. Alexander (ed.) *Durkheimian Sociology: Cultural Studies*. New York: Cambridge University Press.

Alexander, J.C. and Jacobs, R.N. (1998) 'Mass Communication, Ritual and Civil Society', pp. 23–41 in T. Liebes and J. Curran (eds) *Media, Ritual and Identity*. London: Routledge.

Allan, S. (2002a) 'Reweaving the Internet: Online News of September 11', pp. 119–40 in B. Zelizer and S. Allan (eds) (2002) *Journalism After September 11*. London: Routledge.

Allan, S. (2002b) *Media, Risk and Science*. Buckingham: Open University Press.

Allan, S. (2004a) *News Culture*. Maidenhead: Open University Press.

Allan, S. (2004b) 'The Culture of Distance: Online Reporting of the Iraq War', pp. 347–65 in S. Allan and B. Zelizer (eds) *Reporting War*. London: Routledge.

Allan, S. (2005) 'News on the Web: The Emerging Forms and Practices of Online Journalism', pp. 67–81 in S. Allan (ed.) *Journalism: Critical Issues*. Maidenhead: Open University Press.

Allan, S. and Zelizer, B. (eds) (2004) *Reporting War: Journalism in Wartime*. London: Routledge.

Allan, S., Carter, C. and Adams, B. (2000) *Environmental Risks and the Media*. London: Routledge.

Altheide, D.L. (1987). Format and Symbols in TV Coverage of Terrorism in the United States and Great Britain. *International Studies Quarterly* 31: 161–76.

Altheide, D.L. (2003) 'Notes Towards a Politics of Fear', *Journal for Crime and the Media* 1(1): 37–54.

Althusser, L. (1971) 'Ideology and Ideological State Apparatuses' in L. Althusser *Lenin and Philosophy and Other Essays*. New York: Monthly Review Press.

Amin, S. (1976) *Accumulation on a World Scale*. New York: Monthly Review Press.

Anderson, A. (1993) 'Source–Media Relations: The Production of the Environmental Agenda', in A. Hansen (ed.) *The Mass Media and Environmental Issues*. Leicester: Leicester University Press.

Anderson, A. (1997) *Media, Culture and the Environment*. London: UCL Press.

Anderson, A. (2000) 'Environmental Pressure Politics and the Risk Society', pp. 93–104 in S. Allan, B. Adam and C. Carter (eds) *Environmental Risks and the Media*. London: Routledge.

Article 19 (2003) *What's the Story? Results from Research into Media Coverage of Refugees and Asylum Seekers in the UK*. London: Article 19.

Atton, C. (2002) *Alternative Media*. London: Sage.

Azran, T. (2004) 'Resisting Peripheral Exports: Al Jazeera's War Images on US Television', *Media International Australia* 113: 75–86.

Barthes, R. (1977) *Image, Music, Text*. London: Fontana.

Beck, U. (1992) *Risk Society*. London: Sage.

Beck, U. (1995) *Ecological Politics in the Age of Risk*. Cambridge: Polity.

Beck, U. (1997) *The Reinvention of Politics*. Cambridge: Polity.

Beck, U. (2000) 'Foreword', pp. xii–xiv in S. Allan, B. Adam and C. Carter (eds) *Environmental Risks and the Media*. London: Routledge.

Beck, U. (2001) *World Risk Society*. Cambridge: Polity.

Beck, U., Giddens, A. and Lash, S. (eds) (1994) *Reflexive Modernization*. Cambridge: Polity.

Benhabib, S. (ed.) (1996) *Democracy and Difference*. Princeton, NJ: Princeton University Press.

Benhabib, S. (2002) *The Claims of Culture*. Princeton, NJ: Princeton University Press.

Bennett, L. (1990) 'Towards a Theory of Press–State Relations in the United States', *Journal of Communication* 40(2): 103–25.

Bennett, L. (2003) 'New Media Power: The Internet and Global Activism', pp. 17–38 in N. Couldry and J. Curran (eds) *Contesting Media Power: Alternative Media in a Networked World*. Oxford: Rowman and Littlefield.

Bennett, L. (2004) 'Communicating Global Activism: Strengths and Vulnerabilities of Networked Politics', pp. 123–46 in W. Van De Donk, B. Loader, P.G. Nixon and D. Dieter (eds) *Cyberprotest*. London: Routledge.

Bird, E. (1990) 'Storytelling on the Far Side: Journalism and the Weekly Tabloid', *Critical Studies in Mass Communication* 7: 377–89.

Blaisse, M. (1992) 'Reporters' Perspectives', pp. 137–69 in D.L. Paletz and A.P. Schmid (eds) *Terrorism and the Media*. London: Sage.

Boczkowski, P.J. (2004) *Digitizing the News*. Cambridge, MA: MIT Press.

Bohman, J. (2000) 'The Division of Labour in Democratic Discourse: Media, Experts and Deliberative Democracy', pp. 47–64 in S. Chambers and A. Costain (eds) *Deliberation, Democracy and the Media*. Oxford: Rowman and Littlefield.

Bolton, R. (1986) 'The Problems of Making Political Television: A Practitioner's Perspective', pp. 93–112 in P. Golding, G. Murdock and P. Schlesinger (eds) *Communicating Politics*. Leicester: Leicester University Press.

Boyd-Barrett, O. (1977) 'Media Imperialism: Towards an International Framework for the Analysis of Media Systems', in J. Curran, M. Gurevitch and J. Woollacott (eds) *Mass Communication and Society*. London: Edward Arnold.

Boyd-Barrett, O. (2004) 'Understanding: The Second Casualty', pp. 25–42 in S. Allan and B. Zelizer (eds) *Reporting War*. London: Routledge.

Boyd-Barrett, O. and T. Rantanen (eds) (1998) *The Globalization of News*. London: Sage.

Braham, P. (1982) 'How the Media Report Race', in M. Gurevitch, T. Bennett, J. Curran and J. Woollacott (eds) *Culture, Society and the Media*. London: Methuen.

Bromley, M. (2004) 'The Battlefield Is the Media: War Reporting and the Formation of National Identity in Australia – From Belmont to Baghdad', pp. 224–44 in S. Allan and B. Zelizer (eds) *Reporting War*. London: Routledge.

Brown, S. (2003) 'From "The Death of the Real" to the Reality of Death: How Did the Gulf War Take Place?', *Journal for Crime and the Media* 1(1): 55–71.

Brosius, H.B. and Weimann, G. (1991) 'The Contagiousness of Mass-mediated Terrorism', *European Journal of Communication* 6: 63–75.

Bruck, P. (1993) 'Dealing with Reality: The News Media and the Promotion of Peace', pp. 71–96 in C. Roach (ed.) *Communication and Culture in War and Peace*. London: Sage.

Buckingham, D. (2000) *The Making of Citizens: Young People, News, Politics*. London: Routledge.

Bullimore, K. (1999) 'Media Dreaming: Representation of Aboriginality in Modern Australian Media', *Asia Pacific Media Educator* 6: 72–80.

Burgess, J. and Harrison, C.M. (1993) 'The Circulation of Claims in the Cultural Politics of Environmental Change', pp. 198–221 in A. Hansen (ed.) *The Mass Media and Environmental Issues*. Leicester: Leicester University Press.

Butler, D. (1995) *The Trouble with Reporting Northern Ireland*. Aldershot: Avebury.

Butterworth, E. (1967) 'The 1962 Smallpox Outbreak and the British Press', *Race* 7(4): 347–64.

Campbell, R. (1987) 'Securing the Middle Ground: Reporter Formulas in 60 Minutes', *Critical Studies in Mass Communication* 4(4): 325–50.

Carey, J. (1989) *Communication as Culture*. London: Unwin Hyman.

Carey, J. (1998) 'Political Ritual on Television: Episodes in the History of Shame, Degradation and Excommunication', in T. Liebes and J. Curran (eds) *Media, Ritual and Identity*. London: Routledge.

Carey, J. (1999) 'In Defense of Public Journalism', pp. 49–66 in T. Glasser (ed.) *The Idea of Public Journalism*. New York: The Guilford Press.

Carey, P. (1998) *The Faber Book of Reportage*. London: Faber and Faber.

Carruthers, S. (2000) *The Media at War: Communication and Conflict in the 20th Century*. Basingstoke: Macmillan.

Carter, C., Branston, G. and Allan, S. (eds) (1998) *News, Gender and Power*. London: Routledge.

Castells, M. (1996) *The Rise of the Network Society*. Oxford: Blackwell.

Castells, M. (1997) *The Power of Identity*. Oxford: Blackwell.

Castells, M. (2001) *The Internet Galaxy*. Oxford: Oxford University Press.

Cathcart, B. (2000) *The Case of Stephen Lawrence*. London: Penguin.

Chapman, G., Kumar, K., Fraser, C. and Gaber, I. (1997) *Environmentalism and the Mass Media*. New York: Routledge.

Clayman, S. and Heritage, J. (2002) *The News Interview*. Cambridge: Cambridge University Press.

Cohen, S. (1972) *Folk Devils and Moral Panics: The Creation of the Mods and Rockers*. London: MacKibbon and Kee.

Cohen, S. and Young, J. (eds) (1981) *The Manufacture of News: Social Problems, Deviance and the Mass Media*. London: Constable.

Coleman, C. (1995) 'Science, Technology and Risk Coverage of a Community Conflict', *Media, Culture and Society* 17(1): 65–80.

Commission for Racial Equality (1999) *Racial Attacks and Harassment*. London: Commission for Racial Equality.

Committee for the Protection of Journalists (CPJ) (2005) *Journalists Killed in the Line of Duty*. Available at: http://www.cpj.org

Conflict and Peace Forums (1999) *The Peace Journalism Option, Two*. Taplow Court: Transcend Peace and Development Network.

Corner, J. (1995) *Television Form and Public Address*. London: Arnold.

Corner, J. and Richardson, K. (1993) 'Environmental Communication and the Contingency of Meaning: A Research Note', pp. 222–33 in A. Hansen (ed.) *The Mass Media and Environmental Issues*. Leicester: Leicester University Press.

Corner, J., Richardson, K. and Fenton, N. (1990) *Nuclear Reactions: Form and Response in Public Issue Television*. Luton: John Libbey.

Cottle, S. (1993a) *TV News, Urban Conflict and the Inner City*. Leicester: Leicester University Press.

Cottle, S. (1993b) 'Mediating the Environment: Modalities of TV News', pp. 107–33 in A. Hansen (ed.) *The Mass Media and Environmental Issues*. Leicester: Leicester University Press.

Cottle, S. (1997) *Television and Ethnic Minorities: Producers' Perspectives*. Ashcroft: Avebury.

Cottle, S. (1998a) 'Analysing Visuals: Still and Moving Images', pp. 189–224 in A. Hansen, S. Cottle, R. Negrine and C. Newbold (eds) *Mass Communication Research Methods*. Houndmills: Palgrave.

Cottle, S. (1998b) 'Ulrich Beck, "Risk Society" and the Media: A Catastrophic View?', *European Journal of Communication* 13(1): 5–33.

Cottle, S. (1999) 'From BBC Newsroom to BBC Newscentre: On Changing Technology and Journalist Practices', *Convergence: The Journal of Research into New Media Technologies* 5(3): 22–43.

Cottle, S. (ed.) (2000a) *Ethnic Minorities and the Media: Changing Cultural Boundaries*. Buckingham: Open University Press.

Cottle, S. (2000b) 'TV News, Lay Voices and the Visualization of Environmental Risks', pp. 29–44 in S. Allan, B. Adam and C. Carter (eds) *Environmental Risks and the Media*. London: Routledge.

Cottle, S. (2002) 'TV Agora and Agoraphobia Post September 11', pp. 178–98, in B. Zelizer and S. Allan (eds) *Journalism After September 11*. London: Routledge.

Cottle, S. (ed.) (2003a) *Media Organization and Production*. London: Sage.

Cottle, S. (ed.) (2003b) *News, Public Relations and Power*. London: Sage.

Cottle, S. (2004a) *The Racist Murder of Stephen Lawrence: Media Performance and Public Transformation*. Westport, CT: Praeger.

Cottle, S. (2004b) 'Representations', pp. 368–72 in E. Cashmore (ed.) *Encyclopedia of Race and Ethnic Studies*. London: Routledge.

Cottle, S. (2004c) 'Producing Nature(s): On the Changing Production Ecology of Natural History TV', *Media, Culture and Society* 26(1): 81–101.

Cottle, S. (2005a) 'Mediatized Public Crisis and Civil Society Renewal: The Racist Murder of Stephen Lawrence', *Crime, Media, Culture* 1(1): 49–71.

Cottle, S. (2005b) 'Mediatizing the Global War on Terror: Television's Public Eye', pp. 19–48 in A.P. Kavoori and T. Fraley (eds) *Media, Terrorism, Theory: A Reader*. Oxford: Rowman and Littlefield.

Cottle, S. (2005c) 'In Defence of "Thick" Journalism', pp. 109–24 in S. Allan (ed.) *Journalism: Critical Issues*. Maidenhead: Open University Press.

Cottle, S. (2006) 'Mediatized Rituals: Beyond Manufacturing Consent', *Media, Culture and Society* 28(3) (forthcoming).

Cottle, S. (forthcoming) *Global Crisis Reporting*. Maidenhead: Open University Press.

Cottle, S. and Rai, M. (2006) 'Between Display and Deliberation: Analyzing TV News as Communicative Architecture', *Media, Culture and Society* 28(2): 163–89.

Craig, G. (2002) 'The Spectacle of the Street: An Analysis of Media Coverage of Protests at the 2000 Melbourne World Economic Forum', *Australian Journal of Communication* 29(1): 39–52.

Critcher, C. (2003) *Moral Panics*. London: Routledge.

Cumings, B. (1992) *War and Television*. London: Verso.

Curran, J. (1991) 'Rethinking the Media as Public Sphere', pp. 27–57 in P. Dahlgren and C. Sparks (eds) *Communication and Citizenship*. London: Routledge.

Curran, J. and Seaton, J. (1997) *Power Without Responsibility*. London: Routledge.

Curtis, L. (1984) *Ireland: The Propaganda War*. London: Pluto Press.

Dahlberg, L. (2001) 'The Internet and Democratic Discourse: Exploring the Prospects of Online Deliberative Forums Extending the Public Sphere', *Information, Communication and Society* 4(4): 615–33.

Dahlgren, P. (1988) 'What's the Meaning of This? Viewers' Plural Sense: Making of TV News', *Media, Culture and Society* 10(3): 285–301.

Dahlgren, P. (1995) *Television and the Public Sphere*. London: Sage.

Dahlgren, P. and Sparks, C. (1992) *Journalism and Popular Culture*. London: Sage.

Davis, A. (2000) 'Public Relations Campaigning and News Production: The Case of New Unionism in Britain', pp. 173–92 in J. Curran (ed.) *Media Organisations in Society*. London: Arnold.

Davis, A. (2003) 'Public Relations and News Sources', in S. Cottle (ed.) *News, Public Relations and Power*. London: Sage.

Dayan, D. and Katz, E. (1992) *Media Events: The Live Broadcasting of History*. Cambridge, MA: Harvard University Press.

Deacon, D. (1996) 'The Voluntary Sector in a Changing Communication Environment: A Case Study of Non-official News Sources', *European Journal of Communication*, 11(2): 173–99.

Deacon, D. (2003) 'Non-governmental Organisations and the Media', in S. Cottle (ed.) *News, Public Relations and Power*. London: Sage.

Deacon, D. and Golding, P. (1994) *Taxation and Representation*. London: John Libbey.

Debord, G. (1983) *Society of the Spectacle*. Detroit, MI: Black and Red.

DeLuca, K.M. (1999) *Image Politics: The New Rhetoric of Environmental Activism*. London: The Guilford Press.

DeLuca, K.M. and Peeples, J. (2002) 'From Public Sphere to Public Screen: Democracy, Activism and the "Violence" of Seattle', *Critical Studies in Media Communication* 19(2): 125–51.

Deuze, M. (2003) 'The Web and Its Journalisms: Considering the Consequences of Different Types of Newsmedia Online', *New Media and Society* 5(2): 203–26.

Dillon, M. (2002) 'Network Society, Network Centric Warfare and the State of Emergency', *Theory, Culture and Society* 19(4): 71–9.

Dines, G. and Humez, J.M. (eds) (2002) *Gender, Race, and Class in Media*. London: Sage.

Downey, J. and Murdock, G. (2003) 'The Counter Revolution in Military Affairs: The Globalization of Guerrilla Warfare', pp. 70–86 in D.K. Thussu and D. Freedman (eds) *War and the Media*. London: Sage.

Downing, J. and Husband, C. (2005) *Representing 'Race'*. London: Sage.

Dryzek, J. (2000) *Deliberative Democracy and Beyond*. Oxford: Oxford University Press.

Eder, K. (1996) *Social Constructions of Nature*. London: Sage.

Elliott, A. (2003) 'Risk and Reflexivity: Ulrich Beck', pp. 19–42 in A. Elliott *Critical Visions*. Oxford: Rowman and Littlefield.

Elliott, P. (1977) 'Reporting Northern Ireland: A Study of News in Great Britain, Northern Ireland and the Republic of Ireland', pp. 263–376 in UNESCO (eds) *Ethnicity and the Media*. Paris: UNESCO.

Elliott, P. (1980) 'Press Performance as Political Ritual', pp. 141–77 in H. Christian (ed.) *The Sociology of Journalism and the Press*. University of Keele, Sociological Review Monograph No. 29.

Elliott, P. (1986) 'Intellectuals, "the Information Society" and the Disappearance of the Public Sphere', pp. 247–63 in R. Collins, J. Curran, N. Garnham, P. Scannell, P. Schlesinger and C. Sparks (eds) *Media, Culture and Society: A Critical Reader*. London: Sage.

Elliott, P., Murdock, G. and Schlesinger, P. (1996) 'The State and "Terrorism" on British Television', pp. 340–76 in B. Rolston and D. Miller (eds) *War and Words: The Northern Ireland Media Reader*. Belfast: Beyond the Pale Productions.

El-Nawawy, M. and Iskander, A. (2003) *Al-Jazeera: How the Free Arab News Network Scooped the World and Changed the Middle East*. Cambridge, MA: Westview.

Entman, R.E. (2004) *Projections of Power: Framing News, Public Opinion and U.S. Foreign Policy*. Chicago: Chicago University Press.

Ericson, R.V., Baranek, P.M. and Chan, J.B.L. (1989) *Negotiating Control: A Study of News Sources*. Milton Keynes: Open University Press.

Ericson, R.V., Baranek, P.M. and Chan, J.B.L. (1991) *Visualizing Deviance*. Buckingham: Open University Press.

Ettema, J. (1990) 'Press Rites and Race Relations: A Study of Mass Mediated Ritual', *Critical Studies in Mass Communication* 7: 309–31.

Fang, Y-J. (1994) ' "Riots" and Demonstrations in the Chinese Press: A Case Study of Language and Ideology', *Discourse and Society* 5(4): 463–81.

Fawcett, L. (2002) 'Why Peace Journalism Isn't News', *Journalism Studies* 3(2): 213–23.

Fishman, M. (1980) *Manufacturing the News*. Austin, TX: University of Texas.

Fiske, J. (1994a) *Media Matters: Everyday Culture and Political Change*. Minneapolis, MN: University of Minnesota Press.

Fiske, J. (1994b) 'Radical Shopping in Los Angeles: Race, Media and the Sphere of Consumption', *Media, Culture and Society* 16(3): 469–86.

Fiske, J. (1996) *Media Matters: Race and Gender in US Politics*. Minneapolis, MN: University of Minnesota Press.

Frank, A.G. (1969) *Capitalism and Underdevelopment in Latin America*. New York: Monthly Review Press.

Frazer, N. (1992) 'Rethinking the Public Sphere: A Contribution to the Critique of Actually Existing Democracy', pp. 109–42 in C. Calhoun (ed.) *Habermas and the Public Sphere*. Cambridge, MA: The MIT Press.

Frazer, N. and Honneth, A. (2003) *Redistribution or Recognition?* London: Verso.

Galtung, J. (1993) 'Preface', pp. xi–xiv in C. Roach (ed.) *Communication and Culture in War and Peace*. London: Sage.

Galtung, J. and Ruge, M. (1973) 'Structuring and Selecting News', in S. Cohen and J. Young (eds) *The Manufacture of News: Deviance, Social Problems and the Mass Media*. London: Constable.

Gamson, W.A. and Modigliani, A. (1989) 'Media Discourse and Public Opinion on Nuclear Power: A Constructionist Approach', *American Journal of Sociology* 95: 1–37.

Gandy, O.H. (1982) *Beyond Agenda Setting: Information Subsidies and Public Policy*. Norwood, NJ: Ablex Publishing.

Garnham, N. (1986) 'The Media as Public Sphere', pp. 37–53 in P. Golding, G. Murdock and P. Schlesinger (eds) *Communicating Politics*. Leicester: Leicester University Press.

Gauntlett, D. (2002) *Media, Gender and Identity*. London: Routledge.

Gerbner, G. (1992) 'Violence and Terror in and by the Media', in M. Raboy and B. Dagenais (eds) *Media, Crisis and Democracy*. London: Sage.

Giddens, A. (1990) *The Consequences of Modernity*. Cambridge: Polity Press.

Giddens, A. (1994) *Beyond Left and Right*. Cambridge: Polity Press.

Gitlin, T. (1980/2003) *The Whole World Is Watching: Mass Media in the Making and Unmaking of the New Left*. Berkeley, CA: University of California Press.

Gitlin, T. (1998) 'Public Sphere or Public Spherecules', pp. 168–74 in T. Liebes and J. Curran (eds) *Media, Ritual and Identity*. London: Routledge.

Glasgow University Media Group (GUMG) (1976) *Bad News*. London: Routledge and Kegan Paul.

Glasgow University Media Group (GUMG) (1980) *More Bad News*. London: Routledge and Kegan Paul.

Glasgow University Media Group (GUMG) (1985) *War and Peace News*. Buckingham: Open University Press.

Glasser, T.L. (ed.) (1999) *The Idea of Public Journalism*. New York: The Guilford Press.

Glover, J. (2001) *Humanity: A Moral History*. London: Pimlico.

Goldblatt, D. (1996) *Social Theory and the Environment*. Cambridge: Polity.

Golding, P. and Harris, P. (eds) (1997) *Beyond Cultural Imperialism*. London: Sage.

Goldstein, J.S. (2001) *War and Gender*. Cambridge: Cambridge University Press.

Goode, E. and Ben-Yehuda, N. (1994) *Moral Panics: The Social Construction of Deviance*. Oxford: Blackwell.

Gopsill, T. (2004) 'Target the Media', pp. 251–61 in D. Miller (ed.) *Tell Me Lies: Propaganda and Media Distortion in the Attack on Iraq*. London: Pluto.

Gutmann, A. and Thompson, D. (2004) *Why Deliberative Democracy*. Princeton, NJ: Princeton University Press.

Habermas, J. (1974) 'The Public Sphere', *New German Critique* 3 (Autumn): 49–59.

Habermas, J. (1989) *The Structural Transformation of the Public Sphere*. Cambridge: Polity.

Habermas, J. (1996) *Between Facts and Norms*. Cambridge: Polity.

Hacker, K.L. and van Dijk, J. (eds) (2000) *Digital Democracy: Issues of Theory and Practice*. London: Sage.

Hall, J. (2001) *Online Journalism*. London: Pluto.

Hall, S. (1982) 'The Rediscovery of Ideology: Return of the Repressed in Media Studies', pp. 56–90 in M. Gurevitch, T. Bennett, J. Curran and J. Woollacott (eds) *Culture, Society, Media*. London: Methuen.

Hall, S. (1988) 'New Ethnicities', pp. 27–31 in K. Mercer (ed.) *Black Film, British Cinema*, ICA Documents 7. London: British Film Institute.

Hall, S. (1997) 'The Spectacle of the "Other" ', pp. 223–79 in S. Hall (ed.) *Representation: Cultural Representations and Signifying Practices*. London: Sage.

Hall, S. and Jacques, M. (eds) (1989) *New Times*. London: Lawrence and Wishart.

Hall, S., Hobson, D., Lowe, A. and Willis, P. (eds) (1980) *Culture, Media, Language*. London: Hutchinson.

Hall, S., Critcher, C., Jefferson, T., Clarke, J. and Roberts, B. (1978) *Policing the Crisis: Mugging, the State and Law and Order*. Basingstoke: Macmillan.

Hallin, D. (1986) *The 'Uncensored War': The Media and Vietnam*. Oxford: Oxford University Press.

Hallin, D. (1994) *We Keep America on Top of the World*. London: Routledge.

Hallin, D. (1997) 'The Media and War', in J. Corner, P. Schlesinger and R. Silverstone (eds) *International Media Research*. London: Routledge.

Halloran, J., Elliott, P. and Murdock, G. (1970) *Demonstrations and Communication: A Case Study*. London: Penguin.

Hammond, P. (2003) 'The Media War on Terrorism', *Journal for Crime and the Media* 1(1): 23–36.

Hannerz, U. (2004) *Foreign News*. Chicago: University of Chicago Press.

Hannigan, A. (1995) *Environmental Sociology*. London: Routledge.

Hansen, A. (1991) 'The Media and the Social Construction of the Environment', *Media, Culture and Society* 13(4): 443–58.

Hansen, A. (ed.) (1993) *The Mass Media and Environmental Issues*. Leicester: Leicester University Press.

Hansen, A. (2000) 'Claims-making and Framing in the British Newspaper Coverage of the Brent Spar Controversy', pp. 55–72 in S. Allan, B. Adam and C. Carter (eds) *Environmental Risks and the Media*. London: Routledge.

Hansen, A. and Murdock, G. (1985) 'Constructing the Crowd: Populist Discourse and Press Presentation', pp. 227–57 in V. Mosco and M. Wasco (eds) *Popular Culture and Media Events*. Norwood, NJ: Ablex.

Harris, R. (1994) *The Media Trilogy*. London: Faber and Faber.

Hartmann, P. and Husband, C. (1974) *Racism and the Mass Media*. London: Davis Poynter.

Harvey, D. (2003) *The New Imperialism*. Oxford: Oxford University Press.

Hassan, R. (2004) *Media, Politics and the Network Society*. Maidenhead: Open University Press.

Held, D. (1987) 'Power and Legitimacy in Contemporary Britain', in D. Held *Political Theory and the Modern State*. Cambridge: Polity.

Held, D. (2004) *Global Covenant*. Cambridge: Polity.

Held, D., McGrew, A., Goldblatt, D. and Perraton, J. (eds) (1999) *Global Transformations: Politics, Economics, Culture*. Cambridge: Polity.

Henderson, L., Miller, D. and Reilly, J. (1990) *Speak No Evil: The British Broadcasting Ban, the Media and the Conflict in Northern Ireland*. Glasgow: Glasgow University.

Herman, E. (2000) 'The Propaganda Model: A Retrospective', *Journalism Studies* 1(1): 101–12.

Herman, E. and Chomsky, N. (1988) *Manufacturing Consent: The Political Economy of the Mass Media*. New York: Pantheon.

Herman, E. and O'Sullivan, G. (1991) 'Terrorism as Ideology and Culture Industry', pp. 39–75 in A. George (ed.) *Western State Terrorism*. Cambridge: Polity.

Hier, S.P. (2003) 'Risk and Panic in Late Modernity: Implications of the Converging Sites of Social Anxiety', *British Journal of Sociology* 54(1): 3–20.

Hilgartner, S. and Bosk, C.L. (1988) 'The Rise and Fall of Social Problems: A Public Arenas Model', *American Journal of Sociology* 94(1): 53–78.

Hoskins, A. (2004) *Televising War: From Vietnam to Iraq*. London: Continuum.

Howard, R. (2002) *An Operational Framework for Media and Peacebuilding*. Vancouver: Institute for Media, Policy and Civil Society.

Hunt, D.M. (1997) *Screening the Los Angeles 'Riots'*. Cambridge: Cambridge University Press.

Hunt, D. (1999) *O.J. Simpson: Facts and Fictions: News Rituals in the Construction of Reality*. Cambridge: Cambridge University Press.

Husband, C. (2000) 'Media and the Public Sphere in Multi-ethnic Societies', pp. 119–214 in S. Cottle (ed.) *Ethnic Minorities and the Media: Changing Cultural Boundaries*. Buckingham: Open University Press.

Ignatieff, M. (1998) *The Warrior's Honour: Ethnic War and the Modern Conscience*. London: Chatto and Windus.

Ignatieff, M. (2004) 'The Terrorist as Film Director', *The Age* (Melbourne) 20 November p. 2.

Institute of Race Relations (2002a) *Racially Motivated Murders (Known or Suspected) Since 1991*. Factfile. London: Institute of Race Relations.

Institute of Race Relations (2002b) *Racial Violence*. Factfile. London: Institute of Race Relations.

Iskander, A.L. and El-Nawawy, M. (2004) 'Al-Jazeera and War Coverage in Iraq: The Media's Quest for Contextual Objectivity', pp. 315–23 in S. Allan and B. Zelizer (eds) *Reporting War*. London: Routledge.

Jacka, L. and Green. L. (eds) (2003) 'The New "Others": Media and Society Post-September 11', *Media International Australia* 109 (November).

Jacobs, R.N. (2000) *Race, Media and the Crisis of Civil Society: From Watts to Rodney King*. Cambridge: Cambridge University Press.

Jakubowicz, A. (ed.) (1994) *Racism, Ethnicity and the Media*. St Leonards: Allen & Unwin.

Jankowski, N.W. and van Selm, M. (2000) 'Traditional News Media Online: An Examination of Added-Value', *Communications: The European Journal of Communication Research* 25(1): 85–101.

Julian, I. and Mercer, K. (1988) 'Introduction: De Margin and De Centre', *Screen* 29(4): 2–10.

Kaldor, M. (2003) *Global Civil Society*. Cambridge: Polity.

Kawamoto, K. (ed.) (2003) *Digital Journalism*. London: Rowman and Littlefield.

Keane, J. (2003) *Global Civil Society?* Cambridge: Cambridge University Press.

Keane, J. (2004) *Violence and Democracy*. Cambridge: Cambridge University Press.

Keeble, R. (2004) 'Information Warfare in an Age of Hyper-militarism', pp. 43–58 in S. Allan and B. Zelizer (eds) *Reporting War*. London: Routledge.

Kellner, D. (1992) *The Persian Gulf TV War*. Oxford: Westview Press.

Kellner, D. (1995) *Media Culture: Cultural Studies, Identity and Politics Between the Modern and Postmodern*. London: Routledge.

Kellner, D. (2003) *Media Spectacle*. London: Routledge.

Kerner, O. (1968) *Report of the National Advisory Commission on Civil Disorders*. New York: Bantam Books.

Kitzinger, J. (2004) *Framing Abuse*. London: Pluto.

Kitzinger, J. and Reilly, J. (1997) 'The Rise and Fall of Risk Reporting: Media Coverage of Human Genetics Research, "False Memory Syndrome" and Mad Cow Disease', *European Journal of Communication* 12(3): 319–50.

Knightley, P. (2003) *The First Casualty – The War Correspondent as Hero, Propagandist and Myth Maker from the Crimea to Iraq*. London: André Deutsch.

Lang, K. and Lang, G.E. (1953) 'The Unique Perspective of Television and Its Effects: A Pilot Study', *American Sociological Review* 18: 3–12.

Lash, S. and Urry, J. (1994) *Economies of Signs and Space*. London: Sage.

Lash, S., Szerszynski, B. and Wynne, B. (eds) (1996) *Risk, Environment and Modernity*. London: Sage.

Law, I. (2002) *Race in the News*. Basingstoke: Palgrave.

Leith, D. (2004) *Bearing Witness: The Lives of War Correspondents and Photojournalists*. Milsons Point: Random House.

Lemish, D. (ed.) (2005) 'Gender and War' special edition of *Feminist Media Studies* 5(3).

Lester, L. (2005) *Contesting Wilderness: Media, Movement and Environmental Conflict in Tasmania*. Unpublished PhD thesis. Media and Communication Program, University of Melbourne.

Lester, L. (forthcoming) *Media, Wilderness and Protest*.

Lewis, J. and Brookes, R. (2004) 'How British Television News Represented the Case for War', pp. 283–300 in S. Allan and B. Zelizer (eds) *Reporting War*. London: Routledge.

Liebes, T. (1997) *Reporting the Arab–Israeli Conflict*. London: Routledge.

Livingstone, S. and Lunt, P. (1994) *Talk on Television*. London: Routledge.

Lowe, P. and Morrison, D. (1984) 'Bad News or Good News: Environmental Politics and the Mass Media', *Sociological Review* 32(1): 75–90.

Lull, J. and Hinerman, S. (eds) (1997) *Media Scandals: Morality and Desire in the Popular Market Place*. Cambridge: Polity.

Macbride, S. (ed.) (1980) *Many Voices, One World*. Paris: Unesco.

Macpherson, Sir William (1999) *The Stephen Lawrence Inquiry – Report of an Inquiry by Sir William Macpherson of Cluny*. Cm 4262-I. London: HMSO.

Macnaghten, D. and Urry, J. (1998) *Contested Natures*. London: Sage.

Malik, S. (2002) *Representing Black Britain: Black and Asian Images on Television*. London: Sage.

Manning, P. (2001) *News and News Sources: A Critical Introduction*. London: Sage.

Marcuse, H. (1972) *One Dimensional Man*. London: Abacus.

Marr, D. and Wilkinson, M. (2004) *Dark Victory*. Crows Nest: Allen and Unwin.

McAdam, D. (2000) 'Movement Strategy and Dramaturgic Framing in Democratic States: The Case of the American Civil Rights Movement', pp. 117–34 in S. Chambers and A. Costain (eds) *Deliberation, Democracy and the Media*. Oxford: Rowman and Littlefield.

McChesney, R.W. (2003) 'Corporate Media, Global Capitalism', pp. 27–39 in S. Cottle (ed.) *Media Organization and Production*. London: Sage.

McGoldrick, A. and Lynch, J. (2000) 'Peace Journalism: How to Do It'. Available at: http://www.transcend.org

McGoldrick, A. and Lynch, J. (2001) 'What Is Peace Journalism?', *Activate*: 6–9.

McGuigan, J. (2000) 'British Identity and the "People's Princess"', *The Sociological Review* 50(1): 1–18.

McKee, A. (2005) *The Public Sphere: An Introduction*. Cambridge: Cambridge University Press.

McLaughlin, G. (2002) *The War Correspondent*. London: Pluto Press.

McRobbie, A. (1994) 'The Moral Panic in the Age of the Postmodern Mass Media', pp. 198–219 in A. McRobbie (ed.) *Postmodernism and Popular Culture*. London: Routledge.

Media International Australia (1997) 'Panic: Morality, Media, Culture' Special Edition, *Media International Australia* 85.

Mercer, K. (1994) *Welcome to the Jungle*. London: Routledge.

Miladi, N. (2003) 'Mapping the Al-Jazeera Phenomenon', pp. 149–60 in D.K. Thussu and D. Freedman (eds) *War and the Media*. London: Sage.

Miles, R. (1984) 'The Riots of 1958: Notes on the Ideological Construction of "Race Relations" as a Political Issue in Britain', *Immigrants and Minorities* 3(3): 252–75.

Miliband, R. (1973) *The State in Capitalist Society*. London: Quartet Books.

Miller, A.H. (1990) 'Preserving Liberty in a Society Under Siege: The Media and the "Guildford Four"', *Terrorism and Political Violence* 2: 305–24.

Miller, D. (1993) 'Official Sources and "Primary Definition": The Case of Northern Ireland', *Media, Culture and Society* 15(3): 385–406.

Miller, D. (1994) *Don't Mention the War – Northern Ireland, Propaganda and the Media*. London: Pluto.

Miller, D. (1995) 'The Media and Northern Ireland: Censorship, Information Management and the Broadcasting Ban', pp. 43–75, in G. Philo (ed.) *Glasgow Media Group Reader*, Volume 2, London: Routledge.

Miller, D. (ed.) (2004) *Tell Me Lies: Propaganda and Media Distortion in the Attack on Iraq*. London: Pluto.

Miller, D. and Williams, K. (1993) 'Negotiating HIV/AIDS Information Agendas, Media Strategies and the News', pp. 126–142, in J. Eldridge (ed.) *Getting the Message*. London: Routledge.

Miller, D. and McLaughlin, G. (1996) 'Reporting the Peace in Ireland', pp. 421–40 in B. Rolston and D. Miller (eds) *War and Words*. Belfast: Beyond the Pale Publications.

Mohammadi, A. (ed.) (1997) *International Communication and Globalization*. London: Sage.

Morrison, D.E. (1992) *Television and the Gulf War*. London: John Libbey.

Morrison, D.E. (1994a) 'Journalists and the Social Construction of War', *Contemporary Record* 8(2): 305–20.

Morrison, D.E. (1994b) 'From the Falklands to the Gulf', *Sociology Review* February: 21–4.

Morrison, D.E. and Tumber, H. (1988) *Journalists at War – The Dynamics of News Reporting During the Falklands Conflict*. London: Sage.

Mosco, V. (1996) *The Political Economy of Communication*. London: Sage.

Mouffe, C. (1996) 'Democracy, Power and the "Political"', pp. 245–56 in S. Benhabib (ed.) *Democracy and Difference*. Princeton, NJ: Princeton University Press.

Murdock, G. (1981) 'Political Deviance: The Press Presentation of a Militant Mass Demonstration', pp. 206–25 in S. Cohen and J. Young (eds) *The Manufacture of News – Deviance, Social Problems and the Mass Media*. London: Constable.

Murdock, G. (1984) 'Reporting the Riots: Images and Impacts', in J. Benyon (ed.) *Scarman and After*. Oxford: Pergamon Press.

Murdock, G. and Golding, P. (1984) 'Capitalism, Communication and Class Relations', in J. Curran, M. Gurevitch and J. Woollacott (eds) *Mass Communication and Society*. London: Edward Arnold.

Murphy, D. (1991) *The Stalker Affair and the Press*. London: Unwin Hyman.

Myers, M. (1999) *Mediated Women*. Cresshill, NJ: Hampton Press.

Mythen, G. (2004) *Ulrich Beck: A Critical Introduction to the Risk Society*. London: Pluto.

Paletz, D.L. and Schmid, A.P. (eds) (1992) *Terrorism and the Media*. London: Sage.

Paletz, D.L. and Tawney, L.L. (1992) 'Broadcasting Organizations' Perspectives', pp. 105–10 in D.L. Paletz and A.P. Schmid (eds.) *Terrorism and the Media*. London: Sage.

Paletz, D.L., Ayanian, J.Z. and Fozzard, P.A. (1982) 'Terrorism on TV News: The IRA, the FALN, and the Red Brigades', pp. 143–65 in W.C. Adams (ed.) *Television Coverage of International Affairs*. Norwood, NJ: Ablex.

Pedelty, M. (1995) *War Stories: The Culture of Foreign Correspondents*. London: Routledge.

Peters, H.P. (1995) 'The Interaction of Journalists and Scientific Experts: Co-operation and Conflict Between Two Professional Cultures', *Media, Culture and Society* 17(1): 31–48.

Peters, J.D. (1993) 'Distrust of Representation: Habermas on the Public Sphere', *Media, Culture and Society*, 15(4): 541–72.

Peters, J.D. (1999) 'Public Journalism and Democratic Theory: Four Challenges', pp. 99–117 in T. Glasser (ed.) *The Idea of Public Journalism*. New York: The Guilford Press.

Petley, J. (2003) 'War Without Death: Responses to Distant Suffering', *Journal for Crime and the Media* 1(1): 72–85.

Philo, G. (2002) 'Television News and Audience Understanding of War, Conflict and Disaster', *Journalism Studies* 3(2): 173–86.

Philo, G. and Beattie, L. (1999) 'Race, Migration and Media', in G. Philo (ed.) *Message Received*. Harlow: Longman.

Philo, G. and Berry, M. (2004) *Bad News from Israel*. London: Pluto.

Picard, M. (1991) 'News Coverage as the Contagion of Terrorism: Dangerous Charges Backed by Dubious Science', pp. 49–62 in A. Alai and K. Ede (eds) *Media Coverage of Terrorism*. London: Sage.

Porta, D. and Tarrow, S. (2005) *Transnational Protest and Global Activism*. Oxford: Rowman and Littlefield.

Reese, S.D. (2004) 'Militarised Journalism: Framing Dissent in the Gulf Wars', pp. 247–65 in S. Allan and B. Zelizer (eds) *Reporting War*. London: Routledge.

Roach, C. (ed.) (1993) *Communication and Culture in War and Peace*. London: Sage.

Robinson, P. (2001) 'Theorizing the Influence of Media on World Politics: Models of Influence on Foreign Policy', *European Journal of Communication* 16(4): 523–44.

Robinson, P. (2002) *The CNN Effect: The Myth of News, Foreign Policy and Intervention*. London: Routledge.

Rogers, E. (1962) *The Diffusion of Innovations*. Glencoe, IL: Free Press.

Rojecki, A. (2002) 'Modernism, State Sovereignty and Dissent: Media and the New Post-Cold War Movements', *Critical Studies in Media and Communication* 19(2): 152–71.

Rolston, B. (ed.) (1991) *The Media and Northern Ireland*. Houndmills: Macmillan.

Rolston, B. and Miller, D. (eds) (1996) *War and Words: The Northern Ireland Media Reader*. Belfast: Beyond the Pale Publications.

Rosen, J. (1999) 'The Action of the Idea: Public Journalism in Built Form', pp. 21–48 in T. Glasser (ed.) *The Idea of Public Journalism*. New York: The Guilford Press.

Ross, K. (1996) *Black and White Media: Black Images in Popular Film and Television*. Cambridge: Polity Press.

Scalmer, S. (2002) *Dissent Events: Protest, the Media and the Political Gimmick in Australia*. Kensington: University of New South Wales Press.

Schiller, H. (1976) *Communication and Cultural Domination*. New York: International Arts and Science Press.

Schlesinger, P. (1978) *Putting 'Reality' Together*. London: Methuen.

Schlesinger, P. (1990) 'Rethinking the Sociology of Journalism: Source Strategies and the Limits of Media Centrism', pp. 61–83 in M. Ferguson (ed.) *Public Communication*. London: Sage.

Schlesinger, P. (1991). ' "Terrorism", the Media and the Liberal-Democratic State: A Critique of the Orthodoxy', pp. 17–28 in P. Schlesinger *Media, State and Nation: Political Violence and Collective Identities*. London: Sage.

Schlesinger, P. and Tumber, H. (1994) *Reporting Crime: The Media Politics of Criminal Justice*. Oxford: Clarendon Press.

Schmid, A.P. (1992) 'Editors' Perspectives', pp. 111–36 in D.L. Paletz and A.P. Schmid (eds) *Terrorism and the Media*. London: Sage.

Schramm, W. (1964) *Mass Media and National Development*. Stanford, CA: Stanford University Press.

Schudson, M. (1999) 'What Public Journalism Knows About Journalism but Doesn't Know About the "Public" ', pp. 118–33 in T. Glasser (ed.) *The Idea of Public Journalism*. New York: The Guilford Press.

Schudson, M. (2000) 'The Sociology of News Production Revisited (Again)', pp. 175–200 in J. Curran and M. Gurevitch (eds) *Mass Media and Society*. London: Arnold.

Servaes, J. (1995) 'Media and Development: Alternate Perspectives' Module Four, Unit 23 for Centre for Mass Communication Research, University of Leicester.

Servaes, J. (1996) 'Participatory Communication Research with New Social Movements: A Realistic Utopia', pp. 82–108 in J. Servaes, T.L. Jacobson and A.S. White (eds) *Participatory Communication for Social Change*. London: Sage.

Servaes, J., Jacobson, T.L. and White, S.A. (eds) (1996) *Participatory Communication for Social Change*. London: Sage.

Seymour-Ure, C. (1974) 'Enoch Powell's "Earthquake" ', in C. Seymour-Ure *The Political Impact of the Mass Media*. London: Constable.

Shaw, M. (2003) *War and Genocide: Organized Killing in Modern Society*. Cambridge: Polity.

Silberstein, S. (2002) *War of Words: Language, Politics, and 9/11*. New York: Routledge.

Smith, R.R. (1979) 'Mythic Elements in Television News', *Journal of Communication* 29: 75–82.

Solesbury, W. (1976) 'The Environmental Agenda', *Public Administration* 54: 379–97.

Soloski, J. (1989) 'News Reporting and Professionalism: Some Constraints on the Reporting of News', *Media, Culture and Society* 11: 207–28.

Sontag, S. (1979) *On Photography*. Harmondsworth: Penguin.

Sontag, S. (2003) *Regarding the Pain of Others*. New York: Farrar, Straus and Giroux.

Sontag, S. (2004) 'Regarding the Torture of Others', *The New York Times*, 23 May.

Sparks, C. and Tulloch, J. (eds) (2000) *Tabloid Tale*. Lanham, MD: Rowman and Littlefield.

Spencer, G. (2004) 'The Impact of Television News on the Northern Ireland Peace Negotiations', *Media, Culture and Society* 26(5): 603–23.

Spector, M. and Kituse, J.I. (1973) 'Social Problems: A Reformulation', *Social Problems* 20: 145–59.

Sreberny, A. (2000) 'The Global and the Local in International Communications', pp. 93–119 in J. Curran and M. Gurevitch (eds) *Mass Media and Society*. London: Arnold.

Stockholm International Peace Research Institute (SIPRI) (2005) *SIPRI Yearbook 2005*. Available at: http://yearbook2005.sipri.org/

Stovall, J.G. (2004) *Web Journalism*. London: Pearson.

Taylor, C. (1994) 'The Politics of Recognition', pp. 25–74 in A. Gutman (ed.) *Multiculturalism: Examining the Politics of Recognition*. Princeton, NJ: Princeton University Press.

Taylor, J. (1991). *War Photography: Realism in the British Press*. London: Routledge.

Taylor, J. (1998) *Body Horror: Photojournalism, Catastrophe and War*. Manchester: Manchester University Press.

Taylor, P. (1986) 'The Semantics of Political Violence', in P. Golding, G. Murdock and P. Schlesinger (eds) *Communicating Politics*. Leicester: Leicester University Press.

Taylor, P. (1992) *War and the Media: Propaganda and Persuasion in the Gulf War*. Manchester: Manchester University Press.

Taylor, P. (1995) *Munitions of the Mind: A History of Propaganda from the Ancient World to the Present Day*. Manchester: Manchester University Press.

Taylor, P. (2003) 'Journalism Under Fire: The Reporting of War and International Crisis', in S. Cottle (ed.) *News, Public Relations and Power*. London: Sage.

Tester, K. (1994) *Media, Culture and Morality*. London: Routledge.

Tester, K. (2001) *Compassion, Morality and the Media*. Buckingham: Open University Press.

Thompson, J.B. (1984) *Studies in the Theory of Ideology*. Cambridge: Polity.

Thompson, J.B. (1990) *Ideology and Modern Culture*. Cambridge: Polity.

Thompson, J.B. (1995) *The Media and Modernity*. Cambridge: Polity.

Thompson, J.B. (2000) *Political Scandal: Power and Visibility in the Media Age*. Cambridge: Polity.

Thompson, K. (1998) *Moral Panics*. London: Routledge.

Thussu, D.K. (1996) 'Development News' Module Seven, Unit 38b, for Centre for Mass Communication Research, University of Leicester.

Thussu, D.K. (2000) *International Communication*. London: Edward Arnold.

Thussu, D.K. (2003) 'Live TV and Bloodless Deaths: War, Infotainment and 24/7 News', pp. 117–32 in D.K. Thussu and D. Freedman (eds) *War and the Media*. London: Sage.

Thussu, D.K. and Freedman, D. (eds) (2003) *War and the Media*. London: Sage.

Tiffen, R. (1999) *Scandals: Media, Politics and Corruption in Contemporary Australia*. Sydney: University of New South Wales Press.

Tomlinson, J. (1990) *Cultural Imperialism*. London: Pinter.

Tomlinson, J. (1999) *Globalization and Culture*. Cambridge: Polity.

Tuchman, G. (1972) 'Objectivity as Strategic Ritual: An Examination of Newsmen's Notions of Objectivity', *American Journal of Sociology* 77: 660–79.

Tuchman, G. (1978) *Making News: A Study in the Social Construction of Reality*. New York: Free Press.

Tuman, J. (2003) *Communicating Terror*. London: Sage.

Tumber, H. (2004) 'Prisoners of News Values?: Journalists, Professionalism, and Identification in Times of War', pp. 190–205 in S. Allan and B. Zelizer (eds) *Reporting War*. London: Routledge.

Tumber, H. and Palmer, P. (2004) *Media at War: The Iraq Crisis*. London: Sage.

Turner, G. (1996) *British Cultural Studies*. London: Routledge.

Turner, V. (1974) *Dramas, Fields, and Metaphors: Symbolic Action in Human Society*. Ithaca, NY: Cornel University Press.

Turner, V. (1982) *From Ritual to Theatre: The Human Seriousness of Play*. New York: Performing Arts Journal Publication.

Ungar, S. (2001) 'Moral Panic Versus the Risk Society: The Implications of the Changing Sites of Social Anxiety', *British Journal of Sociology* 52(2): 271–91.

Urry, J. (2002) *The Tourist Gaze*. London: Sage.

Urry, J. (2003) *Global Complexity*. Cambridge: Polity.

Van Aelst, P. and Walgrave, S. (2004) 'New Media, New Movements? The Role of the Internet in Shaping the "Anti-globalization" Movement', pp. 97–122 in W. van de Donk, B. Loader, P.G. Nixon and D. Dieter (eds) *Cyberprotest*. London: Routledge.

Van Dijk, T. (1991) *Racism and the Press*. London: Routledge.

Van de Donk, W., Loader, B., Nixon, P. and Rucht, D. (eds) (2004) *Cyberprotest: New Media, Citizens and Social Movements*. London: Routledge.

Van Zoonen, L. (1994) *Feminist Media Studies*. London: Sage.

Volkmer, I. (1999) *News in the Global Sphere*. Luton: Luton University Press.

Volkmer, I. (2002) 'Journalism and Political Crises in the Global Network Society', pp. 235–46 in B. Zelizer and S. Allan (eds) *Journalism After September 11*. London: Routledge.

Waddington, D. (1992) 'Media Representation of Public Disorder', pp. 160–78 in D. Waddington (ed.) *Contemporary Issues in Public Disorder*. London: Routledge.

Wagner-Pacifici, R.E. (1986) *The Moro Morality Play: Terrorism as Social Drama*. Chicago: University of Chicago Press.

Wall, M. (2003) 'Social Movement and the Net: Activist Journalism Goes Digital', pp. 113–22 in K. Kawamoto (ed.) *Digital Journalism*. London: Rowman and Littlefield.

Watney, S. (1987) 'Moral Panics', pp. 38–57 in S. Watney *Policing Desire*. London: Comedia.

Webster, F. (2003) 'Information Warfare in an Age of Globalization', pp. 57–69 in D.K. Thussu and D. Freedman (eds) *War and the Media*. London: Sage.

West, C. (1999) 'The New Cultural Politics of Difference', pp. 256–67 in S. During (ed.) *The Cultural Studies Reader*. London: Routledge.

Williams, R. (1974) *Television, Technology and Form*. London: Fontana.

Williams, R. (1985) *Marxism and Literature*. Oxford: Oxford University Press.

Wilson, C. and Gutierrez, F. (1995) *Race, Multiculturalism, and the Media*. London: Sage.

Wolfsfeld, G. (1997) *Media and Political Conflict: News from the Middle East*. Cambridge: Cambridge University Press.

Wolfsfeld, G. (2003) 'The Political Contest Model', in S. Cottle (ed.) *News, Public Relations and Power*. London: Sage.

Wolfsfeld, G. (2004) *Media and the Path to Peace*. Cambridge: Cambridge University Press.

Wykes, M. (2000) 'The Burrowers: News About Bodies, Tunnels and Green Guerillas', pp. 29–44 in S. Allan, B. Adam and C. Carter (eds) *Environmental Risks and the Media*. London: Routledge.

Wynne, B. (1996) 'May the Sheep Safely Graze? A Reflexive View of the Expert–Lay Knowledge Divide', pp. 27–43 in S. Lash, B. Szerszynski and B. Wynne (eds) *Risk, Environment and Modernity*. London: Sage.

Young, I. (1996) 'Communication and the Other: Beyond Deliberative Democracy', pp. 120–36 in S. Benhabib (ed.) *Democracy and Difference*. Princeton, NJ: Princeton University Press.

Zelizer, B. and Allan, S. (eds) (2002) *Journalism After September 11*. London: Routledge.

INDEX

Related books from Open University Press

Purchase from www.openup.co.uk or order through your local bookseller

Critical Readings
MORAL PANICS AND THE MEDIA

Chas Critcher (ed)

First developed by Stanley Cohen in 1972, 'moral panic' is a key term in media studies, used to refer to sudden eruptions of indignant concern about social issues. An occurrence of moral panic is characterized by stylized and stereotypical representation by the mass media and a tendency for those in power to claim the moral high ground and pronounce judgement. In this important book, Chas Critcher brings together essential readings on moral panics, which he locates in contemporary debates through an editor's introduction and concise section introductions.

The first section discusses moral panic models and includes contributions on the history and intellectual background of the concept. Differences in thinking between British and American moral panic scholarship are also examined. A second section features important case studies, including AIDS, Satanism, drugs, paedophilia and asylum seekers. This is followed by readings that look at themes such as the importance of language, rhetoric and discourse; the dynamics of media reporting and how it affects public opinion; and the idea of the 'risk society'. Finally, readings critique and debate the use and relevance of moral panic models.

Critical Readings: Moral Panics and the Media is a valuable resource for students and researchers in media studies, criminology and sociology.

Essays by: David L. Altheide, Nachman Ben-Yehuda, Joel Best, Theodore Chiricos, John Clarke, Stan Cohen, Chas Critcher, Mary deYoung, Julie Dickinson, Erich Goode, Johanna Habermeier, Stuart Hall, Sean P. Hier, Tony Jefferson, Philip Jenkins, Hans Mathias Kepplinger, Jennifer Kitzinger, Daniel Maier-Katkin, Angela McRobbie, Peter Meylakhs, Suzanne Ost, Bryan Roberts, Liza Schuster, Stephen Stockwell, Kenneth Thompson, Sarah L. Thornton, Sheldon Ungar, Simon Watney, Jeffrey Weeks, Michael Welch, Paul Williams.

352pp   0 335 21807 5 (EAN: 9 780335 218073) Paperback
         0 335 21808 3 (EAN: 9 780335 218080) Hardback

Critical Readings
VIOLENCE AND THE MEDIA
C. Kay Weaver and Cynthia Carter (eds)

The relationship between media representations and real acts of violence is one of the most contentious and hotly debated issues today. This book is the first to bring together a selection of highly influential readings that have helped to shape this area of research. It includes key investigations of how, and with what implications, the media portray violence in the twenty-first century.

Critical Readings: Violence and the Media contains sections examining how media violence and its 'effects' have been theorized; how media production contexts influence the reporting and representation of violence; and how audiences engage with depictions of violence. Violence is analysed in different media formats, including television, film, radio, the news, public information campaigns, comics, video games, popular music, photography and the internet. The readings cover a range of perspectives, including social learning, desensitisation and cultivation theories, 'no-effects' models, sociological, feminist and postmodern arguments. An editor's introduction and section introductions serve to contextualise the readings.

Providing a detailed and theoretically grounded consideration of the cultural and social significance of media violence, *Critical Readings: Violence and the Media* is an essential resource for students of media studies, cultural studies, sociology and communication studies.

Contributors: Alison Adam, Albert Bandura, Martin Barker, Eileen Berrington, Douglas R. Bruce, David Buckingham, David Campbell, Jay Dixit, Lisa Duke, Molly Eckman, David Gauntlett, George Gerbner, Henry Giroux, Jack Glaser, Donald P. Green, Kellie Hay, Annette Hill, Birgitta Höijer, Derek Iwamoto, Ann Jemphrey, Christine L. Kellow, Jenny Kitzinger, Magdala Peixoto Labre, Catherine Amoroso Leslie, Debra Merskin, Jennifer Paff Ogle, Mary Beth Oliver, Valerie Palmer-Mehta, Julian Petley, Charles Piot, Srividya Ramasubramanian, Dorrie Ross, Sheila A. Ross, Medhi Semanti, H. Leslie Steeves.

400pp   0 335 21805 9 (EAN: 9 78 0335 218059) Paperback
          0 335 21806 7 (EAN: 9 78 0335 218066) Hardback